Popular Culture, Geopolitics, and Identity

Human Geography in the New Millennium
Issues and Applications

SERIES EDITOR
Barney Warf, University of Kansas

Human geography is increasingly focused on real-world problems. Applying geographic concepts to current global concerns, this series focuses on the urgent issues confronting us as we move into the new century. Designed for university-level geography and related multidisciplinary courses such as area studies, global issues, and development, these textbooks are richly illustrated and include suggestions for linking to related Internet resources. The series aims to help students to better understand, integrate, and apply common themes and linkages in the social and physical sciences and in the humanities, and, by doing so, to become more effective problem solvers in the challenging world they will face.

TITLES IN THE SERIES

Boundaries of Faith: Geographical Perspectives on Religious Fundamentalism
    Roger W. Stump

Six Billion Plus: Population Issues in the Twenty-first Century (second edition)
    K. Bruce Newbold

Popular Culture, Geopolitics, and Identity
    Jason Dittmer

Popular Culture, Geopolitics, and Identity

Jason Dittmer

ROWMAN & LITTLEFIELD PUBLISHERS, INC.
Lanham • Boulder • New York • Toronto • Plymouth, UK

Published by ROWMAN & LITTLEFIELD PUBLISHERS, INC.
A wholly owned subsidiary of The Rowman & Littlefield Publishing Group, Inc.
4501 Forbes Boulevard, Suite 200, Lanham, Maryland 20706
http://www.rowmanlittlefield.com

Estover Road, Plymouth PL6 7PY, United Kingdom

British Library Cataloguing in Publication Information Available

Library of Congress Cataloging-in-Publication Data

Dittmer, Jason.
  Popular culture, geopolitics, and identity / Jason Dittmer.
    p. cm. -- (Human geography in the new millennium : issues and
applications)
  Includes bibliographical references and index.
  ISBN 978-0-7425-5633-1 (cloth : alk. paper) -- ISBN 978-0-7425-5634-8 (pbk. : alk.
paper) -- ISBN 978-0-7425-6831-0 (electronic : alk. paper)
  1. Geopolitics--Social aspects. 2. Popular culture--Political aspects. 3. Mass
media--Political aspects. I. Title.
  JC319.D4995 2010
  306.2--dc22
                                      2009049395

∞™ The paper used in this publication meets the minimum requirements of
American National Standard for Information Sciences—Permanence of Paper for
Printed Library Materials, ANSI/NISO Z39.48-1992.

Printed in the United States of America

For my grandmother Florence Fitzpatrick,
who always told me to work hard at something I loved.

Contents

Preface   ix

Introduction: Popular Culture—Between Propaganda
and Entertainment   xv

1   Geopolitics: Histories, Discourses, and Mediation   1

2   Popular Culture: Theories, Methods, and Intertextuality   23

3   Representation of Place and the British Empire   47

4   Narration of Nation in the Post-WWII United States   69

5   Affect, Embodiment, and Military Video Games   91

6   The Active Audience and Evangelical Geopolitics   111

7   Hegemony, Subaltern Identities, and New Media   133

8   Conclusion: Identity, Subjectivity, and Going Forward   155

Bibliography   165

Index   173

About the Author   181

Preface to the First Edition[1]

What is the relationship between popular culture and geopolitics? And what does that relationship have to do with you and me? These are the questions that animate this book, and hopefully they will interest you as much as they interest me. I've seemingly always had an interest in popular culture and geopolitics, although it's only relatively recently that I started asking myself these questions. At the risk of self-indulgence, I'd like to walk you through a retrospective of how these twin interests have developed in my life—not to talk about myself (although I rarely need an excuse) but to give an example of how the three main topics of this book, popular culture, geopolitics, and identity, are enmeshed in often very personal ways. Hopefully this will inspire some introspection about how these three things intersect in your own life, and will pique your interest enough to read the rest of the book.

In 1988 I was twelve years old and entering junior high school. It was a brutal time for me, as early adolescence is for most of us, and it didn't help that I was perhaps a bit more bookish than most. My favorite class that year was World Geography, taught by Mrs. Schoenberger. It was an excellent class, and as she told us about various parts of the world I paid close attention; this was the start of a life-long passion for the variety and difference found in the world, in terms of both physical and cultural landscapes (a professional passion most geographers share, I would later discover). The class was, however, not a politically neutral experience. It was, after all, the very end of the Cold War, with the Soviet Union still per-

---
[1] I am an optimist by nature.

ceived as a very real threat. Growing up in a city with three naval bases (Jacksonville, Florida), I had been told from a very young age that if there was a nuclear war we would likely be a target. Mrs. Schoenberger taught us about the various parts of the world, who was with us and who was against us in the global struggle; I distinctly remember hearing about the economic "backwardness" of Eastern Europe and other areas ruled by proxy from Moscow, as well as hearing about Soviet aggression in places like Afghanistan. It was world geography as viewed from a certain place, with certain geopolitical perspectives. Of course, while I had never had a geography class before, none of this struck me as exactly new. While I could not have found Afghanistan on a map prior to that class, I knew the Soviet Union; at least, I knew the type of people who lived there. They were the Klingons.

I, from a very young age, had tuned in to watch the original *Star Trek* series in reruns every weekday. There I watched the exploits of the USS *Enterprise* as it set about exploring the universe. "Its five-year mission: to explore strange new worlds; to seek out new life and new civilizations; to boldly go where no man has gone before." The USS *Enterprise* was thus tasked with the advancement of scientific knowledge, and it was part of Starfleet, itself an extension of the United Federation of Planets, an interstellar coalition of alien races that nevertheless seemed to be dominated by humans from Earth. The Federation resembled, in some ways, the present-day United Nations, from its logo, to its founding in San Francisco, to its focus on peace, progress, justice, universal rights, self-determination, and equality among peoples (see figures 0.1 and 0.2). In other ways, however, it resembled the United States—especially in the apparent existence of American-style civil rights enshrined in law throughout the Federation and in Starfleet's ranks and terminology (note the designation "USS" *Enterprise* as well as the existence of the real-life American aircraft carriers and space shuttles of the same name). *Star Trek* seemed to indicate that in the future racism, poverty, and the Cold War would all disappear; liberal American

Figure 0.1.   The seal of the United Nations (Courtesy of the United Nations)

Figure 0.2.   The seal of the United Federation of Planets from *Star Trek*. Note the similarities to figure 0.1

ideals become universal, expand to incorporate the entire planet, and eventually go even further (a Russian even serves as navigator of the *Enterprise*). A more cynical viewer might note that Starfleet's explorations seemed primarily to colonize new planets and that the *Enterprise*, armed with phasers and photon torpedoes, seemed more like Spanish conquistador Hernando Cortés than pacifist Martin Luther King, Jr. Of course, the twelve-year-old me did not think that way (I also had little idea at the time of the connections between the Federation and the United Nations).

While there were infinitely many humanoid races in the *Star Trek* universe, there was one group that featured more often than others. The Klingons were introduced in a 1967 episode as the main rivals of the Federation. In the original series, the Klingons were portrayed as a savage race of vaguely North Asian appearance. Rather than being a federation like *Star Trek*'s protagonists, the Klingons were an empire, and they ruled by force, with the empire expanding as a result of a seemingly innate need to dominate. It should come as no surprise that Gene Roddenberry, *Star Trek*'s creator, has said that the Klingons were explicitly modeled on the Soviet Union. Thus, the geopolitical conflict that characterized the Cold War had been displaced, leaving the Earth united in a seeming postracial utopia of liberalism but locating the danger of tyranny and aggression elsewhere in the universe, able to be called upon whenever needed to advance the plot. While no one ever told me the Klingons were the Soviets, and the Federation was a loosely defined "us," nobody needed to. They fit together in my twelve-year-old mind, so when Mrs. Schoenberger told me about the Cold War it seemed quite natural to me—after all, the 1988 geopolitical order was largely the same as it had been twenty years earlier when *Star Trek* was made.

In 1994 I graduated from high school and went to college, choosing international studies and political science as my majors. This resulted from the same interest in difference that I had discovered in Mrs. Schoenberger's class. While my own interests were unchanging in their particular inchoate and inarticulate way, the world had rapidly changed in the intervening years. The Berlin wall had been torn down and the Soviet Union had splintered into fifteen different countries. The world seemed to be progressing in the ways that *Star Trek* had predicted: democracy was ascendant and the utopia of the Federation seemed a few steps closer. The Gulf War (1991) had seemed to promise a "new world order" based on collective security, in which violence was occasionally necessary but only for liberal internationalist purposes. My interest in geopolitics began to blossom as I considered my career options in a world characterized by a peace guaranteed via American might and U.N. diplomacy.

Star Trek had similarly been reimagined, with the Klingons in *Star Trek: The Next Generation* no longer the enemy of the Federation, but rather a somewhat subordinate ally (following the collapse of their economy, portrayed with great end-of-Cold War allegory in *Star Trek VI*) quite similar to post-Soviet Russia, which during the Yeltsin era had undergone Western-proscribed "shock therapy" to jump-start its economy and had adopted a Western-style constitution. Rather than just warlike and aggressive, in *The Next Generation* the Klingons were portrayed as dedicated to personal honor above all else. While this is "different" than many Western cultures at the time the show was made, it is seen as an admirable, and understandable, trait, thus showing a way forward for different cultures (the Federation and the Klingons) to coexist peacefully, without enmity.

In 1999 I started my PhD in geography planning to go into the U.S. State Department, but by then the bloom was off the rose. Conflicts in the former Yugoslavia and in Rwanda indicated that a pacific future had not yet arrived, and the present seemed very much one of bloody violence, characterized by the media as intractable ethnic conflict. Further, American power seemed unable (or unwilling) to address these new threats, and utopia could be seen disappearing in the rear-view mirror as mass graves and genocide proliferated. My own role in this future seemed more problematic than before, as the ethical basis for American power seemed shakier than ever.

All of this was, as you by now expect, mirrored in the universe of *Star Trek*. *The Next Generation* had gone off the air when I started college and had been replaced by a new series called *Deep Space 9*. Darker in tone than previous incarnations of *Star Trek*, the story centered on a space station located simultaneously at the border of Federation territory with a cruel race known as the Cardassians and outside a wormhole that provides access to an unexplored part of the galaxy. This provided the basis for a deeply geopolitical narrative that illustrated the ethical tensions found in operating a huge, multicultural enterprise like the Federation. The Klingons and other familiar races like the Romulans feature in a shifting array of alliances with the Federation as new aliens threaten all three from the distant areas found through the wormhole, a parallel to the seeming instability of a unipolar geopolitical order. At the same time, the uneasy relationship between the Federation and the Cardassians is tested by the Maquis, a group of ex-Federation settlers who gave up their citizenship when the colonies they founded were ceded by the Federation to the Cardassians. The Maquis fight a guerilla war against the Cardassians, pulling the Federation into ethical quandaries where action and inaction both seem "right" depending on your geopolitical perspective, paralleling the conflicts over ethnic cleansing in Bosnia and religious settlements in the West Bank. My own cynicism grew in parallel to *Deep Space 9*'s complicated and ambiguous narratives, leaving me unsure of a career in government service and much more comfortable with a more ambiguous position myself—that of the scholar, unattached to an official foreign policy.

While it would be easy to see *Star Trek* as simply reflecting trends in world politics in a crass attempt to cash in on conflict, that would be too simple an analysis. It is important to consider the full cycle of events described above. As a fan of *Star Trek* during the first two decades of my life, I was predisposed to look at the world in ways that *Star Trek* laid out for me. In fact, I was aware of *Star Trek*'s narrative of progress long before I had any formal education about the Cold War—to say that *Star Trek* followed from "real" geopolitics is to miss out on *Star Trek*'s role in formulating my own geopolitical perspective. For me, it *was* geopolitics.

It is this experience, and many others like it, that brought me to study the intersection of popular culture, geopolitics, and identity. This book is an attempt to provide an introduction to the history, concepts, and some of the academic literature that constitute this increasingly popular area of study. Although it is written primarily for advanced undergraduates and beginning graduate students, I hope that it will find its way into the hands of other interested people. After all, everyone has a part to play in the creation of new geopolitical orders—and just because the utopia of *Star Trek* has not yet unfolded does not mean that we should give up on making this universe a better place.

This book begins with an introduction to the topic of the book, which is followed by two chapters that each focus on a different idea: the first chapter is about geopolitics and the second is about popular culture. Each chapter outlines ways in which each idea has been theorized historically, and then goes on to describe key concepts you need to understand the rest of the book. The five chapters following these initial three are case studies, each outlining a key element of the study of popular culture, geopolitics, and identity and then providing an in-depth example of how that element can be used to understand a particular form of popular culture. The final chapter is a conclusion, drawing together the previous seven chapters in order to provide some final thoughts about identity and what you can do to continue an interest in these topics.

ACKNOWLEDGMENTS

I would be the most ungrateful man in the world if I was not to recognize first and foremost the love and support given to me by my wife, Stephanie. She is a partner in everything I do, which unfortunately for her means that the greater part of 2008 was spent hearing me think aloud and moan about the progress of this book. Her regular infusions of love and support made this project happen. Also needing special recognition is Klaus

Dodds, who, beyond helping with the formulation of the book proposal, read *every* chapter and provided useful comments and correctives. Similarly, Paul Adams and Pauliina Raento were major influences at the proposal stage, and Derek McCormack was good enough to preview some of chapter 5. Barney Warf, the editor of this series, read the book in its entirety, and provided very helpful editorial advice. All the remaining flaws are mine and mine only. Thanks are also due to Susan McEachern at Rowman & Littlefield, who was very supportive of the idea for this book even before I had it.

In many ways writing this book has been an education for me, forcing me to systematize my thoughts after many years of, metaphorically speaking, shoving scraps of paper into my head. As such, this book is the result of innumerable encounters over coffee with my amazing colleagues first at Florida State University, where I undertook my graduate education, then at Georgia Southern University, and now at University College London. Of course, it would be a mistake to forget the wider community of scholars interested in critical geopolitics and popular culture, whom have influenced me from afar (and whose hard work I have pillaged to write this book). I am grateful to all.

Introduction

Popular Culture—Between Propaganda and Entertainment

Music has a particular role in our cultural imagination. Most everyone understands that music has power of one kind or another. It has the power to make us tap our toes and perhaps sway or head-bob with the beat, or the power to make us remember things from when that song was new. Music can also provide us with the boost to get us through a day in which we are dragging, or conversely can relax us when we are nervous. We usually like that music has these impacts on us, because it allows us to shape our environment to help us with our day—by boosting our energy, helping us forget our worries, or whatever. However, we feel differently about music if it is not in our control. Even someone singing an advertising jingle near you so that it gets stuck in your head all day can be irritating, and a neighbor's throbbing bass at midnight can lead to the police being called. At the far end of this spectrum, the loud application of objectionable music has been frequently used as a form of torture (Johnson and Cloonan 2008). Even music that you *like* can drive you crazy if played at the wrong time. How can something that gives so much pleasure also be so infuriating and disabling? This ambivalence about music says quite a bit—at a minimum the experience of music is inflected by how in control we are of that experience. Even the most basic experience of music, then, is inflected by power and politics.

So what happens then when we expand the frame to include control over things like lyrics, or types of rhythms? Power and politics have always been an important part of music in that sense. Elvis Presley's hip movements while performing were deemed lurid and objectionable; rock and roll itself was seen as promoting juvenile delinquency. Alice Cooper was met with the same concerns, as was Marilyn Manson, and today it seems to be rap that bears the brunt of public concern over the types of behavior it purportedly induces among its listeners, namely violence, misogyny, and other forms of antisocial behavior. Of course, the naming of these forms of music as dangerous to listen to only makes sense as a way of situating other forms of culture and practice as normal, and not deviant in any way. Similarly, the behaviors that rock and roll and later rap music have been accused of contributing to are likewise left out of an invented "mainstream." Thus, criticism of these forms of music over the years is not just about the music, but about society, and who controls its limits. It is, in short, political. This is not just true of music, but of all forms of popular culture, whether it is television, sports, or fashion. It is a con-tested field, with a lot more at stake than just aesthetics and personal taste.

So how, then, is popular culture *geopolitical*? One word that is often as-sociated with media and geopolitics is "propaganda." Propaganda refers to the intentional use of the media to generate public sentiments that ben-efit the propagandist. However, it is most often used to designate *other* people's attempts to do this, as a way of invalidating the message of the mediated culture. This can be in the form of news stories that are purport-edly "slanted" against another government, or a film in which the villain is a particular nationality, or just a song that inspires martial feelings at a critical moment in diplomatic relations.

The difference between "propaganda" and "truth" often depends on where you stand, and perhaps on the intentions of the producer, which is difficult to assess in the world of popular culture. Therefore, this book will not engage with the idea of propaganda itself, but it is useful as a test—if popular culture was not geopolitical, why would governments contest it? Instead, we have plenty of evidence that they do. For instance, Yuri Zhu-kov (1965, n.p.), writing in the Soviet newspaper *Pravda*, complained of Ian Fleming's James Bond novels:

> James Bond lives in a nightmarish world where laws are written at the point of a gun, where coercion and rape are considered valor and murder is a funny trick. . . . Bond's job is to protect the interests of the property class, and he is no better than the youths Hitler boasted he would bring up like wild beasts to be able to kill without thinking. . . . It is no accident that sham agents of Soviet counter-intelligence, represented in caricature form, invari-ably fill the roll of Bond's opponents, because Bond kills right and left the kind of men that Fleming wants to kill—Russians, Reds and Yellows. Bond is portrayed a sort of white archangel, destroying the impure races.

More recently, the BBC World Service, a branch of the British Broadcasting Corporation that is funded by the UK government to disseminate news from a British perspective around the world, has been repeatedly jammed by the Chinese government to prevent an alternative (British) perspective being heard within its territory (Pinkerton and Dodds 2009). Further, when Kazakhstan protested its treatment as an anti-Semitic and misogynist country in *Borat: Cultural Learnings of America for Make Benefit Glorious Nation of Kazakhstan* (2006) it was publicly scorned by the American public. However, the president of Kazakhstan, Nursultan Nazarbayev, paid for an advertisement in the *New York Times* and subsequently flew to Washington, D.C. to meet with President George W. Bush in order to foster a more "authentic" image for his country. If popular culture does not matter to geopolitics, then a lot of people are going to a lot of trouble to contest it for nothing.

IDENTITIES: BETWEEN THE GLOBAL AND THE INDIVIDUAL

The idea of propaganda, as stated earlier, is often used as an opposite of the self-evidently true position espoused by the speaker. This is true whether talking about national identities or individual ones (or anything in between). Therefore, who we think we are, and who others think we are, is critical to how we evaluate popular culture. In other words, whether popular culture is propaganda or just entertainment is determined not by its content, but rather by the identity of the consumer. Identity thus is a thread that runs through every chapter of this book.

Identity has become a very politicized term since the 1960s, when various social movements (such as the women's liberation, peace, civil rights, and various anti-imperial movements) highlighted the various ways in which it was possible for people to conceive of themselves as located within society. Since then, processes of globalization have not eliminated identity, as some claimed they would, but instead have heightened attention both to it and the efforts needed to bolster stable place-based identities in the face of ongoing processes of migration and other global circulations of people, goods, and ideas. With people's possible identities drawing on numerous overlapping geographical definitions, and with culture being produced and consumed in new and various places, identity has become less of a taken-for-granted concept than in the past. Instead it has moved to the forefront of the study of both popular culture and geopolitics.

Popular culture conveys information about places, and also originates in certain contexts only to be consumed in various others. In this way it is doubly geographical, conveying ideas about places from one place to another. Identity and power are thus invoked in multiple dimensions. Similarly, geopolitics is about the assignment of values to places, and it constructs hierarchies of people and places that matter and those that do not. While geopolitics is usually considered to be conducted in very elite contexts, this book argues that it in fact circulates in everyday contexts through popular culture. The idea that geopolitics is only for elites is itself a way of producing identities—those who are active in shaping the world and those who are passive. Like popular culture, geopolitics is doubly geographic—shaping places in various ways and also demarcating the places and people who do the shaping and those who do not. Identity, then, is key to both popular culture and geopolitics. The juxtaposition of these words in the title of this book is therefore not just a label, but a call to consider each topic in relation to the others. A more detailed explanation of individual identity can be found in the concluding chapter of this book, in a section entitled "Social Constructionism and Subjectivity." However, to facilitate that understanding of identity it is best to work through the intervening chapters. So, let us briefly turn our attention to this book and its subject matter, popular geopolitics.

THIS BOOK

Popular geopolitics is a niche within political geography wherein scholars study the everyday experience of geopolitics. As such, the term refers to both the subject matter (which will be outlined through the rest of this book) as well as to the project devoted to improving our understanding of that subject matter. The latter is interesting in that over the past several decades the project has moved in hitches and starts, as various scholars of geopolitics have decided to engage with it, and then move on. There have been notably few people who devoted themselves to it for years at a time. In fact, one of the defining features of popular geopolitics has been its lack of definition—not as a subject matter, but as a group of people.

However, another key feature of the project thus far has been its links to various other academic fields, such as cultural geography, international relations, and cultural studies. Scholars in these fields often produce work that is easily aligned with the project of popular geopolitics even if they would never label themselves as scholars of popular geopolitics. This is because the past twenty years or so have seen an efflorescence of research on popular culture and identity across academia, much of which is relevant to popular geopolitics even if not couched self-consciously within its terminology. Thus, popular geopolitics can be seen as a tiny niche within political geography (itself a niche within a relatively small discipline) or, perhaps more optimistically, as part of a large interdisciplinary project that spans many different perspectives. This book seeks to position itself within both perspectives; adopting the terminology and theoretical perspectives specifically associated with popular geopolitics but reaching out to surrounding niches for conceptual insights or particularly excellent case study materials.

This book is intended to be used as a textbook for advanced undergraduate students and as a quick guide for beginning graduate students who are hoping to get a sense of popular geopolitics. As such, it is written in a casual, conversational style that uses numerous examples to convey what can be quite complex concepts. A book devoted to popular culture must necessarily leave out vast swathes of the world's popular culture because the book itself is limited in pages and scope and the world's culture is not; rather it is nearly infinite in scope and continually evolving into new forms and practices. Because of this, tough decisions have to be made about what to include and what to exclude. These tough decisions are made somewhat easier by the author's own limits—drawing upon popular culture that is beyond my experience to make examples is a surefire way to undermine the accuracy of this book. Therefore, this book draws primarily on popular culture from North America and to a lesser extent the United Kingdom. Consequently, readers from these regions are more likely to find the examples illuminating, and apologies are due to readers from other parts of the world.

Another limitation in the choice of case studies and smaller examples can be found in the centrality of media to this book. Popular culture itself encompasses a much larger array of practices; these include playing in or attending sports competitions, and making music or going to concerts. These kinds of activities have not gained much prominence in the popular geopolitics literature yet, although they appear to be on the horizon. Perhaps a future edition of this book will be able to incorporate these new literatures. Instead, this book focuses on mediated popular culture, such as books, TV, movies, comic books, and radio. In part this reflects the popular culture literature, which originates from a normative engagement that was originally skeptical of popular culture's value; it also allows overt connections to the geopolitical—it is easier to explain how a song is geopolitical than how playing sports is (although they both are, in different ways—see Foer 2004). With these limitations in mind, this book nevertheless presents a wide-ranging set of theories and case studies that approach the topic of popular culture, geopolitics, and identity from a variety of different perspectives. So what can be expected in the rest of this book?

CHAPTER OUTLINE AND STRUCTURE

The first two chapters set out the history and theorizations of geopolitics (chapter 1), the definitions and theories utilized in the study of popular culture, and methodologies used by current research in popular geopolitics (chapter 2). In these chapters there will be some references to popular culture when discussing geopolitics, and to geopolitics while discussing popular culture, but the two topics are kept relatively separate so as to give the reader a firm grasp of where the disciplinary concepts come from and how they can be seen to overlap in isolation. The subsequent chapters of this book (excepting the conclusion) will be case studies of popular geopolitics, describing some of the most important concepts and trends in the field. Chapter 3 will discuss representation of place, which has been one of the most significant strands of research in popular geopolitics. The British Empire was chosen as a framing device for this chapter because the construction of ideologies of empire in a society based on principles from the Enlightenment has often involved representing places and the people from there as fundamentally different from those in the imperial center. Thus, representation, particularly in regards to race, is critical to understanding how people can justify their (and their government's) treatment of people abroad.

Chapter 4 discusses the role of narrative in national identity, drawing on the post–World War II United States as an example of the importance of narrative because the United States is a nation that more obviously than most is an imagined community, one that is tied to a narrative of progress and innocence. The importance of popular culture in constituting that narrative will be the focus of this case study, drawing mostly on *Captain America* comic books. Chapter 5 introduces the idea of affect, outlining its connections to both cultural studies and psychology. Affect is, in contrast to representation, fundamentally focused inward—dealing with the ways in which popular geopolitics become embodied biologically as adrenaline, passion, and other sites at the interface between the inside and outside of our bodies. The popular culture to be studied in this case study comes from the American video game industry.

Chapter 6 returns to the cultural theory outlined in this chapter, bringing forth the critique that much of chapters 3 to 5 ignores the role of the audience in producing geopolitical knowledge. This chapter will take this idea of the active audience, bringing their own experiences and desires to their readings of popular culture, and apply it to the religious geopolitics of the extremely popular *Left Behind* series of evangelical Christian novels. This is a great example because in the evangelical Christian community differing understandings of scripture have led to differing opinions about modern-day geopolitics. The final case study will be in chapter 7, and will turn away from the hegemonic world of Western popular culture and will instead look at subaltern identities (i.e., those that are marginalized under current geopolitical conditions). Alternate sources of cultural power have emerged, such as Bollywood (the Indian film industry), the al-Jazeera

Arab television news network, and diasporic websites. These forms of resistance to hegemony utilize the technologies and social practices associated with globalization to carve out space for their own identity. This case study is of Salam Pax, an Iraqi blogger who provided insight into life in Baghdad during the 2003 invasion. The final chapter, chapter 8, is not a case study but rather pulls all of these ideas together and more fully theorizes the role of popular culture in shaping individual identities. This chapter will also show interested students where they can go to get more information and also how they can themselves contribute to the practice of popular geopolitics.

Each case study will begin with an introduction to the terminology of the new concept or perspective before briefly outlining any debates in the literature. This section will be followed by an introduction to ideas from media or political geography that are necessary to understand that particular case study. The actual case study will then begin, drawing on the published research and illustrating the relevance of popular culture to the particular understanding of geopolitics highlighted in the chapter. The case study is intended to be both informative and interesting (hopefully you will find it so). Finally, the chapter will conclude with a summary of what has been discussed and other areas in which the concept could be relevant in everyday life.

1

Geopolitics

Histories, Discourses, and Mediation

We live immersed in a world of popular culture. Popular culture is a bewildering array of narratives, images, and sounds that we often plug ourselves into for fun, or just to relax. But it is also more than that: it is a space of geopolitical action. Whether it is Jon Stewart spoofing the U.S. government's efforts in Iraq via his "Mess-o-potamia" segments on *The Daily Show*, Hollywood celebrities agitating for a Free Tibet on the red carpet of the Oscars, or Trey Parker and Matt Stone spoofing that same celebrity advocacy in *Team America: World Police* (2004), it is undeniable that while popular culture is often stigmatized for being a waste of time, it nevertheless feeds off of geopolitical events that are deemed to be important.

The geopolitics of popular culture often operates under our own radar, whether through music in the background (such as Toby Keith's *Courtesy of the Red, White, and Blue*) or advertisements on the television (such as Chevrolet's "An American Revolution"). Both of these examples point to the ubiquity of popular culture; how it is always reminding us of who we are (or are supposed to be). Attention to popular culture usually takes the form of concern over violent video games or over bias in the news media, but rarely do we think about the ways in which popular culture informs us about less controversial topics. For instance, the above examples of Toby Keith's song and the Chevrolet advertisement both illustrate the way in which country music and American car advertisements both utilize and generate nationalist sentiment. While those might seem obvious, popular culture is often seen to have more subtle encodings.

For instance, 2008's *Cloverfield*, a classic monster movie in which a twenty-story alien attacks New York City, was criticized for being insensitive to the September 11, 2001, attack by Al-Qaeda on the World Trade Center. The allusions to 9/11 come in the conceit of a shaky, handheld video camera to film the movie and in the visuals of billowing smoke and skyscrapers leaning against each other. Did the filmmakers intend for the beheading of the Statue of Liberty to represent the loss of civil freedoms after 9/11? Or is the movie instead a commentary on the rise of user-produced media (like YouTube) and Western society's obsession with visual images? Ultimately, that is beyond the ability of the filmmakers to define—once released the movie becomes part of the public sphere, and its geopolitical meaning is entirely open-ended.

Cloverfield is but one example of how popular culture and geopolitics are enmeshed. Many who witnessed the attacks of 9/11 felt compelled to refer to it as "like a movie." *Independence Day* (1996) is just one of many movies in that past that provided a language for talking about the 9/11 attacks when they occurred later. Certainly, the U.S. government believes that popular culture and geopolitics are interlinked—the Pentagon has allocated military equipment to movie shoots that it thinks are sufficiently pro-American in perspective such as *Top Gun* (1986), and in April 2005 the United States Special Operations Command was soliciting contractors to produce comic books aimed at Arab adolescents. "In order to achieve long-term peace and stability in the Middle East, the youth need to be reached. One effective means of influencing youth is through the use of comic books. A series of comic books provides the opportunity for youth to learn lessons, develop role models and improve their education" (U.S. Government 2005, n.p.). Thus, any full understanding of geopolitics requires some attention be paid to popular culture and matters of identity. But what is geopolitics?

WHAT IS GEOPOLITICS?

At the time of writing, there were 264 hits for a Google News Internet search under the term "geopolitics." While some of these are predictably off-base search engine matches, most of the articles seem to key on tightly-knit, succinct phrases, like "the geopolitics of oil," "Russia's muscular geopolitics," and "Middle Eastern geopolitics." The term "geopolitics" seems to be useful to journalists because it has a veneer of tremendous explanatory power: What has led to the rise in tension in Central Asia? Russia's muscular geopolitics. What is driving American foreign policy in the Middle East? The geopolitics of oil. It sounds so helpful, so powerful—like a key opening a lock. It seems like understanding geopolitics could lead to understanding the world.

But what exactly is geopolitics? Upon second glance, those journalistic answers ring a little hollow. Just saying the word "geopolitics" does not really explain anything at all. However, it does refer to *something*—a tradition—a way of thinking that has been highly influential in the twentieth century and, seemingly, one that looks to be key to the current century as well. It is that tradition that provides the tacit explanation that journalists love to harness. In these news articles "geopolitics" seems to refer to hard-nosed assessment of the way the world really is, without any pie-in-the-sky illusions. The world geopolitics describes is a rough place, with limited resources and land and too many people wanting them. So where did this tradition come from?

The Origins of Geopolitics

Geopolitics, as a notoriously slippery idea, can be traced back through time in innumerable ways. However, our narrative starts with Friedrich Ratzel, a German geographer at the end of the nineteenth century. At that time Charles Darwin's theory of natural selection was all the rage, and soon scholars began to try to apply Darwin's ideas to the study of societies—a move now seen as dubious as it reduces humans to making decisions based on what is "natural" rather than what might be moral or ethical. The resulting movement, nevertheless, was known as Social Darwinism. Importantly for our purposes, Ratzel took Darwin's ideas of natural selection and applied them to countries (especially his own, Germany) in what became known as his organic theory of the state. According to this theory, which was published in his book *Politische Geographie* (1897), countries (here known as states) need to grow in order to thrive. Powerful nations, Ratzel claimed, felt a powerful urge to expand the borders of their state in order to have a swath of territory that could reflect and sustain the vigor of their people. The analogies to Darwin's "survival of the fittest" are apparent even here. They are even more obvious when one considers the consequences of Ratzel's ideas if implemented: his theory of the state legitimizes continual war of all against all, as each country must seek the path of least resistance to territorial expansion and must simultaneously defend its territory at all costs—or else begin a downward spiral in which less territory means less national vigor, which means further loss of territory, and so on.

> **Organic theory of the state** Populations draw strength from territory; expansion of the state a sign of strength

Rudolf Kjellén was a Swedish political scientist who studied under Ratzel. It was he that coined the term "geopolitics" in 1899, and his further contribution was, among others, that the state and society should be viewed synergistically. This notion, together with Ratzel's coining of the now infamous word *"Lebensraum"* and his legitimation of the violence inherent to it, prefigures the rise of the Nazi party and its foreign policy. The explicit link between the works of Ratzel and Kjellén and the rise of the Nazi party comes through another man—Karl Haushofer. A major general in the German army, Haushofer retired after World War I and began a new career as a political geographer, where he gained familiarity with the ideas of geopolitics, or *"Geopolitik"* as it is known in German.

> **Lebensraum** "Living space" taken by strong culture from weaker ones

Haushofer became the founding editor of the *Journal of Geopolitics* in 1924, and as such he provided the intellectual basis of what would become Nazi foreign policy. During the early 1920s his former aide-de-camp from the army, Rudolf Hess, participated in the Beer Hall Putsch (the first Nazi attempt to take power in Germany) and was thrown in jail. It was while visiting Hess in prison that Haushofer met Adolf Hitler. During World War II, Haushofer's propaganda value far exceeded his policy influence, as it was falsely rumored in the United States during the war that he headed an institute with over a thousand geopolitical scientists plotting the perfectly scientific path to world domination. However, Haushofer was never a Nazi himself, and never shared their view on the importance of race. In fact, his son was executed by the Nazis for plotting to assassinate Hitler.

Although geopolitics, in the history relayed above, appears to be purely a Central European invention, and a dubious one at that, it is not necessarily so (see Atkinson 2000 for the role of Italian geopolitics in this era). Parallel to the Central European intellectual lineage was another strand of geopolitical thought, this one Anglo-American. In 1890, about the same time that Ratzel was conceptualizing his ideas about political geography, an American admiral named Alfred Mahan published *The Influence of Seapower upon History, 1660–1783*. In this book Mahan, a scholar of naval history, argues strongly that control of the sea was pivotal to victory in battle, as ships could move troops and resources faster than land-based methods of travel. Mahan further argues that control of commerce is key to survival during wartime, and this means that the successful navy must be able to achieve decisive victory over the enemy's fleet, thus protecting their own commerce and exposing that of their enemy to attack. This geostrategy dominated thinking for decades following the book's publication and in fact was the philosophy behind Japan's attack on Pearl Harbor in 1941, proving that ideas soon escape the intentions of those who originate them.

Mahan's ideas found fertile soil with influential British geographer Halford Mackinder, who was variously a scholar at the University of

Oxford, director of the London School of Economics, cofounder of the University of Reading, and Member of Parliament. Mackinder argued that the expansion of railroad networks was fundamentally reworking the political geography of the world by giving land-based powers the ability to move troops and resources with the ease of sea-based powers. Further, because Europe, Africa, and Asia together could be controlled by a strong land-based power, yet Central Asia could never be successfully invaded by a sea-based power as it was so far from the sea, naval powers such as the United Kingdom (Mackinder was a major proponent of British Empire) and the Mahan-influenced United States should ensure that Russia (the occupier of this sea-power immune tract of land in Central Asia) remained contained (see figure 1.1). This idea was originally published in 1904, and then updated in 1919 and 1942. Mackinder's strategy, like Mahan's, proved highly influential, providing among other things an intellectual basis for President Truman's Cold War doctrine of containing the Soviet Union.

Environmental Determinism and the Decline of Geopolitics

Thus, there were strands of what we can call geopolitical thinking occurring on both sides of the Atlantic prior to World War I. From these thinkers we can begin to decipher what geopolitics meant at this time. Common to all of these thinkers is an effort to systematize political life,

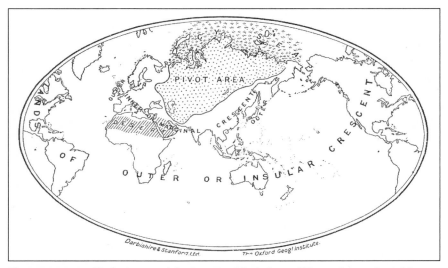

Figure 1.1.   Mackinder's map of the "geographical pivot of history"; how does this map make some places seem more important than others?

providing order and creating general rules that are seemingly "natural." At this point it is worth noting that the discipline of geography has tradi-tionally incorporated both physical and human geography, and the scientific meth-ods associated with the physical sciences were at this time dominant in human geog-raphy. Just as physics attempted to derive the rules by which matter and motion oper-ated, human geography attempted to de-rive the rules associated with the social en-vironment. Thus, the efforts of these geopolitical thinkers to derive fundamental rules was not unusual for the time. Both the German and Anglo-American strands of geopolitics were heavily influenced by environmental deter-minism—the belief that human societies and their cultures are largely a product of the environment in which they develop. This can be seen in both Mack-inder's focus on land and sea powers as somehow naturally opposed to each other, and also in Ratzel's focus on territory and resources as determinative of national power.

> **Physical and human geography** Primary division within geography; physical geography emphasizes environmental processes while human geography focuses on social processes

> **Environmental deter-minism** Theory that the environment determines cultural behavior

The problem with environmental determinism is that the rules derived in its name invariably turn out to be less than universal. For instance, environmentally deterministic scholars have argued simultaneously that the intellectual developments in classical Greece were because the land-scape of mountains inspired loftier thoughts—and that America was similarly drawn to greatness because of its wide open plains, which led inhabitants to "think big." Of course, these are simplistic formulations and environmental determinism can be quite sophisticated, as in the work of Jared Diamond (1999). Nevertheless, all forms of environmental deter-minism suffer from a lack of attention to what people think and do. In-deed, it is becoming increasingly apparent that, while the environment obviously influences what people do, what people do is increasingly modifying the environment through climate change and other processes.

What is also true of these writers is that, although they sought to derive the *objective* truth about how the world of politics and states works, they all approached it from a *subjective* standpoint. Mahan's "universal" naval geostrategy was composed in the milieu of a newly industrializing coun-try with two long coastlines. His proscription for a strong navy is further contextualized by Mahan's position as a naval officer—his claims can be viewed as a strategic maneuver within the long-running interservice ri-valries of the U.S. armed forces. Mackinder's geopolitical vision similarly deals entirely with the anxiety of maritime nations being overwhelmed by land-based powers. As an avowed imperialist, Mackinder was personally particularly keen to prevent Russia from severing the link between Great Britain and India (Russia and the United Kingdom engaged in a long rivalry for domination of Central Asia during the late 1800s, often referred to as the "Great Game"—see figure 1.2). Haushofer's Geopolitik was oriented toward justifying conflict with the purpose of regaining the territory that Germany lost in World War I, a war in which he fought and which he viewed as lost by geopolitically unsavvy national leaders. Thus, every one of these writers approached geopolitics from their own national, and sometimes personal, perspective. It is important to note that this is not a personal flaw—it is impossible for anyone to abstract themselves from their subjective identity in order to conduct objective research. The problem here is that they did not acknowledge their own perspective and reduce the scope of their claims. Instead, their universal theories of how the world works were aimed directly at their national policy makers; political geographer Isaiah Bowman even went to Paris as an American negotiator for the treaties that concluded World War I. In the hands of

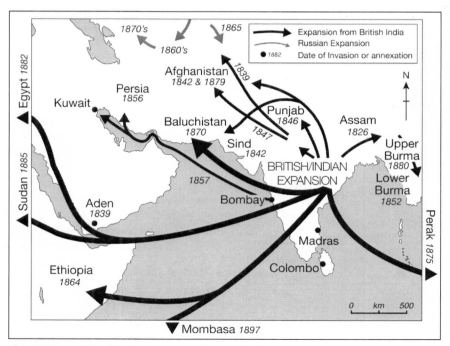

Figure 1.2. Map of Central and South Asia during period of the Great Game (UCL Drawing Office)

these scholars, geopolitics was formulated as a kind of applied political geography—academic knowledge bent to the purposes of the state.

In the aftermath of World War II, Geopolitik was seen as corrupted by its association with Haushofer and Hitler's ambitions. With it went the English version of the word; Isaiah Bowman even wrote an article claiming to differentiate between the supposedly neutral, objective science of American geography and the ideological perversion that was German geopolitics. Geopolitics became a dirty word—described by American geographer Richard Hartshorne as an intellectual poison (Hartshorne himself had worked for the Office of Strategic Services, a forerunner of the CIA, so he was hardly neutral himself).

The Return of Geopolitics

From shortly after the end of the war until about 1970, geopolitics was not the subject of serious academic study, although the word did persist somewhat in the journalistic sense described at the beginning of this chapter, and political geographers such as Saul Cohen continued to study politics at the global scale. This, however, does not mean that geopolitical thinking came to an end. Indeed, the onset of the Cold War brought global, geopolitical thinking to the fore in a way that had never happened before. With two global superpowers seemingly locked in conflict, the entire world had to be rendered understandable for leaders and citizens of the major powers. This was a distinctly geographical project—both in regards to constructing a geostrategy and making populations feel like their security hinged on events in distant parts of the world. It is impossible to understand Truman's containment policy (which justified permanent military commitments like the North Atlantic Treaty Organization [NATO]) and the later Domino Theory (which justified the Vietnam War) as anything but applied political geography. Indeed, political geographers such as Saul Cohen were involved early on, but the term "geopolitics" never reared its head until Henry Kissinger become involved in U.S. presidential politics. As national security advisor and secretary of state, Kissinger advocated just the sort of faux-objective calculation in American for-

NATO North Atlantic Treaty Organization; alliance founded to fight against the Soviet Union during the Cold War

Domino Theory Belief during the Cold War that if one country becomes Communist its neighbors will as well

Henry Kissinger National security advisor and secretary of state in the Nixon and Ford administrations

eign policy that the journalistic usage of "geopolitics" today refers to, and it is perhaps to him that we owe this lingering meaning. While not directly referencing (or exonerating) the pre–World War II usage of the term, he nevertheless seemed to lift the veil by implying that the study of geopolitics could work for the United States.

A new generation of scholars began to look at geopolitics—lending diversity to the geopolitics described by Saul Cohen in the 1960s and 1970s. However, just as Ratzel, Mackinder, and Haushofer were rooted in their time, so were these scholars. The 1970s in geography were a time dominated by a type of analysis that became known as spatial science. The spread of computing technology facilitated understandings of geographic phenomena as geometric relations across

> **Spatial science** Form of geography associated with quantitative analysis of locations and distributions

space that could be objectively measured, with foreign policy made on this rational basis. Generally speaking, this abstract form of geopolitics envisioned the world as a Cartesian plane, with geopolitical actors (states) located at specific coordinates and weighted according to their power, resources, etc., allowing models to be built. Much like prior formulations of geopolitics (the work of American geographer Nicholas Spykman in particular foreshadowed this approach, with his notions of power degrading with distance from its epicenter), this "new" geopolitics assumed an anarchic, violent world in which the gain of territory and resources is the main motivating force in action.

> **Cartesian plane** 2-D surface with location-finding grid associated with it

However, this reincarnation of "objective" geopolitics was quickly joined by a radical refiguring of geopolitics led by the French geographer Yves Lacoste. Where the quantitative form of geopolitics was related to the technological innovation of the 1970s, Lacoste's more openly partisan geopolitics reflected the Marxism and radicalism of that same decade. His 1973 paper on the geography of U.S. bombing patterns near Vietnam's Red River exposed the United States's attempt to destroy the dike system that maintained the region's agricultural system. This paper was followed by a pamphlet entitled *The purpose of geography is, above all, the making of war!* that made clear the relationship between professional geographers and the maintenance of inequality around the world. Indeed, historically geography has been in the first instance about mapping places to be colonized

> **Marxism** Political-economic theory and practice that argues that economic exploitation is at the root of society

and later about teaching imperial subjects about the extent of their domain. Further, as we have seen, the history of geopolitics in the twentieth
century is one fraught with dubious forays into imperialism and warfare.
While linguistic differences, among other things, have kept Lacoste from
being more integrated with the Anglophone geopolitics community, his
interventions marked a turning point in the way geopolitics was conceived of in the Anglophone world.

CRITICAL GEOPOLITICS

> **Poststructuralism** Body
> of thought that takes
> meaning as not pregiven

In the late 1980s, the Anglophone political
geography community began to belatedly
incorporate intellectual currents that were
already existent elsewhere in the social sciences. These currents were collectively
known as poststructuralism, and they
downplayed (but did not disparage) the role of economic and political
structures in social life. Those involved in poststructuralism generally
advocated the importance of language and culture, alongside those economic and political structures, in understanding social outcomes. Those
actively incorporating poststructuralism into geopolitics, such as Gearóid

> **Critical geopolitics**
> Intellectual movement
> dedicated to questioning
> the geographic assump-
> tions of global politics

Ó Tuathail (1996), John Agnew (1994), and
Simon Dalby (1991), sought to refashion the
subdiscipline as something more contemporary and dynamic than the static geopolitics of the past. Hence, their project—
dubbed critical geopolitics—focused on
discourse.

Discourse

Discourse is a term that refers to the way in which we talk about things.
Discourses are key to any understanding of the world—geopolitical or
otherwise. A short example of geopolitical discourse can be found in the
oft-used phrase "Middle East" to describe the region around today's
countries of Iraq, Israel, and Saudi Arabia (among others). This term,
upon consideration, is meaningless without a center point against which

> **Discourse** A way of
> talking and thinking about
> a subject

the Middle East is being measured—if
something is the "East" it must be east of
something in particular. That center point
is Britain, which dominated the region after World War I. Using this term then tac-

itly accepts the British claim to be the center of the world (which is cartographically mirrored by their successful mapping of the prime meridian to go right through the outskirts of London). This may seem innocent enough, but consider the Iraqi citizen who self-identifies as a Middle Easterner—they have accepted a term that reinforces their own geopolitical marginality. That someone could view themselves as anything other than the center of their own world illustrates a fundamental tenet of the poststructuralist turn—that words, and discourse, have great power. It is worth remembering that "geography" can be translated from the Greek as "earth-writing." This term comes from geography's early definition as the science of mapping and dividing the world up into natural regions. However, today it lends a new meaning as increasingly geography is about studying the ways in which we inscribe meanings into places—literally dividing the world up into spaces with which we associate values.

So, where classical geopolitics sought to root its analyses in "the way the world is," critical geopolitics interrogates how and why we have come to think of the world (or parts of it) in a certain way. This is a very useful intellectual move, as it calls into question all sorts of received wisdom, including that which we produce now. For instance, if we view classical geopolitics as a discourse rather than the truth about the world, we can identify several features of international politics that are neglected, and several that are overemphasized. For instance, every classical geopolitical thinker from Ratzel on assumes the primacy of the state in global affairs. Indeed, for these thinkers it was their job to advance their own state among the others. The world is seemingly naturally composed of these states, which unproblematically reflect cultural and historical divisions among humanity. One term, still used today to great advantage by politicians because of its geopolitical heft, is "the national interest." By terming something the national interest a leader can rhetorically undercut any opposition, who by definition are then against what is best for the country (subtly identifying the opposition as traitors is a time-honored tactic in democratic politics). However, that term elides a great many distinctions between the people of the nation. Is free trade in the national interest of the United States? Perhaps for the executives who run Abercrombie & Fitch, but perhaps not for North Carolina textile workers. By adopting the state as the only frame through which geopolitical decisions can be legitimately made (a notion called state-centrism), less powerful groups and individuals are literally erased from consideration.

> **State-centrism** The assumption that states are the natural unit of analysis in geopolitics

The Role of Cultural Authority and the Media

Related to this idea of the national interest is the question of cultural power—which is key to being able to convince others that your idea of the national interest is what their idea of the national interest should be. Traditionally, this job was assumed by scholars (like Mackinder and Mahan) and by politicians. In either case, it was usually older male elites who used their positions in authority to silence alternatives. In the case of Mackinder, Mahan, and other classical geopolitical scholars, their claim to a comprehensive, scientific understanding of the world gave their views significance. For today's politicians that significance comes from their access to experts, intelligence agencies, and the like. In either case, the assumption of greater understanding that comes with these positions masks the potential abuse of that position to frame geopolitical knowledge in ways that are beneficial to those doing the framing. This does not have to be intentional: everyone's perspective on the world is partial and situated: this means that we cannot help but see the world through our own eyes, and this necessarily introduces biases. Hence, critical geopolitical scholars try to avoid grand, sweeping statements about the way the world works. Instead these scholars try to show how the world looks differently from these different perspectives, and how those with greater cultural power shape the overall geopolitical order.

This necessarily involves studying geopolitical perspectives and traditions associated with people and groups other than the traditional elite. A good example of this expanded view of geopolitics would be the attention paid to the media in critical geopolitics. One of the foundational works in this regard was written by Joanne Sharp (1996; 2000), who analyzed the ways in which the magazine *Reader's Digest* produced a Cold War–based discourse in which the United States was the polar opposite of the Soviet Union. Sometimes taking an even tougher stance on the Soviet Union than contemporary presidential administrations, the publishers of *Reader's Digest* exercised their cultural power in an effort to shape the overarching discourse of the day. To many of the media-savvy readers of this book the idea that the media have ideological "slant" might seem obvious—but it would never have received any attention from classical geopolitical scholars, who would see no relevance in the media. This illustrates just how far geopolitics has changed during the twentieth century.

One of the ways in which critical geopolitics has been very successful is through focusing on the ways in which power and discourse circulate and reinforce each other. As the example of *Reader's Digest* shows, those with cultural power can exercise influence over those with less cultural power. However, very few people (if any) have the power to *impose* their view on everyone else. Rather, discourses only become successful if they intersect with, or are co-opted by, a range of people's interests. In other words, if the publisher of *Reader's Digest* had promoted the idea that America and the Soviet Union were not so different after all, the magazine might have been investigated by Senator Joseph McCarthy's House Un-American Activities Committee and shut down by J. Edgar Hoover's FBI. Both of those men made their careers out of so-called red-baiting (trying to "out" suspected Communists). As it was, *Reader's Digest* simply reinforced discourses of anti-Communism that were circulating in the highest levels of the U.S. government. Tracing these connections is key to understanding how the anti-Communism that was seen as "the national interest" became known as such.

Formal Geopolitics

Scholars of critical geopolitics have identified three different types of geopolitical discourse. These are very broad categories and some discourse seems to bridge these categories rather confusingly. Nevertheless, the categories are quite useful in day-to-day usage (see table 1.1). The first category is "formal geopolitics." This is geopolitical discourse produced by academics, either in university settings or in more overtly political think

> **Think tanks**
> Organizations dedicated to policy analysis

tanks like the Heritage Foundation or the Brookings Institution. A think tank is an institution that is funded to conduct research to advance the policy goals of its supporters. Thus, all of the classical geopolitical thinking that was described at the beginning of this chapter can be described as formal geopolitics. Despite our focus here on critical geopolitics, we should not lose sight of the fact that much of the work done in political science and international affairs is done within the tradition of classical geopolitics— the tradition of scholars informing policy makers about "how the world is" and telling them what to do to maximize the state's power. For instance, President George W. Bush's second secretary of state, Condoleezza Rice, was a professor of political science at Stanford University who initially gained the ear of the Reagan administration and subsequently the

Table 1.1. Definitions of Formal, Practical, and Popular Geopolitics (adapted from Ó Tuathail 1996)

Type of Geopolitics	Definition
Formal Geopolitics	Discourse associated with academics and think tanks
Practical Geopolitics	Discourse associated with policy makers
Popular Geopolitics	Discourse associated with everyday people

George H. W. Bush administration, serving as an expert on the Soviet Union. From this example we can see that formal geopolitical discourse is generally formulated to feed into government decision making.

Practical Geopolitics

The move of Dr. Rice into government symbolizes our segue into the second type of geopolitical discourse, "practical geopolitics." This is the discourse used by politicians and policy makers. While it often follows from formal geopolitical theorizing, it frequently takes on a life of its own as politicians seek to frame debate to advantage themselves. A classic example of practical geopolitical rhetoric would be the 2002 presidential proclamation of an "axis of evil." In his State of the Union speech, President George W. Bush proclaimed that Iraq, Iran, and North Korea "constitute an axis of evil, arming to threaten the peace of the world. By seeking weapons of mass destruction, these regimes pose a grave and growing danger. They could provide these arms to terrorists, giving them the means to match their hatred." The description of these countries as an "axis" has subsequently been critiqued as being misleading in that there was no evidence of any cooperation between the three countries (in fact, Iraq and Iran are, in recent times, enemies). Nevertheless, by conjuring up an image of an alliance and naming that alliance after the Axis powers of World War II, Bush was able to simultaneously position the United States discursively as an "Allied" force for good and also implicitly make an argument for a preemptive strike against these countries (as the popular consensus is that the Allied powers should have stood up to Hitler earlier rather than wait for the 1939 invasion of Poland). Practical geopolitics may seem to be the most important form of geopolitical discourse; it is certainly the "business end" of geopolitics, as the words of politicians can unleash death and destruction on the objects of their discourse. However, it is not necessarily the most common. That honor is held by the third type of geopolitical discourse, popular geopolitics.

Popular Geopolitics

Popular geopolitics refers to the everyday geopolitical discourse that citizens are immersed in every day. In a democratic society (which is not a given, of course) popular consent is necessary to some degree for the conduct of foreign policy. If President Bush had come on television after the attacks on the World Trade Center and Pentagon in 2001 and said "we know who did this; the terrorists are based in Canada," and subsequently began to bomb Canada the way the United States in actuality began to bomb Afghanistan, there would have been a huge public outcry and it is hard to imagine how the war could continue to be prosecuted. Now this is of course an outlandish scenario—but it is worth thinking about why it is outlandish. Part of what critical geopolitics does best is denaturalize what appears to be commonsense geopolitical knowledge. Of course the American population would never stand for the bombing of Canada. But why, then, does it stand for, and indeed broadly speaking support, the continued bombing of Afghanistan?

The answer lies in the ways in which Canada and Afghanistan are positioned within popular geopolitical discourse in the United States. To make a gross generalization (usually to be avoided), most Americans think of Canada as cheerful, polite neighbors to the north. It is a country of hockey, beer, and other overly simplistic but generally amiable associations. As for Afghanistan, most Americans had (in 2001) very few associations with the country. While Canadians might object (rightfully) to being reduced to beer-guzzling hockey fanatics, I would argue it is certainly more advantageous than the image of Afghanistan as a far-away, exotic, and dangerous (and, of course, Islamic) locale that most Americans simultaneously held. Fundamentally, Canadians would be seen as more similar to Americans than Afghanis are. Thus, when President Bush told the American people that the terrorists were in Afghanistan, it slipped convincingly into the relatively blank slate associated with the country in popular American discourse. It *seemed* like the kind of place that terrorists might be hiding. Indeed, it was—none of this is meant to undermine that fact. However, remember that discourse is how we talk about the world; while it is separate from "what really is," it is impossible to understand "what really is" without reference to language and discourse. How did Afghanistan come to be understood this way? That, by and large, is the subject of the rest of this book. Why do we think of the world the way we do? What processes feed into these understandings?

Popular geopolitics involves the study of the media in virtually all its forms. We use the word so often just referring to the news media that we often forget the root meaning of it—media are avenues through which information is *mediated* to us. Any formal or practical geopolitical discourse needs to be broadly disseminated if it is to become a popular geopolitical discourse. In addition, it is important to remember that geopolitical discourses can be formulated "from below" by grassroots discussion. Those, too, would have to be mediated to a larger audience to become truly popular. The focus of popular geopolitics on the media includes the news media (newspapers, TV journalism, etc.) and, most importantly for this book, popular culture, such as comic books, television shows, novels, movies, music, and the Internet. We live in a mediated world—all that we know about the world beyond our personal experience comes to us via various media, whether it is the printed word, the televisual, radio, or something else entirely. The media even colonize our personal experiences; it is almost impossible to go somewhere without preconceived notions of what to look at and how to feel about it. What would it be like to experience a place, not having read about it or seen it on screen? Thus, the media play a major role in not only how we see the world, but also how we make sense of it.

This mediation of the world is geopolitical because it occurs in ways that associate values and behaviors with various parts of the world, which in turn influences the ways in which people interact. For example, during the Reagan administration there was a steady flow of anti-Communist action films, including *Red Dawn* (1984), in which the Soviets, Cubans, and Nicaraguans launch an unlikely invasion of Colorado only to be turned back in part by a group of American teenagers who refuse to collaborate, and *Rocky IV* (1985), in which the "Italian Stallion" defeats a much bigger, steroid-enhanced Soviet boxer through sheer American hard work and willpower. In the latter movie, the final match takes place in Moscow and the crowd is so convinced that Rocky deserves to win by what they see that they begin to chant his name—even the Soviet leader (a Mikhail Gorbachev look-alike) is compelled to stand and applaud Rocky's superiority.

Although both movies are somewhat comical in retrospect now that the Cold War is long over, they served to reinforce what was common sense to me at the time—the Soviets wanted to defeat (and possibly kill) Americans if they could, and would utilize underhanded trickery to do so (the steroids), but the United States would always triumph because of innate traits that made us successful in geopolitics (and boxing, apparently). Later, completely different villains would take the place of the Soviets with, nevertheless, similarly derogatory characterizations. There is plenty more that could be discussed about these movies but we will have to limit our discussion here to providing an example about how popular culture serves to mediate popular geopolitical discourse about who "we" are and what "our" position in the world is vis-à-vis those who are different than us.

BASIC CONCEPTS OF POPULAR GEOPOLITICS

Imagined Communities

Now it is worth taking a moment to study some of the work outside of geopolitics that has been very influential in the popular geopolitics we will be focusing on for the rest of the book. The first of these ideas is that of the imagined community. In order to understand this idea, you have to understand the difference between "states" and "nations." While in everyday language we use the term "nation" to mean "country," in the world of academia "state" actually means "country." This is particularly confusing in the United States, where "state" colloqui-ally refers to a smaller component of the country. For the purposes of this book, however, we will use the academic terms—

> **Imagined communities**
> Societies brought into existence by the use of common literature and media

with "state" meaning a full-fledged country (like France) and "nation" referring to a group of people who primarily identify with each other (like the French people). Sometimes these two terms roughly coincide (as in France), but you can always find people within the state who belong to another nation and you can always find members of the nation outside the state. Benedict Anderson (1991, 6–7) calls nations "imagined commu-nities" because they are different from regular communities in that they are not based on face-to-face contact:

> It is *imagined* because the members of even the smallest nation will never know most of their fellow-members, meet them, or even hear of them, yet in the minds of each lives the image of their communion. . . . It is imagined as a *community* because, regardless of the actual inequality and exploitation that may prevail in each, the nation is always conceived as a deep, horizontal comradeship.

According to Anderson, these imagined communities sprang into exis-tence shortly after the invention of the printing press. It was then that profit-minded capitalists began to publish in the vernacular languages of particular regions in an effort to boost sales beyond that which the Latin-reading elites (the church and aristocracy) could provide. This had three effects. First, it began to standardize regional dialects, creating a group of people with a recognizably common cultural characteristic (language). Second, it undermined the power of the Latin-reading elites by providing access to religiously and politically sensitive texts to the masses. Finally, and crucially for popular geopolitics, it created an avenue (or medium) through which consumers of popular texts and culture could gain com-mon understandings of what was going on in the life of this new com-munity, this new nation.

However correct Anderson might be, the story does not end there. Very few people would be willing to kill or be killed in the name of an "imag-ined community" that results from common reading material. Neverthe-less, thousands (if not more) die every year under the banner of national-ism. This is because nations are not popularly understood the way that Anderson has described them—in most of the world nations are seen as primordial entities, with roots back in the mists of time. For example, to-day's Irish are envisioned by advocates of primordial nationalism as a branch of the Celtic race that has existed as long as there are written records. This theory carries with it associations of racialism, but its eigh-teenth-century proponents were more interested in language as an indica-tor of identity. Unlike Anderson, who sees language as a commonality that links otherwise disparate people together, the primordialists like Jo-hann Herder believed that, because people in different nations thought in different languages, they would innately think different things (and peo-ple in the same nation would think similar things). Thus, there is a funda-mental difference between people of different nations. You can see how it is a short trip through German philosophy from the language-based na-tionalism of Herder to the organic state of Ratzel described at the begin-ning of the chapter. It is this view of the nation that has become popu-lar—as something hardwired and fundamental. Even among groups where a primordial perspective on the nation seems somewhat abhor-rent—like the United States—the fundamental importance of the nation to an individual's identity remains.

Geopolitical Imaginations

Once we see nations not as fundamental, always-existing identities but rather as identities contingent on relatively recent historical processes and our relationship to common media, we can start to see how a focus on discourse, and everyday practices such as saluting the flag, is neces-sary for explaining why people continue to feel this strongly about their nation well after its "imagining." Part of the reason for this is that the imagined community of the nation serves as a foundation point for what Edward Said (1978) referred to as "imagined geographies." Anyone at-tempting to make sense of the world must resort to exactly the kind of generalities that are inherent to the idea of the nation. Imagined geogra-phies are collections of facts and stereotypes about places in the world that together compose an individual's (or a group's) worldview. In a way we already discussed imaginary geographies when we discussed the difficulty of fitting Canada into Americans' conceptions of terrorism and the relative ease with which the Bush administration was able to bomb Afghanistan.

Another example would be Said's classic term "Orientalism," which he used to refer to a way of thinking about the Middle East. While he was specifically referring to British and French imaginary geographies of the Arab world, his term has been used by others to refer to any imaginary geography of "the East" that stereotypes the people there as exotic, premodern, emotional, and indo-lent. This stereotype was used to describe

Orientalism Belief that there is a fundamental distinction (and opposi-tion) between Western and Eastern societies

Arabs and Muslims anywhere in the region, eliding the differences between, for example, the people of Oman and the people of Algeria. It became politically useful to think of "the Orient" as lazy and backwards because it justified the intervention of the British and French (and, later, the Americans) in the region as being "for their own good." In the discipline of geography, the phrase "imaginary geographies" has usually been inverted to become "geographical imaginations" (e.g., Gregory 1994), and in this book we will twist it yet further, referring more often to "geopolitical imaginations," a phrase that heightens the sense of the power and danger that is mediated along with these discourses.

> **Geopolitical imagination**
> A person's (or society's) constellation of taken-for-granted truths about the world and the way in which power should be utilized in that world

Banal Nationalism

Geopolitical imaginations are often, though not always, conceived in largely national terms. Whereas Anderson's concept of imagined communities focused on the ways in which the first nations were formed, Michael Billig's concept of banal nationalism (1995) refers to the ways in which nationalism is perpetuated. Instead of conceiving of nationalism

> **Banal nationalism**
> Everyday ways in which citizens are reminded of their national affiliation; a reservoir that can be drawn on in times of crisis

as something extreme and peripheral to everyday life (as in the oft-cited examples of nativist political parties or separatist movements), Billig suggests that we look at our own daily existence and how already-established nations are reproduced over time (i.e., why people continue to believe in them). This is an important corrective to the notion that nationalism is something "out there" while the modern West has become effectively postnational, and therefore is more rational and less emotional than other parts of the world (see the discussion of Orientalism above). Billig makes effective use of the example of flags (indeed, he refers to banal nationalism as the "flagging" of everyday life). He points out that, if you see a crowd on television at a rally, all waving national flags, you recognize that as nationalism. However, citizens of the West see innumerable flags of their own country every day but they go unremarked because they are "unwaved." These flags include those on public buildings, postage stamps, used car lots, bumper stickers, t-shirts, politicians' lapels, and television weather maps.

Of course, banal nationalism does not have to entail actual flags—rather, any instance when citizens are encouraged to think of themselves using national categories. This can be overt, such as in the Olympics, which has transcended its intentions as a movement to promote peaceful coexistence among nations through amateur athletics to become a platform for nationalist competition, complete with national medal counts. The American broadcasts of the Olympics, for example, drip with flags and personal narratives of the American athletes with competitors from other nations largely serving as narrative foils, hoping to crush American Olympic dreams. The transnational empathy that the Olympics were originally intended to foster has seemingly been extinguished by nationalism. However, just as the Olympics only occur every four years (or every two years if you count summer and winter games), nationalism is not always overtly on display in the countries that Billig studies (like the United States, the United Kingdom, France, etc.). These nations are generally understood to exist, to be stable, and are not in imminent danger. Thus, there is not a huge need to be demonstrative about the nation, and in fact by avoiding overt nationalist displays it is possible to feel superior to the emotionalism of nations that do not have the luxury of sublimating their nationalist displays. Having said that, banal nationalism sustains that identity until it is needed in a more overt form. Consider for instance what occurred in the United States following the attacks on September 11, 2001. Flag manufacturers (generally located in China) were unable to keep up with the soaring demand for American flags following those attacks, leading to flag shortages. Similarly, a wave of patriotic magnets soon adorned seemingly every car in the United States, as consumers went out of their way to demonstrate their commitment to the nation through public display. It was obvious to all who saw this that American nationalism was alive and strong.

Since one of the goals of critical geopolitics is to question the state-centric nature of geopolitics, it is important to consider these processes that lead us all to think of ourselves as national citizens. Why are these national identities so entrenched? Answering that question is one of the goals of the rest of this book—but, in short, the answer lies in concepts like banal nationalism that root our identities in the everyday popular culture in which we are immersed. Further, the way our identities connect to other peoples' identities is of the utmost importance—as is indicated by our example of the Middle East above. Some scholars have expanded Billig's concept to include not just nationalism but also imperialism (Flusty 2007). Imperialism is a complex term, referring generally to the domination of one group by another. Thus, banal imperialism refers to the ways in which domination, a concept that most people find morally abhorrent, is naturalized within the realm of geopolitics and is thus rendered acceptable (see chapter 3).

CHANGING THE WAY GEOPOLITICS WORKS

Both banal nationalism and banal imperialism are about everyday geopolitics. Geopolitics is fundamentally about who "we" are, and what other people are like. Much to the chagrin of geographers and other academics who feel they can answer those questions best, those lessons are increasingly taught via everyday popular culture, whether through films such as *300* (2007) or the user-driven content of the so-called Web 2.0 (blogs, YouTube, Facebook, MySpace, etc.). This book will provide you with the tools to understand the ways in which geopolitics and popular culture intersect in your lived experiences. This raises the question, however, of "why bother?"

The academics who crafted the formal theories of classical geopolitics would not have had to worry about this. They had a clear objective: to uncover the hidden truths about geography and politics and use those truths to advantage their own states and nations. There were lives, resources, territory, and treasure on the line and academics were part of the national repertoire of weapons in an ongoing competition with other states and nations. Critical geopolitics, however, seeks to establish a different relationship between academia and power. Critical geopolitics, as a project, is extraordinarily well-aware of the discipline of geography's complicity in past imperialisms. Indeed, the mapping of new territories in the post-Columbian era (1492–present) has usually been followed by the marching of armies. Critical geopolitics then is not about being aligned with state power, which is sometimes a politically unpopular position to take. Although most scholars of critical geopolitics would love for their ideas to be taken up by policy makers, I suspect most doubt they ever will be. For instance, the probability of a state's government voluntarily dissolving, having been convinced of their own state's lack of historical underpinnings, is probably next to nil.

However, academic ideas such as those espoused in this book do filter through the political/cultural system, as we outlined earlier in the case of formal, practical, and popular geopolitics. For instance, a recent article by journalist Ian Black (2007) in *The Guardian* (a British newspaper) focused on the claim by King Abdullah of Jordan that a "Shia Crescent" was emerging in the Middle East, an evocative phrase describing the rise of sectarian conflict within the Islamic world between the Shi'a and the Sunni (the two major sects within Islam). The story details how the term was perceived to be: "simply too frank; it was simplistic, too, smoothing over local factors of ethnicity and nationalism to provide a single, overarching explanation." The Jordanian intelligence chief who devised the turn of phrase was later fired because of the adverse reaction. In a region that has borne the burden of conflict associated with past phrases such as

"Axis of Evil" and "Arc of Crisis" (see Sidaway 1998), perhaps this public rejection of the reductionism found in these sound bites marks a turning point. Of course, it would be ridiculous to claim that critical geopolitics, as a group of people involved in an academic movement, is solely responsible for this event. However, it is not ridiculous to think that critical geopolitics played a part.

While it is fair to be skeptical that critical geopolitics can "save the world," it is not so wrong to hope that it can make it a better place, and even manage to improve some lives here and there by exposing the discursive and material bases for conflict. In regards to popular geopolitics, this requires a new, critical appraisal of popular culture and its role in helping constitute geopolitical imaginations. It is to that task that we now turn.

2

✛

Popular Culture

Theories, Methods, and Intertextuality

The study of popular culture is a relatively recent phenomenon in academia, generally dating back to the 1960s and the founding of the Centre for Contemporary Cultural Studies at the University of Birmingham (UK). However, the study of culture has a long and privileged position within the academy—one need only think of the literature courses that are usually required in any liberal arts curriculum, or the art and music history courses that usually supplement them. For the most part, these courses are the result of early ideas about what going to college should be about: educating young men (women of course, largely being barred at the time) so that they can become gentlemen in society. According to Oxford poet and cultural critic Matthew Arnold (1869), culture was about "the best that has been thought and said in the world." A basic knowledge of that canon of cultural tradition was seen as a civilizing influence that could bring about social cohesion, inasmuch as knowledge of these topics brought with it authority over those who did not have that knowledge. Thus, the study of culture was limited to the "highlights," and was limited to forms of culture that were associated with social elites (painting, sculpture, classical music, etc.). This book, however, is primarily concerned with popular culture. So what is the difference?

DEFINING POPULAR CULTURE

Popular vs. High Culture

Most definitions of popular culture involve mass consumption—that is, popular culture is available to most people in a society relatively easily.

This includes a wide variety of goods and activities, such as magazines, television shows, sports activities, the cinema, comic books, novels, and the Internet. Popular culture, as described above, is framed as the opposite of *high culture*, or the culture of elites. Popular culture was first conceived of, and deemed a threat, with the invention of the printing press in the 1400s, which began to shift cultural authority away from elites to new sources of cultural production. Geopolitically, this was visible with the Protestant Reformation, which sparked several wars in the 1500s and early 1600s as the authority of the Catholic Church to interpret scripture was devolved to "the masses" by the proliferation of Bibles in popular languages (rather than Latin).

> **High culture** Culture distinguished by its connection to cultural elites

That was just the beginning, however, and ever since then authority figures (from national governments to parents) have anxiously wondered what their "subjects" were reading, listening to, or seeing. Governments have often been concerned with other sources of information "contaminating" their citizens, and indeed the social sciences' first foray into studying the content of messages came during World War II as the Allies became concerned about German propaganda efforts (Severin and Tankard Jr. 1992). Similarly, recent news stories about the effect of MySpace/Facebook culture or R&B music on adolescents mirror earlier concerns with "propaganda" in their anxiety about the mediated messages in which youth are immersed.

The rise of popular culture primarily aimed at young people stems from the rise in post–World War II prosperity in North America and Western Europe, where for the first time most households could have a television and young people had their own spending money, either from parental allowances or from their own part-time jobs (which, also for the first time, did not have to be used for household purposes). This increase in disposable income led in turn to the growth of companies dedicated to mass consumerism, particularly the growth of Hollywood studios, record companies, and other corporations that cater to the youth demographic.

This notion of popular culture as degraded (or degrading) lingers, and can be heard in every moan and groan from the intelligentsia over the amount of time spent in the press discussing the antics of celebrities such as Britney Spears and Lindsay Lohan. However, the line between popular and high culture is not as distinct as advocates of high culture (or popular culture) would like to imagine. Producers of each form of culture draw inspira-

> **Pop Art** Visual art that reuses pop culture commodities to make high culture art

tion from the other side. For instance, the Pop Art movement of the 1950s and 1960s illustrated the fuzziness of the borders between high and popular culture. This fuzziness has only grown, with popular authors like Stephen King now under more scholarly

> **Paris Review** An elite literary magazine in which many successful novelists first appeared

scrutiny (e.g., Badley 1996) and opera stars like the late Luciano Pavarotti even performing on *Saturday Night Live,* collaborating with rock bands like U2, and singing at the opening of the 1990 World Cup. Further, the cultural authority that used to belong to the literati like the *Paris Review* is now increasingly shared with popular culture institutions like *Rolling Stone* magazine and MTV. From all this hybridity of popular and high culture we can see that there really is not a clear divider between the two; instead we are left with the issue of aesthetics. High culture is ultimately defined as being of "higher quality" than popular culture, but as quality is an element of personal taste this divide is ultimately indefensible.

Popular vs. Folk Culture

Popular culture has also been defined through its opposition to folk culture, rather than high culture, particularly within the discipline of geography. Folk culture can be defined as traditional culture linked to a particular place and people. Folk culture has historically been understood within geography in relation to the pressures supposedly put upon it by globalization. Globalization is another slippery concept (like geopolitics), but for the purposes of this discussion we will define it as an intensification of global connectivity, driven in part by revolutions in transportation and telecommunications over the last thirty years. The effect of these revolutions has been called time/space compression, which refers to the decrease in relative distance between places.

> **Folk culture** Culture associated with a specific place, often one deemed premodern

> **Globalization** Intensification of spatial interactions associated with revolutions in transportation and communications

> **Time/space compression** Decline of relative distance caused by globalization

Time/space compression has significant implications for local economies, however, as goods and services now circulate around the globe with increasing ease. Some view this as a good thing, with cross-fertilization of culture providing opportunities for greater international understanding, embodied in popular culture such as "ethnic" restaurants, "world music," and the recent yoga boom in the United States and Western Europe. Others view this negatively as the commodification of difference, with elements of folk culture being stripped of their local meaning and sold to Western consumers who use it to project a cosmopolitan, modern identity predicated on their worldliness. This practice is clearly linked to the Orientalism described in the previous chapter, with the West defined by its progress and universality and the East (or, here, the rest of the world) defined by its exotic traditional folk culture, which is linked to the past as well as particular to a specific region (and, thus, particular rather than universal). Because of this, popular culture is thought of in many parts of the world as a steamroller, incorporating into itself the parts of folk culture that Western consumers want but destroying the rest in a blitz of modern Western commodities and entertainment.

In particular, this charge is often leveled at American culture, in part because the United States is the chief proponent of free trade around the world (but, as with the inclusion of folk culture into popular culture, only on its own terms). Further, the United States dominates many of the culture industries, like Hollywood and the music industry. This domination is sometimes referred to as cultural imperialism, which is the deliberate attempt to supplant local culture and make a people consumers of your culture rather than producers of their own (Tomlinson 2001). As we shall see in the following chapters, producing your own culture is important because it allows local control of the discourses through which your identity is formulated and circulated (or at least local *influence*—see especially chapter 7).

Cultural imperialism
Promotion of one country's culture in another country's territory

However, others have seen this hypothesis of increasing homogeneity as misleading. An assumption of the "cultural imperialism" hypothesis is that popular culture is limited to material goods, and excludes cultural practices. Put another way, you are what you consume. In fact, many American (and other Western) goods take on entirely different meanings when used in non-American or non-Western contexts. For example, one classic study analyzed the meanings that audiences in the United States, Israel, and Japan found in the consumption of the equally classic television soap opera *Dallas*, and found that each audience took something different from the show because each audience *brought* something different to the show (Liebes and Katz 1990). Thus, while globalization might cause goods to circulate more widely, it will not erode the differences that make places distinct.

The similarities between the "popular culture vs. high culture" and "popular culture vs. folk culture" paradigms is instructive. Both paradigms are ultimately definitions of popular culture, in which popular culture and its polar opposite constitute each other (i.e., it would be impossible to have "popular culture" if there was no high culture or folk culture with which to contrast it). In both definitions popular culture is defined as threatening: high culture is conceived of as a bulwark of civilization, and folk culture is similarly conceptualized as the difference within the world that makes life interesting (for those with the resources to partake in it). However, the power imputed to popular culture in that act of threatening is in some ways negated by the dim view that many cultural authorities (and those aspiring to that authority) take of popular culture. Rarely do critics say that orchestra audiences are smaller and aging rapidly because *American Idol* is better. Equally rarely do we hear that Hollywood films do better than art house foreign cinema because they are better. Instead, we hear that the fault lies with the audience—"they just don't get good culture." This shift from the quality of the popular culture to the quality of the audience is instructive. It tells us that popular culture/high culture/folk culture is closely linked to identity—that of the people who produce it, the people who consume it, and the people who use it to their own ends. It is through popular culture (at least in part) that we decide who we are, who we want to be, and how we want people to understand us. Hence, as we saw in the preceding chapter, popular culture and geopolitics are intertwined in this field of popular geopolitics. So, how do we move forward from this understanding to theorize the relationship between popular culture and geopolitics?

THEORIZING POPULAR CULTURE

As we have seen, early ideas about the nature of popular culture stemmed from the anxiety that many elites held of the effect of popular culture on the masses and the maintenance of the social hierarchy. This anxiety could not be expressed as such, and so indulging in popular culture was pathologized, with some claiming that popular culture aficionados were endangered by their behavior. The following 1965 critique of jazz fans is now commonly directed at video gamers and their compatriots: "looking through magazines and newspapers and listening to jazz music does not merely fail to help him [the pop culture fan, apparently male by default], it prevents him from normal development" (Leavis 1965, 104). However, this conservative critique mirrored earlier engagements with popular culture by left-leaning academics, most obviously the Marxist-inspired Frankfurt School.

The Frankfurt School and Classical Marxism

The Frankfurt School refers to a loosely associated group of scholars that coalesced around the Institute for Social Research at the University of Frankfurt in the early 1930s. These scholars were all influenced to some extent by the ideas of Marxism. According to Marxist thought, popular culture is only understandable through analysis of the economic structure that produced it. Therefore, while you might consider the aesthetic or other qualities of a Hollywood blockbuster like *Wedding Crashers* (2005), a proper analysis requires a fundamental understanding of the circumstances that originally made Hollywood cinema popular. Max Horkheimer, Theodor Adorno, Walter Benjamin, and other Frankfurt School scholars took that classical Marxist view of popular culture and tried to update it to explain the flowering of popular culture in the twentieth century. Adorno and Horkheimer (1979) argued for the understanding of popular culture as the result of the "culture industry," a monolithic, faceless element of the capitalist economy that sedates the masses with pleasure, causing them to ignore their own economic alienation and subordination. In much the same way that capitalism produces desires that might be achieved in the short to middle term (e.g., buying a dream car or taking a cruise), thereby convincing workers to participate in the capitalist system rather than creating a new system that might be more advantageous in the long term, capitalism produces popular culture that makes workers consider only the pleasures that can be achieved soon—like watching your favorite television shows or seeing *Wedding Crashers*. By stringing workers along in this way popular culture is part of a system that keeps workers from rising up and doing something more politically meaningful.

This is a very popular concept today among the cultural critics, because it allows them to reinforce their own class status by disdaining popular culture in favor of high culture, which as we have seen above is a common *modus operandi*. However, most of these people are not Marxists—rather they have appropriated the critique for their own purposes. For example, there has been much annoyance lately in certain circles (e.g., Kohut and Parker 2007) over the amount of press coverage that the results of reality television competitions receive, in contrast to, among other things, the

> **Frankfurt School**
> A collection of dissident Marxists who studied society from the 1930s onward

> **Culture industry** In Frankfurt School, monolithic source of popular culture believed to dominate workers' consciousness

wars in Iraq (2003–present) and Afghanistan (2001–present). Without being Marxist, this critique enables popular culture to be designated as that which distracts from "real" issues. The common denominator

> **Agency** Ability to effect change

between the Frankfurt School and the more contemporary use of their ideas comes in their theorization of popular culture consumers. Here the term "consumer" takes on something of a literal meaning in that consumers of popular culture are denied any agency—the effects of the popular culture are encoded in the moment of production, leaving consumers in the role of zombies, internalizing the preferred meanings of the popular culture with which they are presented. While the intent of the Frankfurt School was to explain that the working classes were not rebelling because of the machinations of capital, it effectively blamed the working classes for not being able to resist popular culture in favor of more authentic, revolutionary culture.

(Post)Marxism and Consumption: Gramsci, Foucault, and de Certeau

In contrast with the classical Marxist critique just described, a second tradition has emerged and has become entrenched in academia under the term "cultural studies." Whereas the Frankfurt School was associated with German scholars (who largely migrated to the United States), this particular perspective originated in the United Kingdom, although it draws from an international group of theorists who would not have necessarily thought of themselves as part of cultural studies (these influences will be discussed below).

> **Cultural studies**
> Academic movement, begun in Birmingham (U.K.), that seeks to connect the issues of culture, agency, and power

The leading names of early cultural studies included Stuart Hall, Richard Hoggart, Raymond Williams, and others. Together they launched a new way of thinking about popular culture. Rather than viewing popular culture as degraded or deviant, they saw it as just another part of the multitude of ways in which people come to share meaning in their lives. By this I mean that the consumption of similar elements of popular culture provides a common cultural framework for seeing, interpreting, and ultimately finding meaning in the world:

> Culture, it is argued, is not so much a set of things—novels and paintings or TV programmes or comics—as a process, a set of practices. Primarily, culture is concerned with the production and exchange of meanings—the "giving

and taking of meaning"—between the members of a society or group. . . . Thus culture depends on its participants interpreting meaningfully what is around them, and "making sense" of the world, in broadly similar ways. (Hall 1997, 2)

Thus, popular culture can be something good (or bad). It can be something essential, it can provide social cohesion and common understanding.

This formation of cultural studies as an intellectual movement occurred in the wake of the Soviet invasion of Hungary in 1956, which saw disillusioned Marxists in the West abandoning communist orthodoxy and looking for new theories that were nonetheless critical of capitalism. One inspirational figure to arise in this rethinking of Marxism was Antonio Gramsci, who had died decades before in relative obscurity. Gramsci was a founder and one-time leader of the Italian Communist Party who, like many of his colleagues, found themselves in real jeopardy when the Fascists took over in 1922. In 1926 he was jailed and remained in prison until he died from poor health in 1937, but during this time he committed many of his most influential ideas to paper.

Gramsci's starting point was that it was impossible for capitalist elites to coerce the working classes into doing the elites' will because there were simply too many workers if they were united as a result of attempted coercion. Instead, the domination that Gramsci saw around him could only come as a result of a reframing of the debate. His *Prison Notebooks* (1992) famously outlined his concept of hegemony, which is the process by which class is deemed beyond politics. The key to the prevention of a workers' revolution, according to Gramsci, lay in making the elites' culture hegemonic throughout society. Because of this, the working class no longer saw its own best interest, but rather viewed its interests as coinciding with those of the elites. Examples of this false consciousness at work include working-class nationalism and the liberal belief in the primacy of the individual, both of which are broadly visible in today's society and contribute to the erosion of working-class solidarity. Thus, Gramsci argued that Marxists should first attempt to gain hegemony over working-class culture by loading it with their own anticapitalist ideology, and only then should an actual revolution take place (with the terms of conflict back in the Marxists' favor).

> **Hegemony**   Concept that describes the ways in which elites colonize workers' culture, but must adopt some elements of working-class culture as well; now not strictly used in relation to class

> **False consciousness**
> State of not being aware of your own best interest

It is easy to see the similarities between Gramscian hegemony and the Frankfurt School, but there are a few key differences. Hegemony implies not monolithic domination of workers' minds, as the Frankfurt School does, but rather the co-optation of workers' culture through an almost infinite number of daily social interactions. The consequence of this co-opting is that the elites must make their culture more recognizable by the working class as their own in lots of miniscule, everyday ways. Recent examples from American electoral politics spring to mind, as candidates traditionally fall all over themselves to appear like "one of the people": President George W. Bush's ritualistic brush clearing at his Texas ranch, Michelle Obama's revelation on *The View* that their family eats bacon for breakfast, and John Kerry's less successful attempt in 2004 to connect with the voters via windsurfing. Hegemony does not exactly involve "meeting in the middle," but nevertheless does require some flexibility on the part of elites. This theorization not only imputes more agency to the working class than the classical Marxist perspective (it shows that they have, in effect, negotiating power—even if the end result is that they participate in their own alienation) but it also puts culture (and particularly popular culture, as the most everyday form of mass culture) front and center in an understanding of politics.

The ideas of Gramsci, like most ideas, soon escaped the intentions of their author. Gramsci's focus on culture as a major component of power and politics has been widely understood and adopted by right-wing movements that would have been anathema to Gramsci himself. The association in the United States of the Democratic Party with unions, and thus the white working class, has long roots, but it has been widely recognized over the past couple of decades by many commentators that the Republican Party has sought to shift the debate from a class-based politics to one that emphasizes nationalism and culture, such as debates about immigration and gay marriage (see for example Frank 2004). This has been generally successful since 1980 as a strategy for fusing two disparate economic interests—social conservatives (often working and middle class) and fiscal conservatives (often middle and upper class)—into a working coalition. Another example of this strategy at work at the global scale, rather than the national, is the Cold War itself, which can be interpreted in Gramscian fashion as the muddling of the economic interests of the developing world by the introduction of faux-ideological conflict (effectively sculpting global conflict as east-west rather than north-south). This had the added benefit for the state's ruling class of uniting (virtually) all Soviets and Americans under their particular nationalist banners. But, as Gramsci would predict, that co-optation required concessions in elite political culture. In the case of Western Europe this concession came in the form of the welfare state, and in the case of the United States this came in

> **Welfare state**   State in which there is redistribution from wealthy to poor

the form of a watered-down welfare state. The U.S. version can be differentiated from some of the Western European versions (there are several) by more minimalist government role, such as subsidies for the poor and elderly and regulation of markets. In both forms, however, the welfare state enabled mass consumerism by redistributing some wealth to the working class. This mass consumerism is in many ways the very basis of popular culture.

Another perspective that has been highly influential in cultural studies is the work of Michel Foucault (1974; 1977; 1989). His work seems superficially very similar to that of Gramsci, but there are some key differences which will be drawn out here. Foucault was one of the main theorists in the poststructuralist tradition (see the preceding chapter's discussion of the beginnings of critical geopolitics), and as such he was primarily concerned with discourse and meaning. Because he saw meaning as essentially unhinged from language, he believed that meanings were constantly in flux as different people with varying degrees of power struggled to make their meaning hegemonic—the influence of Gramsci is clearly there. However, unlike Gramsci, Foucault did not adopt the Marxist assumption that economic production and class are at the root of social reality. To paraphrase the two scholars, Gramsci viewed discourse (and popular culture) as the way in which reality was artificially masked from the working class; Foucault would have seen Gramsci's claim as itself a discourse that sought to become hegemonic, no different than the elite discourses against which Gramsci was arguing: "In Foucauldian terms, discourses are not simply reflections or (mis)representations of 'reality'; rather they create their own 'regimes of truth'—the acceptable formulation of problems and solutions to those problems" (Lees 2004, 102–103).

It is the popularity of Foucault's poststructuralism that moves cultural studies away from a strictly Marxist perspective—into something that has been referred to as post-Marxist (Chang 1986). Post-Marxism is a perspective that acknowledges the tremendous insights into economy, culture, and oppression that mainstream Marxism has made over the past century and a half, but denies the Marxist assumption that the only form of oppression that ultimately matters is class-based (all other forms of oppression being also rooted in capitalism). Therefore, Foucauldian analysis of popular culture often focuses on the ways in which popular culture discourses contribute to the creation of hegemony, whether that is patriarchy (gender-based hegemony), bigotry (race-based

> **Post-Marxism**   Beliefs that derive from Marxism but do not share Marxism's focus on economics

hegemony), heteronormativity (sexual preference–based hegemony), or other forms of hegemony. Foucault also provided a boost for the study of popular culture because, like Gramsci (although Foucault usually gets more credit for this), he directs attention away from the massive, depersonalized economic structures of Marxism toward the everyday, banal forms of discourse that permeate daily life.

Foucault's ideas, unlike Gramsci's, have not been adopted by right-wing commentators, which in some ways is interesting because, while Gramsci was an avowed Communist, Foucault was quite apolitical in the traditional sense (although he did advocate for social change). This seeming paradox results from Foucault's belief that there is no truth, but only truth effects, which are quite transitory. As an example, the debate in many parts of the United States about teaching evolution or the "intelligent design" hypothesis in public schools is viewed by both sides in a Gramscian manner—"truth" being on their side, with the other side trying to obfuscate that truth. Foucault would likely see it differently, as two essentially political positions (evangelical Christianity and secular rationalism, both seeking to be the hegemonic philosophy of the United States) trying to legitimate their perspectives—with "truth" being the effect of each side's relative ability to harness the discourse of science to their own ends (and deny that legitimacy to their opponent). Thus, Foucault's ideas are difficult to adopt for traditional political campaigning or criticism because they not only deconstruct your opponent's position but also undermine your own. Foucault remains wildly popular however in academic circles, where his poststructuralist form of hegemony remains incredibly helpful for explaining the political world around us because of its focus on the way in which truth claims are mobilized.

Rounding out our discussion of the theoretical influences on cultural studies is another French theorist, Michel de Certeau. The theorists mentioned thus far in this chapter have been ordered such that they are increasing in the amount of interest they have in the act of consumption—the Frankfurt School paid very little attention to it, Gramsci slightly more, etc. Foucault in particular envisions hegemony as emerging out of the everyday cultural consumption among and between large numbers of people in specific localities. One step further on this spectrum is de Certeau, who in his book, *The Practice of Everyday Life* (1984), theorized about the ways in which consumption occurs. His focus is on the ways in which we perform our everyday, routine lives, often without conscious concern for how we do so. The most influential parts of this work for cultural studies deal with de Certeau's division between tactics and strategies.

Strategies, in de Certeau's formulation, are the hegemonic practices and discourses of institutions, bureaucratically entrenched in particular places and procedures. Because they are institutional, they are powerful but

Table 2.1: **Advantages and Disadvantages of Strategies and Tactics (adapted from de Certeau 1984)**

	Advantages	Disadvantages
Strategies	• Powerful • Vast resources	• Slow • Expensive to maintain
Tactics	• Fast • Cheap	• Weak • Vulnerable

slow, with great resources but also great overhead costs. *Tactics* refer to the practices of individuals who are decentralized, lack power, but are infinitely more flexible than strategic-acting institutions. Subversive and slippery, tactics are incapable of revolutionizing the system but are only strong enough to prevent the crushing of the individual by the institutions and their strategies (see table 2.1 for a summary). The virtue of tactics vis-à-vis strategies is that tactics are utilized in a covert way, avoiding outright confrontation, which is also why it is difficult for social theorists to witness them being used (this in part also explains why the consumption of popular culture is historically undertheorized in comparison to production).

An example of tactical engagement with institutional strategies can be found in the work of Jonathan Leib. He has analyzed license plates for automobiles as governmental strategies to disseminate their favored geopolitical image (e.g., Leib, forthcoming). For example, in 1961 the plates of the Dominican Republic were marked "Era de Trujillo" across the top of the plate. This referred to the decades-long rule of strongman Rafael Trujillo, who dispensed with elections shortly after taking office. When he was assassinated in 1962, however, Leib has noted that drivers quickly dispensed with the top part of their license plate, in what is clearly a tactical maneuver to reshape the discourse of national identity (figure 2.1). This kind of focus on consumption is key to any study of popular geopolitics.

Lacan and Psychoanalysis

Another form of cultural theory has emerged that is quite separate from the work associated with cultural studies, drawing instead from the discipline of psychology. Specifically, it spins out from the practice of psychoanalysis, most generally associated with the work of Sigmund Freud. The theorist most associated with the study of popular culture, however, is Jacques Lacan, who expanded

Psychoanalysis Study of human psychology and behavior

Figure 2.1. Altered Dominican license plate; the unaltered plate has "Era de Trujillo" across the top (Photo: Jonathan Leib)

upon Freud's ideas by linking them with the poststructuralist focus on language and discourse.

Freud (2000) linked sexuality and human development in a narrative that eventually leads to the sublimation of desire into the unconscious. This narrative begins with infancy, when sexuality is undeveloped but in which pleasure nevertheless crystallizes around specific parts of the body. This occurs at a moment prior to the formation of the infant's sense of identity. Later, when gender and identity begin to become significant, children are taught to deny themselves these pleasures, whether because of moral codes, religion, or social propriety. This desire for pleasure, however, does not go away as it is fundamental to humanity—resulting in the development of the unconscious, a reservoir of unacknowledged desire and potentially self-destructive energies.

Lacan (1998) focused his work on the stage in which gender and identity become significant, because he believed that it was during this stage that the unconscious was produced through language (a focus, you might recall, of poststructuralism). One of

Mirror stage
Psychoanalytic concept that describes the moment of identity formation

Lacan's major contributions to psychoanalysis was his description of the mirror stage, in which children begin to recognize the image in the mirror as not actually themselves but just an image, thus composing a coherent subjectivity for themselves where just prior there had been a prelinguistic feeling of unity with the world. This shift from the prelinguistic world (or imaginary, in Lacan's words) to the linguistic (or symbolic) world is critical for the formation of our own identity, but nevertheless creates a gap between the new subject and the old sense of unity with the world that was ruined by the introduction of language and identity. This sense of alienation becomes sublimated (as in Freud)—thus

> **Subjectivity** An individual's sense of self, including perspective, thoughts, emotions, etc.

driving a subconscious desire to seek pleasure in a return to a unified, prelinguistic self. The ability to recognize ourselves in the mirror is key to the formation of subject identities—but it does not have to literally be a mirror. The mirror can be other people or, crucially for the study of popular culture, characters in movies. Lacan is especially popular in film studies because the cinematic screen metaphorically serves as the mirror and the dim lights promote the audience's connection to the movie, enabling a childlike forgetting of ourselves, and a pleasurable return to the presubjective self (consider how often someone who sees a good movie describes it as so good that they forgot where they were).

If Lacan seems a bit far removed from the subject of geopolitics, I believe most scholars of popular geopolitics would agree with you. However, Lacan and psychoanalytical readings of popular culture have become quite popular in the subdisciplines of cultural geography and media geography. Further, Lacan's focus on identity holds out potential for making inroads in the field of geopolitics, where as we have seen identity is key to the construction of geopolitical discourses. Further, the role of the visual gaze in the mirror stage dovetails nicely with the increasing focus on visuality in geopolitics, and the centrality of gender and sexuality to psychoanalysis with the growth of feminist perspectives on geopolitics, so it is perhaps only a matter of time until psychoanalysis becomes a full part of the popular geopolitics repertoire of theories (for some possibilities see Nast 2003).

METHODOLOGIES OF POPULAR GEOPOLITICS

Methodology refers to a set of research practices that should flow naturally from the study's research questions and theoretical assumptions. In other words, how you study popular culture stems from what you hope to learn about it and how you think it works. Gillian Rose (2007) outlines three different sites at which culture can be studied, and three different modalities that can be studied at each site. While she is primarily interested in visual culture, her schema can be adapted for popular culture broadly defined.

> **Methodology** Research methods and the assumptions that are associated with them

Sites and Modalities

Rose's schema is generally rooted in the cultural studies paradigm, which focuses on the poststructuralist view of culture's meaning as fundamentally in process throughout its existence (although she does include psychoanalysis, which has in this book been separated from cultural studies). Thus, she argues that there are three sites at which this meaning is negotiated. The first site is that at which the popular culture is produced—this could be a Hollywood studio, a college radio station, a blogger's basement sanctum sanctorum, or anywhere else where an object or trend originates. Here, the work of the producer crystallizes into the object or practice under study. The second site is the location of the object or practice itself, which can be analyzed and considered in relationship to other objects and practices. The third site is where the popular culture is consumed (either literally or metaphorically) by fans of popular culture.

By way of example, consider a pop music single. We could begin with the site of production, beginning by questioning the meaning of the song for the songwriter, or the ways in which the single was produced to be particularly radio-friendly in order to sell the entire album, making profits for the record company. We could then move to the site of the song itself, inquiring about the key of the song and its potential impact on listeners' emotions, or about the difference between the way the song sounds when heard live in concert versus as a disembodied, heavily produced song on the radio. The final site is that of the audience, where meaning and judgment is ultimately negotiated by listeners. Questions to be asked at this site include what meaning audiences attribute to the song (in contrast to what the songwriter thought it was about) and in what context audiences hear it (is it heard in nightclubs or is it heard at weddings?). These are all questions that are relevant to understanding the meaning of a song, but they all focus on different sites at which the song is encountered. Bruce Springsteen's "Born in the USA" (1984) can be used to trace the importance of these sites. The song was purportedly written about the negative effects of the Vietnam War on returned veterans (and those who did not return). However, the song itself could be described as a bouncy, cheerful anthem in tone, and so it is often understood to be a patriotic song, most famously by President Ronald Reagan when he was running for re-election in 1984.

Rose defines the three modalities as aspects of the processes found at each site. The first of these processes is the technological. When considering this modality a researcher focuses on the medium through which the popular culture is experienced, from the very generic (i.e., is it printed, televisual, auditory, etc.?) to the very particular (i.e., is a song played on a vinyl record or on an MP3 player?). The second of these processes is the compositional, which pays particular attention to the formal characteristics of the popular culture. For example, in regards to movies, scholars have often paid attention to the framing of shots, which literally shape the perspective of the viewer. One example is the movie *Children of Men* (2006), which utilized an amazing 454-second continuous shot (i.e., there were no cuts in the scene as the camera followed the action) to show the movie's protagonist slipping into, and searching through, a building that was under assault by heavy artillery and machine-gun fire. The effect is impressive, providing a sense of realism that inserts the viewer in the movie in a particular way (at one point "blood" spatters on the camera lens and the scene continues unabated). The final aspect of the processes found in each site is the social. This refers to the context in which popular culture is embedded, and thus this changes over time. Popular culture is notoriously short-term in its expected life (as an example look at fashion magazines, which focus on six-month "seasons" as the shelf life of their products), but one does not have to wait very long before older popular culture becomes "retro-chic." Thus, the time and place in which popular culture is produced and consumed matters a great deal in the processes of meaning-making. The combination of sites and modalities allows for several different entry points for researchers to begin a study of popular geopolitics, depending on which sites and modalities they think are theoretically most important for their subject matter.

Research conducted on popular geopolitics has, despite the wide-open possibilities implied by these sites and modalities, often been quite conservative and limited in the types of method used. For reasons of space, this section will focus on the methods that have dominated popular geopolitics, but current research is increasingly thinking "outside the box" and considering the possibilities beyond the previous practices that are described in Rose's book and in other sources on methodology.

Archival Research

Archival research entails a search of historical documents, and can be used in conjunction with any of the research methods detailed below in order to provide the contextual information that is critical to understanding the relationship between popular culture and geopolitics. However, archival research can also be a method unto itself. For example, Klaus Dodds (2005) used archival research to study the role of movie producers in sculpting the geographies of the early Cold War through the settings of the James Bond films (more on this in the next chapter). He did this by comparing the locations found in the earlier novels by author Ian Fleming with the locations chosen for the movies in the mid-1960s to fit the producers' perceptions of the geopolitical moment. The archival research utilized the papers of

> **Archival research**
> Method associated with historical research on documents and other, often bureaucratic, media

Richard Maibaum, the chief screenwriter for thirteen Bond films, in order to find the reasons for changes as well as to document the creative process and the power relations involved in it. Archival research is particularly useful in studying the site of production, as Dodds does, and can speak to all three of Rose's modalities.

The actual practice of archival research is quite idiosyncratic, depending on what archives you are studying and what kind of information you are looking for. Archival research can encompass many different types of data, whether textual, numerical (historical statistics, tables, etc.), visual (advertising, etc.), or auditory (music, oral histories, etc.). However, there are numerous guides available within geography that can help minimize the uncertainty of starting a new project (e.g., Baker 1997; Clifford and Valentine 2003).

Compositional Analysis

Compositional analysis refers to a set of research practices that focus on the compositional modality. An example of this method can be found in the work of Sean Carter and Derek McCormack (2006), who analyze the movie *Black Hawk Down* (2002) in this way. Their analysis focused on the way in which the narrative unfolded, the more technical elements of filming, and how those two elements unite in the "sublime aesthetics of combat" (237). This aesthetic evokes both the unreality of combat and the random-

> **Compositional analysis**
> Organization of elements within a media artifact

ness of events within the frame. The aesthetics of combat in turn impact the audience of the film, enmeshing them in a visceral experience similar to the continuous shot described above in *Children of God*.

The technique of conducting compositional analysis is dependent on the type of popular culture you are analyzing. Further, this type of analysis requires a fairly technical understanding of the type of popular culture that you are analyzing in order to produce a coherent result, as there are significant bodies of knowledge that filmmakers, musicians, writers, fans, and the like utilize when producing or consuming popular culture. These include genre conventions, history of the medium in question, etc. Some grounding in those knowledges is key to compositional analysis because producers of popular culture include homages, in-jokes, and the like in many of their creations that consumers may, or may not, be expected to understand. Beyond requiring technical expertise, compositional analysis can be a limiting method because it does not speak to the sites of production and audiencing because it is so relentlessly focused on the popular culture itself. However, in combination with other methodologies it can be quite powerful.

> **Genre**   Category of media that includes common conventions

Content Analysis

Content analysis is a quantitative method developed to study textual data, and has been most commonly applied this way in popular geopolitics, especially (but not exclusively) in the study of newspapers and other textual media (like news magazines). This method dates back to the Frankfurt School–influenced period after World War II when interest in propaganda led to the development of techniques with which to assess the meaning found in large amounts of text. Because this originated in the social sciences rather than in the tradition of the humanities, it relies on the scientific paradigm, which requires quantification and the rigorous application of specific methods to create generalizable results. Thus, unlike the preceding two methods (which come out of the humanities paradigm), content analysis has a specific set of procedures associated with it. First, the scope of what you will study needs to be set. Much like methodology itself, this should flow from the questions that you want to answer. Second, the researcher must consider seemingly objective and nonoverlapping categories according to which the data will be categorized. These categories should also follow from your research questions. Third, the data should be coded using the categories devised prior. Finally, the actual analysis

> **Content analysis**   Quantitative study of textual or other data

> **Coding**   Regimented process of quantifying textual or other data

occurs, in which the codes are counted and used to answer the research questions.

As an example, Garth Myers, Thomas Klak, and Timothy Koehl (1996) conducted a content analysis of newspaper coverage of conflicts in Rwanda and Bosnia from six major American newspapers in order to compare the ways in which the media framed the conflicts that dominated those countries in the mid-1990s. They identified key categories (language associated with civil war, savagery, and ethnicity/tribalism) that appeared in the newspaper stories and compared their relative frequency to see how conflicts that could be conceptualized as similar were instead constructed as different. This research was one of the first in popular geopolitics to assess the role of the media in shaping geopolitical discourse. While the quantification reduces the richness of the data, it does permit patterns to emerge that might be unexpected by the researcher. The danger in this reductionism though is that every instance of a word being used counts the same, whereas in "real life" we know that there is a real difference between, for instance, a local newspaper describing something and the agenda-setting *New York Times* saying something the same way. One turn of phrase is likely to descend into obscurity and the other is likely to matter a great deal in political opinion. Further, content analysis, like compositional analysis, deals only with the text under consideration and ignores the sites of production and consumption.

Discourse Analysis

Discourse analysis is strongly connected to the ideas of Michel Foucault, discussed earlier in this chapter. It is also related to content analysis, although it eschews the quantitative method that focuses on the actuality of words themselves in favor of a more qualitative perspective that focuses on the uses to which empowered people put words. Thus, the first part of any discourse analysis is (similarly to content analysis) to select the source material for your analysis. However, dissimilarly to content analysis, there

> **Discourse analysis**
> Qualitative study of
> textual or other data

is no need for these materials to all be comparable. Because discourses can stretch across media, discourse analyses can do the same. For example, if you are interested in studying discourses of race, a number of popular culture artifacts could be useful, from old *Tarzan* movies to magazine advertising. However, it is also important to limit your study to the sources that you think will be most instructive *because* these discourses are so ubiquitous. Can you imagine trying to study everything in popular culture inflected by race? It would be a never-ending quest. Following the selection of sources, the researcher must engage in two processes. First, the researcher must examine the way in which the claims of a discourse are made, contributing to a critical analysis of the logic that identifies the flaws and absences in the discourse. Second, the researcher must investigate the power and positionality of those constructing the discourse so that they may be contextualized.

An example of this research method in popular geopolitics can be seen in the work of Joanne Sharp (1996; 2000), who opened up the study of popular culture in geopolitics with her seminal study of *Reader's Digest* over the span of the Cold War (which was also mentioned in the previous chapter). *Reader's Digest* is a magazine that claims to take the best magazine articles in circulation and condense them down to a more manageable length for middle-class consumers. In this study she focused on the power of the editors to promote anti-Communist discourses while simultaneously promoting an "American" can-do attitude of personal action and achievement, not only through the "condensing" process but also through the initial article selection. Sharp was also able to identify changes in these discourses over time, especially as the Cold War ended.

Discourse analysis of this kind is focused on the site of the popular culture itself, but the Foucauldian concern with the source of authority means that the site of production gets attention as well. Further, the focus of discourse on intertextuality (see the end of this chapter) means that the social modality also receives significant attention. Finally, the Foucauldian interest in power and authority makes this a natural fit for scholars of geopolitics who are ultimately also interested in power. Hence, the majority of works in popular geopolitics can be identified as discourse analyses.

Ethnography, Focus Groups, and Interviews

The last of the commonly used methodologies is a series of related methods that are linked through their engagement with audiences of popular culture. These are relatively recent developments within geopolitics which, as was discussed in chapter 1, has historically been studied at the macro-scale. Actually talking to people about what they think about geopolitics (excepting, of course, elites) would not have occurred to an earlier generation of

> **Feminist geopolitics**
> Criticism of critical
> geopolitics that shifts
> attention from the global
> scale to the individual

scholars. However, in the late 1990s feminist geographers began to critique critical geopolitics for perpetuating this classical geopolitical mistake (e.g., Hyndman 2001; 2004). The focus of critical geopolitics on discourse left geopolitics abstract and disembodied—literally devoid of people—and generally unwilling to consider alternatives. Feminist geopolitics, as an engagement with geopolitics that was parallel to critical geopolitics (at the time of writing the two are more enmeshed than in the past decade), has brought methodological diversity to popular geopolitics.

The methodologies associated with feminist geopolitics are key to popular geopolitics because the study of popular culture has, as we have seen earlier in this chapter, increasingly moved away from the notion that popular culture affects its audiences in ways that are somehow predictable by studying the popular culture itself. Thus, just as critical geopolitics was critiqued as "geopolitics without people," popular geopolitics could be critiqued as "culture without people." These methods help to alleviate this concern.

Ethnography refers to the immersion of the researcher into a community, within which social practices are not only witnessed, but participated in, by the researcher. This enables the researcher to participate in the everyday life of the group, perhaps noticing things that even the group could not tell the researcher were he or she to ask in an interview. The researcher is, to a certain extent, implicated in the research to a greater degree than the other methods about to be discussed because the researcher is a participant observer—often working alongside the group at a task, both to put the group at ease and also to better understand the group dynamics. As an example, Nick Megoran (2008) gained insight into the role of pop music

> **Ethnography** Research method that entails holistic description of a group of people and their practices

and music videos in affirming the government of Uzbekistan's claims of danger from neighboring Kyrgyzstan by living in the borderlands between the two countries. There he met people who were able to attest to the power of the music in their lives. This account of geopolitics at the scale of individual people told a vastly different story than would have been available through other methods, and reflected the personal commitment of the scholar (Megoran learned two local languages so that he could socialize with his new neighbors).

Interviews and focus groups are also attempts to study at the scale of the individual but are more formalized than ethnography in that they involve sitting down with an individual (or group of individuals in the case of a focus group) and discussing a topic of interest. It differs from ethnography in that it does not have the "everyday" observational quality, but it does allow for more overt questions by the researcher, which may be necessary.

> **Focus groups** Groups of people gathered together for in-depth discussion about a topic of interest

For instance, in the case of popular culture, participating in a group watching a movie will render a great deal of information about *how* the movie is *consumed*, but will be unlikely to give insight into *what* an audience thought the movie *meant*. Of course, there is considerable flexibility in these methods, and often ethnography's participant observation entails some semiformal questioning, and equally often interviews and focus groups produce data that is beyond what the respondents literally said (researchers often note their own observations about respondent mood, gestures, etc.).

This research is now quite common in feminist geopolitics, for example in the work of Anna Secor (2001), who has participated in women's political groups in Istanbul and thus has witnessed how Islamic women, who are portrayed in Western discourses as unable to influence politics, nevertheless do. This kind of work is also being done in popular geopolitics, although only just so. Klaus Dodds (2006) updated his previous work on James Bond by observing audience feedback from *Die Another Day* (2002) on the Internet Movie Database (http://www.imdb.com). This kind of online ethnography is different from traditional ethnography in that it can be done with no "footprint" by the researcher, but it also means that there is a consequent lack of knowledge that could be gained through full participation. Of course, scholars could participate in the Internet forum they are studying should they wish, thus generating more information but also being more personally implicated in the research.

> **Intertextuality**
> Relationship between texts' meanings

This tour of the methodologies used in popular geopolitics is only a brief introduction to the ways in which knowledge within the field is constructed. For more detail, there are numerous books explicitly about methodology in the social sciences, and increasingly about methodology in geography specifically (e.g., DeLyser, Aitken, Herbert, Crang, and McDowell 2009).

Intertextuality of Popular Culture and Geopolitics

It is worth taking a moment before beginning these case studies to remember that the structure of the book (as outlined in the introduction) reinforces the idea that these ideas, and case studies, are all independent. For instance, the theories of geopolitics and popular culture are separated into two chapters for clarity, but were both developed in the same world, with the same events swirling around them. Similarly, the case studies serve to, for example, isolate representations of the British Empire from the affective media of the United States—nevertheless this is also an illusion.

The term for this enmeshing of ideas and texts is *intertextuality*, in which authors borrow from, or refer to, other texts to create a totality that is referred to in academic thought as the "literature." It soon becomes impossible to chart these influences chronologically (i.e., who influenced whom) and instead we must approach the literature as always in process. For example, when President George W. Bush told the media that he wanted Osama bin Laden "dead or alive" in December 2001, was he purposefully harnessing the macho mythology of the American Western movie genre to look tough for the electorate? Or, conversely, does the Western movie genre shape American geopolitical culture in such a way that Bush was expressing something that felt natural to him? Ultimately, the answer is both. This synergy of ideas, actions, and speech is at the root of geopolitics.

3

✣

Representation of Place and the British Empire

THE CONCEPT: REPRESENTATION

Ideas

It is striking how much of our understandings of the world are taken on faith from other sources, and how vague those understandings can be. The job of a geography instructor is to stand up in front of a class and represent places, many of which he or she has no direct experience, to a group of students who (hopefully) write down what is said as if it were reliable information. More accurately, the instructor is re-presenting *representations* that he or she had previously consumed—whether in geography classes from his or her own student days, or through popular culture, news media, etc.—even when he or she is teaching about places to which he or she has personally been (one person's experience of a place being far too partial from which to generalize). The power of geographers and

> **Representation** Claim about a place's characteristics, nature, etc.

other academics to represent the world in lectures, books, and maps, and therefore to construct realities that may or may not be recognizable to the people in the places represented, has historically led to a variety of outcomes for those people—some positive, some negative. So, you can imagine that the discipline of geography itself has had to do quite a bit of soul-searching regarding its role in representing other places in ways that are ethical.

Concern over practices of representation within geopolitics goes back to the origins of the critical geopolitics movement, but geography (and geopolitics) as a whole has long been *about* representing places. As was mentioned in chapter 1, the word geography comes from the Greek, roughly translating as "the writing of the earth." As Mary Gilmartin (2004, 282) writes:

> Earth writing takes the world as we experience or understand it, and translates it into images. The forms of these images vary: they can be written, visual or oral and aural, and within each of these categories there exists a wide range of possibilities. Written representations include academic texts, newspapers, magazines, travel writing, novels, plays and poetry. Visual representations include maps, photographs, posters and films. Oral and aural representations include music, film soundtracks and audio recordings, as well as the stories we tell about the relationship between people and places.

Of course, these types of popular culture are just one way in which places are represented. Since its inception in ancient times, geography has been implicated in "earth-writing." For example, cartography, the art and science of map making, is about taking the complexity of the world (or at least a section of it) and graphically rendering it for the viewer to understand. This involves deciding what is important about a place (should the roads found in a place be included, or the location of murders?) and then drawing the map in such a way that people will understand. This is a simple example of how geographic representations are political—of the two maps just mentioned as possibilities, which one is likely to be appreciated (and funded) by the local tourism commission? Geographers have also represented the world through the writing of textbooks, academic articles, policy proposals, etc., often to great controversy. For example, geographer Isaiah Bowman's post–World War I geography textbook *The New World* (1921) was roundly condemned in Germany for naturalizing the post–Treaty of Versailles geopolitical order, including territorial losses for Germany and the break-up of the Austro-Hungarian and Ottoman Empires.

Cartography Art and science of map making

Treaty of Versailles Treaty that ended World War I

The ubiquity of geographic representations, once you start looking for them, can lead to feelings of disorientation—which images are real and which are false? Or perhaps we are immersed in a media-saturated world in which nothing is "real," and instead we are fed sensory misinformation by our alien overlords, à la *The Matrix* (1999)? That is a possibility that is impossible to discount. However, rather than fall into the trap of believing nothing is real and therefore not bothering with the world, it is more fruitful to consider the ways in which representations are selectively deployed in ways that have real impacts on the "real world." After all, the villains in *The Matrix* were not just having a few laughs at our collective expense—they created their computer-generated world for political purposes (to use humanity as batteries). So, the trick for many geographers has been to use their awareness of the power of representations to create a more just world. As Gilmartin (2004, 282) again writes: "We operate within broader social and political contexts that attempt to delineate fact from fiction and right from wrong. Representation, therefore, is central to what we as geographers do."

What, then, is representation? It is not an easy question to answer, not least because to talk about representation is to try to isolate a nearly ubiquitous phenomenon. It is very similar to the concept of discourse (discussed in chapter 1), but, since in the context of this chapter we are limiting our discussion to representation of places and peoples, it is possible to conceive of representation as a narrower concept than discourse—as operating *within* specific discourses. Representation makes claims about the way the world is, and as such it is "a powerful world-disclosing and world-changing technology" (Castree and Macmillan 2004, 471). By "world-disclosing" Castree and Macmillan argue that representation claims to unveil the world to us. By "world-changing" they add the notion that representations can have material consequences.

Representation works through the comparison of one thing to another. There is no way to independently describe somewhere, it can only be done through the use of analogy to other ideas, places, and peoples. Even if you describe a place as "hot" or "polluted," you are analogizing that place to either your personal reference point (home, perhaps) or to a mythical "average" place. Further, representations tend to treat their objects as unchanging—the representation assumes that there is something stable and essential about its object to be represented. "Representation is constitutively inadequate therefore; it is always *exceeded* by the world it seeks to 'capture'" (Castree and Macmillan 2004, 476).

Nevertheless, despite the inadequacy of all representations they are necessary parts of our everyday lives. Not talking about places does not seem to be a viable alternative, although it is the only way to avoid misrepresenting those places and peoples in some way. While the authenticity of a representation is always something to be aimed for, equally important is attention to the effects of particular representations. Authenticity is difficult to assess, because the very excess of a place can provide evidence for multiple competing representations, all of which may be true in their own way. Thus, critical geographers have often

MisRepresentations = Jersey Shore MTV

looked at the political impacts of specific representations, i.e. whom they advantage and whom they hurt, or whom they include and whom they exclude.

Debates

The study of representation has sparked debate within geography since its inception. As alluded to above, representation called into question, in

> **Realism**   Philosophy that says there is a knowable reality

many ways, the discipline's conception of itself as the authoritative source of authentic earthly knowledge. By problematizing geography's role in the production of knowledge, the study of representation brought into conflict two different groups within the discipline—those scholars associated with the philosophy of realism and those associated with social constructionism.

> **Social constructionism** Philosophy that says reality is the product of social interactions

- Realism refers to the perspective that there is a knowable reality out there and that the role of academic geographers is to gather objective knowledge about that reality, create theories about how that reality works, etc. (this is a vast simplification, but will do for these purposes).
- Social constructionism calls into question the idea of objective knowledge itself, and argues that "reality" is not real, but rather the product of a web of representations spun by sources deemed authoritative.

It is clear how conflict would emerge between these two positions. The social constructivist geographers viewed the realist geographers as part of a larger coalition of empowered groups who represented certain places, and the peoples who live there, for example, in ways that contributed to colonial domination. Although popular geopolitics (and, consequently, this book) obviously adopts a more social constructivist perspective than a realist one, it is easy to sympathize with the realists, who are generally motivated by a genuine desire to improve the world through the generation of new knowledge—an Enlightenment-era notion of progress that has a great deal of appeal (and has often generated great achievements). To the realists, questions of representation appeared like an attempt to undermine the possibility of that progress, and further they had the feel of a personal attack, given the realists' personal investment in their work.

Nevertheless, the social constructivists were on to something—the history of geography is replete with what are now obviously quite partial

representations of place. Further, it would be prideful to think that geographers *used* to be biased, but now we have conquered that aspect of ourselves. Rather, it seems obvious that within even the span of just a few years we can become aware of how cultur-
ally situated our past thoughts are. So, how was this debate concluded? Rather than one side crushing the other, a set of compromises seem to have been made. It is hard to find any pure realists in geography anymore, as most seem to have shifted to a position called critical realism. Critical realism refers to the belief that there *is* a reality

> **Critical realism**   Philosophy that says there is a reality but we will never completely understand it because of our flawed perception

out there, and it can be studied, *but* the researcher must strive to be aware of his or her own cultural positioning when conducting that research. Likewise, social constructivists have moderated their position a bit, generally rejecting the notion that reality is nothing but representation.

Having thus arrived at an almost-consensus about the role of representation in geography, the 1990s and early 2000s were the heyday of studies of representation in geography. The astute reader will recall that this coincides (but not coincidentally) with the rise of critical geopolitics as a corrective to the "realist" impulses of classical geopolitics (see chapter 1). Much of the work discussed in the case studies in this book emerges out of this period. However, representation itself has recently been problematized. This is not because it is no longer considered important, but because the domination of geographic (and geopolitical) thought by representation has been so thorough that other ways of understanding (and, importantly, experiencing) place have been occluded.

Nonrepresentational theory (Thrift 1996) is the term that has emerged as an umbrella under which several criticisms of representation have been grouped. Here we will focus on two. The first criticism is that analysis of representation positions scholars at a critical distance from events in the real world. This sense of detachment reinforces the perception of the scholar as occupying a privileged position, able to see representations for what they are, rather than being duped by them like the rest of humanity. Ironically, it was exactly this sort of criticism of objectivity that the social constructivists had leveled at the realists—only now the same critique is being made from within. The second criticism is that repre-

> **Nonrepresentational theory**   Social theory that downplays cognition and representation vis-à-vis other elements of social life, such as practice and affect

sentation privileges certain forms of experiencing the world: the cognitive, the textual, and the visual. Indeed, as we have seen (and will see in later chapters as well), popular geopolitics has been "mesmerized" (Thrift 2000, 381) by texts and inordinately focused on geopolitical maps, films, and other envisionings of the way the world works. This criticism of popular geopolitics is beginning to be addressed, and we will pick up with this element of nonrepresentational theory in chapter 5.

There is, nonetheless, a lot of good reason to continue paying attention to representation. Despite new interests in discovering nonrepresentational engagements with the world, representing is still a key strategy knowingly or unknowingly utilized by virtually everyone every day. For scholars of popular geopolitics to stop paying any attention to representation while, for example, the entertainment industry continues to churn out highly politically charged television shows such as *24* (which has widely been used to justify torture during interrogation), would be to, in part, abandon an important role for academics as critics of society. On that note, this chapter now shifts to a discussion of the ways in which literature and film have represented places in ways that provided justification for empire.

INTRODUCTION TO EMPIRE

Representation was selected as the first concept to be discussed among the case studies in this book because it is so fundamental to geopolitics specifically, and geography more generally. The British Empire from the

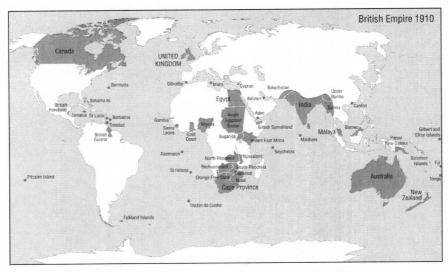

Figure 3.1.   A map of the British Empire in 1910 (UCL Drawing Office)

nineteenth century until the present provides a case study through which we can look at this concept in action because it provides a rich array of representations of various parts of the world (see figure 3.1), and because it is so well documented in popular culture. Prior to beginning this case study though, we must spend a moment discussing empire, and why representation of place is so important for it.

There are, essentially, two forms of empire. These forms are not opposed to each other, but roughly approximate the evolution of the idea of empire over time. As such, they overlap quite a bit, with both forms being found simultaneously in various parts of the world over the past several hundred years. Nevertheless, the historical emphasis has shifted from the first form of empire, which in this book will be referred to as colonialism, to the second form of empire, which we will call imperialism. It should be noted that other scholars use different labels, such as "imperialism" and "neo-imperialism," for these same concepts, but this book uses these labels because they emphasize the most important elements of each, as shall be described below.

> **Colonialism** Invasion, occupation, and adminis-tration of a foreign land for economic or other gain

> **Imperialism** Maintenance of unequal economic relations through (generally) nonmilitary means

Colonialism

Colonialism refers to the control of territories by a foreign power in an explicit attempt to enrich itself through preferential access to the colony's resources. In the modern era (i.e., leaving aside for now the Roman Empire and other ancient empires), colonialism emerged from the economic theory known as mercantilism. Mercantilism, simply put, was the belief that a country's relative wealth was governed by its balance of trade. That is, if a country was exporting more than it was importing (in terms of value, not actual quantity), then wealth would accumulate within the country. One strategy that emerged from this theory was colonialism. By conquering a foreign place (preferably one that had resources the colonizer needed) and imposing a colonial administration, it was possible to restrict to whom the colonized could sell their resources (thereby lowering the cost, by lowering the demand for the resources) and simultaneously monopolize the supplying of markets in the colony (thus rais-

> **Mercantilism** Economic theory that argues for protectionism and a trade surplus

ing prices for the colonizer's goods by restricting the supply in the colony). Therefore, the balance of trade would shift in the colonizer's favor, with high-value goods being sold to the colonized, who could only pay for those goods by exporting more and more of their own low-value goods. This is a highly simplified description, but it provides the most important elements.

As an example, the American colonies provided many different resources to the United Kingdom, such as corn, flax, and wheat. By the 1700s, mercantilism had largely been made redundant by the vast economic changes associated with the Industrial Revolution. The Industrial Revolution led to a change in the global division of labor, with workers in Western Europe (the hearth of the Industrial Revolution) increasingly focusing on industrial labor (manufacturing things cheaply, aided by nonhuman power sources, like coal) and the rest of the world increasingly relegated to supplying the natural resources that fed into the industrial processes in Western Europe. Thus, colonies like South Carolina were founded and settled as a collection of commercial plantations to grow cotton and other crops that could be used in textile mills in the midlands of England. Why did the colonies not build their own textile mills and convert their cotton into high-value cloth? They did not do so because they were barred from industrializing by colonial authorities. This, among other grievances, like the lack of political freedom and perceived overtaxation, led to the American Revolution—the first successful rebellion against colonial control (beginning in 1775)—and helps explain why the United States still does not represent itself as an imperial power despite having taken up that role in the twentieth century. It would be followed by a series of revolutions: throughout Latin America in the eighteenth century (against the Spanish and Portuguese Empires) and throughout Africa and Asia in the twentieth century (against the British, French, Dutch, German, Italian, and Belgian Empires).

> **Industrial Revolution**
> Economic shift from manual labor to other forms of power in manufacturing

However, these later revolutions were not just expressions of patriotism and a desire for political independence; they were also laden with national hopes of economic advancement, to be realized by breaking the restrictive trading patterns imposed by the colonizers and competing on the open market. However, just as France supported U.S. independence as a way to weaken its rival, the British Empire, other powerful (and industrial) countries supported the end of the Spanish Empire in the 1800s and the British and French Empires in the 1900s because they thought it would be advantageous for themselves.

Imperialism

Imperialism refers to the maintenance (or expansion) of national power at the expense of other, less empowered, countries through methods of governance at a distance (rather than imposing colonial rule). This governance at a distance reflects the fact that conquering far-flung parts of the world and maintaining military control in the face of imperial rivals and increasingly embittered populations is an expensive (and probably impossible) proposition (see for example the struggle by the United Kingdom to prevent the Japanese takeover of their Asian colonies in World War II). An ever-changing set of ephemeral strategies rather than a specific action (like colonization), imperialism can best be seen in its effects, such as the continued economic peripherality of most places of the world that were colonies for any substantial amount of time. For instance, most of Latin America, which has been politically independent for almost two hundred years, still lags behind the United States and Western Europe in virtually every economic category. This reflects their economic resubjugation by first the United Kingdom, and later the United States, in the period following their political independence.

So how does this imperialism work? In Latin America it is possible to identify three interlinked imperial strategies. The first strategy is the promotion of *free trade*. When the British became the world's leading industrial power they soon recognized that with their built-in advantages they could out-compete countries that were just emerging from the colonial experience, thereby relegating those newly independent countries to the economic tasks that the United Kingdom did not want to specialize in (because of their generally low profit), such as agriculture, mining, etc. Thus, the British advocated the global adoption of free trade—a set of trading rules that ostensibly eliminate any tariffs, quotas, or preferences by one country for another. The same thought process led the United States to support the dismantling of the British and French Empires after World War II—and led to U.S. support for free trade principles in Latin America that lasts to this day (except in areas in which the United States is economically disadvantaged, like agriculture).

The second imperial strategy used in Latin America is support for friendly political regimes. While the idea of foreign intervention in U.S. elections is anathema to U.S. citizens (see for example the spectacularly backfiring attempt by British citizens to urge Ohio voters to vote for John Kerry in 2004), the United States has a long history of overt intervention in Latin American politics. This strategy takes various forms, from having U.S. ambassadors campaign for specific candidates (Nicaragua), to requiring countries to amend their constitution (Cuba), to sponsoring the assassination of democratically elected presidents (Chile), to funding and arming pro-U.S. rebellions (Guatemala, Nicaragua, Cuba). The governments supported by the United States, either via active military and financial aid or by passive nonintervention, generally support the United States in international forums and promote free trade policies, often in the face of their own population's desires.

The third imperial strategy is traditional military intervention, similar to colonialism. However, under imperialism, military intervention is much more likely to be short-term. The goals are to achieve a quick resolution to an imperial problem (often regime change) and to demonstrate the empire's potential to intervene elsewhere in the hopes of getting what it wants elsewhere without actually having to exercise military might. Examples of U.S. intervention in Latin America that follow this pattern include invasions of the Dominican Republic (1916, 1965), Grenada (1983), Panama (1989), and Haiti (1915, 1994). It should be noted again that during this period (and still today) it is not acceptable in American political discourse to describe the United States as an empire, although in many other parts of the world this is a common representation.

Empire and Enlightenment Principles

Now, most of the strategies just mentioned, associated with both colonialism and with imperialism, do not sound very pleasant. In fact, most of them would probably be considered by most people in the abstract to be immoral. Even the seemingly least offensive of these strategies, free trade, essentially comes down to the imposition of policies on other countries that leads to millions of people suffering material deprivation. Most of the strategies are perceived as far more obviously immoral than that. That is because they fly in the face of a set of abstract principles that were derived during the Enlightenment and remain very important today in the countries that are most often associated with imperialism. These principles include human equality, conflict resolution through a fair legal system, and the universality of human rights. In the abstract, these are principles in which most people in imperial countries believe. So, then, how is it possible that there have been imperial interventions all over the world, for as long as there have been modern empires? The answer lies in how those interventions are represented—ultimately morality is seen to lie in the particulars of each intervention rather than in general principles. Those particulars are, in turn, framed through processes that represent the people and places of imperial intervention in certain ways. Now this chapter will turn to the specific case study of the

> **The Enlightenment** Era in which reason was held up as the ultimate arbiter of truth

British Empire, using examples from literature, film, and cartoons to illustrate how the world was represented through popular culture in ways that served the growth and maintenance of empire.

CASE STUDY: THE BRITISH EMPIRE

Literature and Colonialism

One of the most influential thinkers regarding culture and its relationship to British colonialism and empire was Edward Said, and it could be argued that the entire field of popular geopolitics owes its existence to his influence. We have discussed his idea of imagined geographies in chapter 1, where we also outlined his concept of Orientalism, in which the spatial categories of East and West are constructed as mutual opposites. As such, he was intimately concerned with processes of representation: "Representation itself has been characterised as keeping the subordinate subordinate, the inferior inferior" (Said 1993, 95).

By juxtaposing culture and imperialism (as in the title of his 1993 book), Said hopes to illustrate the constitutive relationship between the two— how the latter cannot occur without the former. "The idea of overseas rule—jumping beyond adjacent territories to very distant lands . . . has a lot to do with projections, whether in fiction or geography or art, and it acquires a continuous presence through actual expansion, administration, investment and commitment" (Said 1993, xxv). Thus, Said recognized the relationship between the discursive (culture) and the material (imperialism), and he then explored specific cases where literature constructed the colonized in particular ways.

One of his subjects was Jane Austen's *Mansfield Park* (1814), which was written just as the United Kingdom was about to go into its greatest period of geopolitical significance, as Napoleon's France had been dispatched and the United Kingdom had no major rivals, save Russia's ambitions in Central Asia. Austen's work has become increasingly popular, and is now read in college literature courses and is the subject of many film adaptations. This particular novel is the story of a poor girl named Fanny who is taken into her aunt and uncle's prosperous British estate (Mansfield Park). The estate's wealth (and, broadly at this time, Britain's) comes primarily (if tacitly) from the production of crops in the colonies (in this case, sugar production in the Caribbean), but Said notes that this is rarely mentioned in the narrative. At one point Fanny inquires about the treatment of slaves but her questions are met with silence. Further, the structure of the narrative incorporates a lesson about life, embodied in young Fanny. Said (1993, 88) quotes this passage from *Mansfield Park*, in which Fanny returns to her childhood home:

Fanny was almost stunned. The smallness of the house, and thinness of the walls, brought everything so close to her, that, added to the fatigue of her journey, and all her recent agitation, she hardly knew how to bear it. Within the room all was tranquil enough, for Susan [her sister] having disappeared with the others, there were soon only her father and herself remaining; and he taking out a newspaper—the accustomary loan of a neighbour, applied himself to studying it, without seeming to recollect her existence. The solitary candle was held between himself and the paper, without any reference to her possible convenience, but she had nothing to do, and was glad to have the light screened from her aching head, as she sat in bewildered, broken, sorrowful contemplation.

She was at home. But alas! it was not such a home, she had not such a welcome, as—she checked herself; she was unreasonable. . . . A day or two might shew the difference. *She* only was to blame. Yes, she thought it would not have been so at Mansfield. No, in her uncle's house there would have been a consideration of times and seasons, a regulation of subject, a propriety, an attention towards everybody which there was not here.

Said's commentary on this passage (1993, 88) illustrates how the book's narrative, in which Fanny reaches her potential only after coming out into the globally connected (via colonialism) Mansfield Park, is itself supportive of the U.K.'s colonial project:

In too small a space, you cannot see clearly, you cannot think clearly, you cannot have regulation or attention of the proper sort. The fineness of Austen's detail ("the solitary candle was held between himself and the paper, without any reference to her possible convenience") renders very precisely the dangers of unsociability, of lonely insularity, of diminished awareness that are rectified in larger and better administered spaces.

Thus, *Mansfield Park* (and most British literature of the time, Said argues) not only naturalized colonial exploits by making the positive effects of colonialism visible (through the opulent lifestyle of the characters) and masking the negative impacts, but it also constructed the notion that personal (and national) progress could only be found through increasingly large impositions of organization over larger and larger spaces.[1]

James Bond and Imperial Decline

Just as Orientalism not only constructed the spatial category of the Orient but also the Occident, the long-running James Bond movie franchise (since 1962) not only represents the United Kingdom, but also represents the various "exotic" locations in which the scenes are set. These films:

---

[1] It should be noted that this is not an uncontested view on *Mansfield Park*. For a contrarian perspective, see Fraiman 1995.

drew on current fears in order to reduce the implausibility of the villains and their villainy, while they also presented potent images of national character, explored the relationship between a declining Britain and an ascendant United States, charted the course of the Cold War, offered a changing demonology, and were an important aspect of post-war popular culture, not only in Britain but also more generally, particularly after the Americans created and financed the filmic Bond. (Black 2004, 292)

Indeed, these films provide a lens for watching changes in geopolitical representation over time, with twenty-four films (as of 2008's *Quantum of Solace*) produced since 1962's *Dr. No*.

Following World War II, the United Kingdom faced the implosion of its empire, with its "jewel in the crown," British India, fragmenting into two new states (India and Pakistan—and later Bangladesh). The 1950s and 1960s marked a more complete collapse, with Sudan, Iraq, Ghana, Malaysia, Nigeria, Tanzania, Sierra Leone, Cameroon, Uganda, Jamaica, Trinidad and Tobago, Kenya, Zambia, Malawi, Barbados, Guyana, and various others (this list is necessarily shortened) departing from the British Empire. Britain attempted to maintain some of its imperial prestige, however, forming the Commonwealth as an organization intended to maintain the patriarchal relationship between the postcolonial states and their former ruler. However, as time has gone on that relationship has become increasingly hollow, with the United Kingdom able to exert very little power over its former colonies (as evident from recent history in Zimbabwe). Bond, however, ignores most of this. "One of the ideological functions of the Bond narrative is to construct an imaginary world in which Pax Britannia still operates. Thus, Britain is presented as being in the frontline of the conspiracies directed against western civilization" (Chapman 1999, 39).

> **The Commonwealth of Nations** Organization founded as a successor to the British Empire

This representation of the United Kingdom as a global power requires Bond to project that power around the world, effectively creating a hierarchy that consists of countries that act, and those (postcolonial states) that are acted upon. Or, to describe this hierarchy more callously, some countries play chess, others are the chessboard. As Klaus Dodds (2003, 132) points out, the places in which Bond movies are set were not necessarily in the British Empire, but are places "that British audiences could nonetheless imagine as centers of intrigue and where they could take pleasure in witnessing their secret agent triumph against the odds." To see this geography, see table 3.1. Jeremy Black (2004) has argued that there are massive geographical absences in the Bond corpus, with the intelligence agencies of continental Europe not figuring at all even when Bond is working in their countries, despite being nominally on the side of the British. Similarly, when Bond goes to Africa (which he rarely does—in this case nonrepresentation is itself a form of representation), South America, or Asia, the local authorities never impede his mission. "Non-alignment means non-existence for the local government. It is as if these countries are non-governed, ripe for exploitation by international megalomaniacs, and waiting for the order (and purposeful glamour) brought by Western intervention in the shape of Bond" (Black 2004, 300).

Dodds (2003) focuses his geopolitical analysis of the James Bond phenomenon on Istanbul, arguing that its geographical location at the edge of the Soviet-influenced zone of the Balkans, as well as its traditionally Orientalist and exotic representation by Europeans, make it the perfect set-

Table 3.1:   Bond Films and Their Locations (updated from Dodds 2003, 132)

Movie	Locations
Dr. No (1962)	Jamaica
From Russia with Love (1963)	Turkey, Italy, Yugoslavia
Goldfinger (1964)	Switzerland, USA
Thunderball (1965)	Bahamas
You Only Live Twice (1967)	Japan, Hong Kong
On Her Majesty's Secret Service (1969)	Switzerland
Diamonds Are Forever (1971)	USA, Netherlands
Live and Let Die (1973)	USA, San Monique
The Man with the Golden Gun (1974)	Thailand, Hong Kong
The Spy Who Loved Me (1977)	Austria, Egypt, Sardinia
Moonraker (1979)	Italy, USA, Brazil
For Your Eyes Only (1981)	Greece/Corfu, Italy
Octopussy (1983)	India, Germany
A View to a Kill (1985)	USA, France
Never Say Never Again (1986)*	Monte Carlo, North Africa, Bahamas
The Living Daylights (1987)	Austria, Czechoslovakia, Afghanistan, Morocco, Gibraltar
License to Kill (1989)	USA, Central America (Isthmus City)
GoldenEye (1995)	Russia, Cuba, Monte Carlo
Tomorrow Never Dies (1997)	Vietnam, China, Germany
The World Is Not Enough (1999)	Spain, Azerbaijan, Turkey
Die Another Day (2002)	Cuba, Iceland, the Korean DMZ
Casino Royale (2006)	Czech Republic, Madagascar, USA, Montenegro, Italy
Quantum of Solace (2008)	Austria, Haiti, Italy, Bolivia

*Not produced by Eon Productions/United Artists.

ting for Cold War intrigue. In *From Russia with Love* (1963), Bond is sent to Istanbul to retrieve a decoding device from a Soviet female agent. In his search for the device, he is paired up with a local informant, Karim Bey, who guides Bond's path through such "Oriental delights" as the Grand Bazaar and ancient Byzantine ruins. Bond also witnesses a somewhat erotic fight between two Roma (known as "Gypsies" in the film, a now outdated label) women over who will marry their tribal chief's son (the British Board of Film Classification required the scene to be shorn of its most revealing images). Perhaps unsurprisingly, Bond manages to escape Istanbul with the decoder (and the Soviet agent) on the famous Orient Express. The representation here is of a pleasure-filled city fundamentally rooted in its history, while the Soviet Union and the United Kingdom are locked in a conflict of global significance that requires their agents to sneak into other countries, like Turkey, to steal and kill.

In *The World Is Not Enough* (1999), Bond once again returns to Istanbul. The plot centers on a new oil pipeline from the Caspian Sea to bypass Russian dominance in oil transport. To avoid "dangerous" places like Iraq, Iran, and Syria, the new pipeline ends on the Turkish coast just south of the Black Sea (see figure 3.2). The primary villain in the film, a mercenary known as Renard, plans to explode an ex-Soviet nuclear submarine in the waters of Istanbul (laden with stolen radioactive materials) to cut off the waterways to the Black Sea, leaving oil from the Russian pipeline with no way to be shipped globally. Thus, secondary villain Electra (who owns the new Turkish pipeline) comes to hold the monopoly of oil transportation, with all the power that implies. Bond, of course, prevents the detonation of the submarine and the subsequent geopolitical upheaval.

This plot summary may sound like it is grounded in hard geopolitical facts but it is nevertheless a representation. Turkey has multiple geopolitical identities. Debate over Turkey's "European" credentials has been in the news a lot over the past decade as Turkey has made a bid to join the European Union (EU), only to be stymied by opposition from within the EU, much of which seems to center on perceived cultural differences. Indeed, as we have said, Bond movies tend to play up the exotic elements of their locations, and Istanbul is no different. Instead, in *The World Is Not Enough* Turkey is situated within an exotic Central Asian/Black Sea region that, while represented as culturally distant from life in the United Kingdom (see again the exotic representation of *From Russia with Love*), is seen as critical to the maintenance of world order because it is the source and/or transit point for petroleum supplies necessary to keep British consumerist lifestyles afloat.

It should be noted that the Bond movies often paired the hero up with American agents (like perennial also-ran colleague Felix Leiter), and Bond often gets backup from U.S. troops (as in 1979's *Moonraker*). However, in

Figure 3.2. A map including Turkey and the Caspian Sea region (UCL Drawing Office)

these scenarios it is always Bond who is smarter, smoother, and more critical to the successful resolution of the crisis. Thus, the special relationship between the United States and the United Kingdom is represented as being reciprocal—Britain gets the money and brute force that the United States can offer, while the United States gets British intelligence, subtlety, and panache. This representation of Britishness is expanded in the work of Paul Stock, who reverses Dodds's focus on Bond's adventures overseas and instead focuses on the one place in the United Kingdom that Bond is always pictured returning to: the office of his boss, M. "It is a place where ideology, iconography, and office fittings converge; where changes and challenges to that 'office space' are juxtaposed; and where cognitive maps and the resonance of a British signifier on the margins of Empire can be examined" (2000, 35).

> **The special relationship**
> Term coined by Winston Churchill to reflect the diplomatic, cultural, and other ties between the United Kingdom and the United States

Stock identifies M's office as the historical memory of bygone empire, but it is also the nerve center of ongoing attempts to maintain global power. It remained virtually unchanged from 1962 to 1995. Laden with leather armchairs, polished wood walls, paintings of sailing ships, replica cannons, busts of historical figures, and perhaps most anachronistically, a globe with the British Empire still colored in pink, M's office served as a museum to

Britain's lost maritime empire, or perhaps as a denial of that loss. Humorously, when M meets Bond on a submarine in *You Only Live Twice* (1967), his entire office has been crammed into a small cabin on board, as if Britain's maritime past enables M to be at home at sea as in London. M's office within the British intelligence services is located, tellingly, within a "front" corporation called Universal Exports, which dovetails nicely with our earlier discussion of empire and its relationship to commodity trading. Indeed, when Bond is undercover he often travels as a salesman, the conceit being that British businessmen overseas are so natural, so expected, that he can go anywhere in the world and not seem unusual.

GoldenEye (1995) marks the first appearance of Dame Judy Dench in the role of M, part of a general move to make the often misogynist Bond more acceptable in a postfeminist (and post–Cold War) era. Gone was the gentlemanly social club atmosphere of Universal Exports and the trappings of empire. Now M overtly worked in a modern building in London, well enough known by Bond's adversaries for it to be blown up in *The World Is Not Enough*. Her office is bereft of the wood and brass, and is instead a modern business office, with vertical blinds, leather swivel chairs, and a few pictures hanging on the walls. The shift in office adornment parallels the shift from colonial to imperial administration (as those words were defined in the earlier section). Thus, the James Bond films can be seen as illustrating shifts in Britain's relationship to the world from colonial to imperial, while nevertheless remaining consistent in its representation of that world as exotic places in which British power remains critical and British geopolitical actions are to be carried out.

The Falkland Islands and the Reassertion of Empire

While the James Bond movies represent exotic locations from the developing world as the chessboards on which the United Kingdom battles for its national interests, the real United Kingdom was faced with a real imperial war in April 1982, defending the Falkland Islands colony (known in Argentina as the Malvinas) in the South Atlantic Ocean from an Argentinean assault. This war was easily described with the language of classical geopolitics—two states competing over territory in traditional war. However, as Dodds (1996) points out, the war was represented in the news media in different ways, with the Falklands themselves morphing in the geopolitical imagination as one representation gave way to another.

The first version of the Falklands was one of a distant place threatened by an aggressive Fascist government (Argentina was, at the time, ruled by a military government). This representation transformed the Falklands into another Czechoslovakia or Poland, countries threatened by Nazi Germany at the beginning of World War II. Given that the battle against

Nazi Germany is to this day a keystone of British national identity, this representation had powerful resonance. Key to this representation was the description of the Falklands as about the size of Wales, with the climate and landscape of Scotland (both being constituent parts of the United Kingdom). By describing the islands in terms familiar to British residents, the eight thousand miles between London and Port Stanley (the capital of the Falklands) were collapsed and an imagined connection between the islands was forged. However, an alternative representation of the Falklands was as a reminder of the immoral imperial past of the United Kingdom. Like the contemporaneous conflict in Northern Ireland (in which Irish Republicans fought to oust the British from the region, and sought reunification with the rest of the island), the Falklands could be another bloody battlefield from which the United Kingdom could not gracefully extricate itself, penance for an illiberal imperial past (and present). Thus, an individual's stance on the war was linked to how they conceived of the Falklands—if you adopt one representation as "true," the political course to be taken appears self-evident. While the representations of Argentina as a Latin American Nazi Germany and of the Falkland Islanders as strong island stock whose way of life was threatened by aggressive militarism (like the United Kingdom in World War II) ended up becoming the hegemonic representations, they were not uncontested.

Klaus Dodds has studied the work of British political cartoonist Steve Bell (who publishes his work in *The Guardian* newspaper) to see how Bell visualized the war in the Falkland Islands. Dodds argues that Bell has a "critical geopolitical eye," which he defines as "a way of looking at international politics that does not accept the conventional approaches to representing and understanding warfare" (1996, 573). While many would dismiss political cartoons as a distraction from "real politics," Dodds recognized the incisive power of the political cartoon. Able to be read either at a glance on the way to catch the morning bus, or more lingeringly while drinking coffee at the breakfast table, the single-frame cartoon can pack a great deal of punch in a small amount of printed space. While reading an editorial or other type of political commentary in a newspaper requires some time and quiet to focus on the text, the visuality of a cartoon allows for references to be quickly understood.

One example of this phenomenon comes from the long-running American cartoon *Doonesbury*, in which cartoonist Garry Trudeau portrays President George W. Bush as an asterisk wearing a frayed Roman legionnaire's helmet, representing him as imperial and prone to militarism and simultaneously as fundamentally insubstantial. The asterisk is supposed to represent his contested initial election in 2000 (see figure 3.3). Without reading anything "Bush" says or does, the viewer can quickly appreciate Trudeau's perspective on Bush. What makes this doubly effective is the power of humor to deflate the pretensions of politics (and politicians). The success of Comedy Central's *The Daily Show* in the United States is testament to this, and another example of Dodds's concept of the critical geopolitical eye. Comedian Jon Stewart (host of the show) has emerged as a (geo)political commentator in his own right, and is perceived by many as the key to getting support from young voters.

Bell's cartoons about the Falkland Islands War perform a similar function to that of *The Daily Show* and *Doonesbury*. All three provide a forum for quick-hitting humor that can quite effectively call into question the assumptions on which geopolitical action is predicated. In this case (and as is often the case on *The Daily Show*), Bell consistently calls into question the separation between partisan domestic politics and the supposedly nonpartisan realm of foreign policy, which is a long-standing conceit of international relations. In the United States, this conceit is often phrased as "politics stops at the water's edge," implying that anyone who seeks to gain partisan advantage through manipulation of foreign affairs is not acting in the national interest (the national interest, as was discussed in chapter 1, is itself a conceit).

Bell's criticism of the Margaret Thatcher Government (in power in the United Kingdom from 1979 to 1990) stems from the simultaneity of the

Figure 3.3. Doonesbury's George W. Bush (DOONESBURY Copyright 2006 G. B. Trudeau. Reprinted with permission of UNIVERSAL PRESS SYNDICATE. All rights reserved)

Falkland Islands War and high unemployment in the United Kingdom. Bell understands the war to be a diversion of national attention away from domestic suffering toward imperial glory during a time when the Thatcher Government was in danger of being swept from office. Thus, Bell views the representation of the Falklands as a smaller version of Britain on the other side of the Atlantic as simply the most politically useful for Thatcher out of the many possible permutations, with the connection to a purported reality totally unnecessary for its widespread promotion.

The ability to promote this representation of the Falklands was in part because of a prior *lack* of representation of the Falklands. Most British people simply did not know of them. Dodds quotes two humorous stories about this: the first a British paratrooper (who later fought in the war) who, when notified of the Argentinean invasion, initially thought that the Falklands were just off the coast of Scotland, and the second a British sea lord in a top-level government meeting about defending the Falklands from potential Argentinean invasion who, with great confidence, circled the wrong islands when asked where the Falklands were located. Even the cartoonist Bell admitted that he had little idea what the Falklands were like, and in fact he had little interest in adopting any realistic representation. Rather, to illustrate in his cartoons his view of the war as an absurdity, "the realities of the Falkland Islands [were] subsumed beneath a fantasy space of popular English icons and symbols of national identity" (Dodds 1996, 585). This air of fantasy was produced by portraying a flying penguin (penguins of course being a flightless bird) circling over the combat in Bell's cartoons. At one point one of these flying penguins provides the cynical antihero of the invasion, Kipling, reason to fight on, having been taught some limited English and thus substantiating the Britishness of the islands. However, only this penguin, alone among the many portrayed caught up in the combat, is remotely British (see figure 3.4). Bell's ultimate refusal to portray the Falklands as anything but an absurd battlefield of domestic politics eroded the authority of the British government's representational claims.

Figure 3.4.   Steve Bell's vaguely British Penguin (Courtesy of the artist)

CONCLUSION

Summary

In this case study of the British Empire, we have caught a glimpse of the complex web of representations that help compose our geopolitical imaginations. While *Mansfield Park*, James Bond, and Steve Bell's cartoons could never be said to encompass the whole spectrum of popular culture that represents the British Empire or the rest of the world, they provide a sample of the methods used to naturalize empire (or, indeed, to argue against it). Said's critique of *Mansfield Park* was twofold: that it left unspoken the social relations that enabled Fanny's wealthy uncle to provide such opulence for his family, and that the unfolding of the narrative itself denigrates the local, favoring regional and global scales of organization (like empire). Thus, empire is tacitly promoted even as it is left unspoken (often literally, in the case of Fanny's question to her uncle). The James Bond movies both portray the United Kingdom (through the changing decor of M's office) and the global geopolitical spaces that the United Kingdom acts within (most especially Istanbul, but also other "exotic" places), but both of those specific representations construct an overarching representation of the United Kingdom as a global power, unchanged from the empire's heyday (à la *Mansfield Park*). Finally, Steve Bell demolishes this key distinction between the United Kingdom's domestic and foreign spaces with his absurdist cartoons portraying the war in the Falklands. By illustrating (literally) that the war was intended to be a distraction from domestic politics, Bell deployed his sense of humor to deflate the geopolitical pretensions that surrounded the war (e.g., the image of World War II as a just war, and with the Falklands as a mini–United Kingdom and Argentina as Nazi Germany).

The failed attempt by Steve Bell to undercut the drive to war in the South Atlantic raises several important questions. Why do some representations "take root" in the public consciousness and others are pushed aside? That is a very complex question, but generally speaking the answer can be found in power. Power is itself a complex notion, but is generally understood as the ability to influence. Rather than being something people (or things) have, it is best understood as being relational (i.e., power is not an object to be held or expended, but a relationship between people, see Allen 2004). The relationship here is between the producers of representations and the consumers, with competition between producers being the area in which power is exercised. For

> **Power** Relationship between two entities that features unequal agency between them

instance, it could be concluded that Steve Bell was not as powerful as the creators of the James Bond movies, because his "critical geopolitical eye" was unable to stave off war, while the latent imperialism of the James Bond genre clearly carried the day. However, this would be overly simplistic. As we will see in more detail in chapter 6, consumers of representations also have power (remember that power is always held in relation to someone or something else). Thus, the emergence of one representation as more significant than others not only has to do with the relative power of the producers but also the power of consumers to adopt one representation over others. This may be because the representation fits into a discourse that they favor (e.g., it is "scientifically authentic") or because it justifies or supports an advantageous belief (e.g., the belief that imperial subjects are too lazy to work without a firm colonial administration). Perhaps it just makes those accepting the representation feel good about themselves (e.g., Orientalism). In any event, for a representation to emerge as hegemonic it requires the audience to believe it—it is ultimately a collaboration.

Extensions in Your Life

When going through heavily mediated everyday life (and education), it is worth considering the role of representation in constructing personal worldviews. While it is impossible to do without representation, a little daily awareness about it can go a long way.

- In the last action movie you saw, where did the villains come from, and what was that environment like?
- Where did the hero or heroine come from, and what was their "home" space like?
- What images would be representative of everyday life in *your* country?
- Would everyone in your country be likely to agree with you about those images?

4

✛

Narration of Nation in the Post-WWII United States

THE CONCEPT: NARRATIVE

Ideas

Related to the idea of representation is the concept of narrative, which has storytelling at its core. This is, at first glance, an idea that sounds very far from the foundation of academic knowledge, since for most of us when we think of storytelling we think of tall tales, fiction, or at least embellishment of the facts, and we like to think of academia as being about the exact opposite of that: truth, and the unvarnished version at that. However, since the 1970s academics have generally agreed that much of knowledge production is really the construction of narratives (White 1973).

If representation frequently involves places, and what they are like (or are perceived like), then narrative is about time: about events unfolding in a way that makes sense to the reader or listener. A good way to begin considering this is with a fundamental question: is the world getting better, getting worse, or staying the same? Each answer is an indicator, at base, of a kind of historical narrative about the world. If someone thinks the world is getting worse, he or she will read news stories of tragedy and see proof that he or she is right, and if he or she thinks the world is getting better, he or she will sort for the positive and feel equally validated by the very same world events. Just as people will ignore evidence that contradicts the geographic representations they believe in (as in "she's not like other [insert nationality]"), people sort through evidence for that which substantiates their master narratives.

Chapter 4

Narrative paradigm
Notion that people perceive and organize reality through practices of storytelling

Logos Logic and reasoning

Mythos Story and narrative

Narrative rationality
Confirmation of a narrative's validity by comparison with personal experiences

Walter Fisher (1987) has argued (in what has become known as the narrative paradigm) that people do not think only in terms of reason (what the Greeks referred to as *Logos*) but also through *Mythos*, or story. In other words, while traditional models of human behavior indicate that we make decisions based on the rationality of arguments with which we are presented, Fisher argues that we make decisions based on the coherence of the stories with which we are presented. The measure of a story's coherence is how well it meshes with our experiences of the world. Thus, a "good" reason to believe something is if it is fundamentally linked to our own life stories: what we have experienced, and how we have made sense of our own personal narratives. Traditional notions of rationality can then be understood as relying on outside, objective measures of validity, while narrative rationality relies on an audience's subjective judgment of how well the story hangs together and validates their own experiences. Of course, even decision-making based on traditional rationality is also rooted in a specific narrative of scientific progress. Most importantly, audience members' identities are in part constructed through which narratives they invest in personally.

Beyond questions of personal identity, narrativity gives us tools to understand the world and our location within it. Because a narrative unfolds over time, it shows us that it is impossible to understand events in isolation. Rather, they should be understood as episodes in a larger narrative. Within a narrative a plot serves as the internal logic that holds the episodes of a narrative together. A plot is a series of relationships (some causal) between people and things that are grounded in both history and geography. It is only through an elemental understanding of a narrative's plot that people know which details to pay attention to as life unfolds: "in the face of a potentially limitless array of social experiences deriving from social contact with events, institutions, and people, the evaluative capacity of emplotment demands and enables *selective*

Plot Relationships in space and time that promote an understanding of narrative

appropriation in constructing narratives" (Somers 1994, 617, emphasis in original). In other words, what someone thinks is important in a narrative shapes the stories he or she tells (and experiences). If he or she is interested in women's rights, his or her history of the United States will be very different from one interested in military history. Both selectively appropriate the episodes in history that speak to their narrative.

There are three scales to narrativity of which it is worth being aware (Somers 1994). The first is ontological narrativity, which refers to the narratives that compose us at the scale of the individual. They define who we think we are and therefore inform our actions, which in turn add to the narrative. Thus, the narrative, and our sense of self, is always in a process of becoming. What are the five most important events in a person's life? They might be when he or she met someone special, when he or she realized they could do something they did not know they could, a completely random event (like winning the lottery), or perhaps when he or she lost someone important. Once that is answered, it is possible to think about why the events were selected and glimpse that individual's ontological narrative.

> **Ontological narrativity**
> Personal narratives of who you are and how you got here

People have a location in the plot of their ontological narratives that informs their current behavior. Some of these narratives are incredibly personal; others are shared among vast groups of people. These collective myths might be termed public narratives, and they are the second scale of narrativity. An example might be the Holocaust, which is a touchstone for many younger Jews who did not even live during that time. These narratives are shared by at least a few people, and often millions. They are often promoted by powerful institutions, like governments, parents, corporations, etc., that aim to structure the perspectives of those within a collective identity. An example would be the narratives of American identity that help shape collective responses to new experiences. There are many of these narratives, from Manifest Destiny, to America as the culmination of human progress (i.e., a "new Jerusalem" or a "shining city on a hill"), to individualist narratives of the American Dream ("anybody can make it").

> **Public narratives**
> Communal narratives of history, inclusion, and exclusion

The third scale of narrativity is metanarrativity. Metanarratives are the overarch-

> **Metanarrativity**
> Overarching narratives about the way in which history is unfolding and will continue to unfold

ing theories and concepts that we see as unfolding in all times and places. An example could be the notion of human existence as slowly improving (see the beginning of this chapter), or human existence as a timeless conflict between East and West (see Said's notions of Orientalism from chapter 1), or human existence as a battle between our animal natures and our civilizing humanity (with various people located in different roles within that plot).

These narratives, then, are all linked through their provision of plots that not only structure the way in which we view the world but also the way in which we view ourselves. "Narratives help to construct personal and social identity, provide sense and order to experience, and frame and structure action" (Roberts 2006, 710). As structures, though, they are incredibly resilient, especially as a result of the selective appropriation of experiences that fit an individual's ontological and public narratives. However, confusion reigns when our narrative rationality cannot make sense of an anomalous experience. For instance, after the 11 September 2001 attacks many Americans asked themselves and others, "why do they hate us?" because the narrative of American innocence that dominated within the United States did not prepare them for an attack like that. For these reasons, the narrative paradigm has a lot to say about how we understand geopolitics and react to changing circumstances.

Debates

This idea of narratives, as mentioned earlier, is somewhat anathema to a lot of traditional views of the social sciences. It was originally associated solely with history, which was itself seen as fundamentally about describing the world rather than explaining it. The social sciences, in contrast, were defined by their quest to abstract and theorize the world, while historical narratives were perniciously particular and specific. By the 1960s and 1970s, even historians began to question the validity of narratives. Thus, the first debate about narratives revolved around their very legitimacy as an object of study. In the 1970s, however, both historians and other scholars interested in the study of people rediscovered narratives and radically refigured why they were important. Whereas originally narratives were descriptive (e.g., "this is what happened"), narratives were reconfigured as being constitutive: "all of us come to *be* who we *are* (however ephemeral, multiple, and changing) by being located or locating ourselves (usually unconsciously) in social narratives *rarely of our own making*" (Somers 1994, 606, emphasis in original).

A second point of contestation about narrative revolves around what is called essentialism. Essentialism refers to the treatment of people as simply members of categories. This is exemplified in what has become known since the 1990s as identity politics. Identity politics is the implementation of political strategies meant to improve the condition of a social group that is considered oppressed. This highlighting of oppressed groups calls into question the universality of some public narratives. This is sometimes controversial as dominant groups often view identity politics as an attack on their own way of life, affluence, and capacity to shape public narratives. They may also consider themselves oppressed *as a result of* identity politics—some groups are best served by the idea of the universal experience. Identity politics connects to public narratives because these groups often contest the history of the nation in which they coexist with other groups because they feel ignored or underrepresented. For instance, in the United States, Black History Month has elicited controversy by promoting African American history during the month of February. The month is intended to counteract the white-centric history that supporters claim is taught in schools. Some critics argue that it is wrong to single out one ethnic group in the United States for special treatment; others argue that it is tantamount to segregation—an excuse to keep history classes focused on white history for the other eleven months out of the year.

> **Essentialism** Treatment of an individual as primarily a member of a category

> **Identity politics** Politics organized around the promotion of a particular category of people

At the other end of the political spectrum, many neo-Confederate groups contest the dominant historiography of the American Civil War, arguing that the Civil War was not about slavery but instead was about liberty and the ability of the Confederate states to secede from the Union when they felt that their interests (usually related to taxation and trade policy) were not being addressed. This renarration of the story of the Civil War has not emerged as strongly in popular culture as has the reinvigoration of African American history, but many bumper stickers reflect this view throughout the American South and beyond.

In any event, what is at root here is a recognition that narratives matter—and the traditionally taught history of the United States is not recognizable by at least some of its citizens as telling the history of their people. Popular culture has gone some way to acknowledge these absences. For instance, *Glory* (1989) was the tale of the first all–African American group of army volunteers to fight in the Civil War. *Unforgiven* (1992) is a Clint Eastwood western featuring Morgan Freeman as an African American cowboy, which was a common sight in the historical West that has been systematically ignored by early cinematic westerns (Goss 2004). Similar inclusiveness can be seen in other forms of popular culture, such as literature, TV, advertising, etc., and also for other population groups. The movie *Windtalkers* (2002), for example, highlighted the role of Native Americans in World War II. Note that all of these movies locate these marginalized groups in key landscapes and moments of American history that are seen as fundamental to national identity. Thus, the idea of national unity can be seen to fragment as other identities exist alongside national identities. National identities do not cease to exist in identity politics, but they become just one loyalty that people have among many (and perhaps for many still the strongest).

These renarrations of American history were done in reaction to an essentializing narrative that claimed a particular experience and public narrative as "American." However, making a movie about "the black experience" is also essentializing—claiming a particular experience and public narrative as "black" and ignoring the possibilities for diversity within it. While it is certainly a step in the right direction (the "black American" experience being a more specific one than just "American"), it nevertheless creates a box and puts a variety of people, experiences, and narratives into it.

It is perhaps best to imagine people's identity as being produced through a variety of public narratives, all intersecting in one ontological narrative. Which of those narratives seems most relevant at any given moment is a product of many contingencies. As an example, in the 2007–2008 Democratic primary, many African American women had to choose between two candidates who represented huge potential landmarks in public narratives with which they affiliated: Hillary Clinton, potentially the first female president, and Barack Obama, potentially the first African American president. Different women chose differently, because each of them had ontological narratives that made one candidate signify more to them than the other did. Of course, many based their decision on *Logos* more than *Mythos* and focused on specific issues rather than identity. Therefore, we must be careful not to essentialize people and their decisions by assuming they will act a certain way because they are categorized a certain way.

INTRODUCTION TO THE NATION

Nations are, in many ways, the fundamental building blocks of our geographic imaginations. Generally speaking, nations are the largest-scale collective identities to which we are strongly attached. For example, many Americans identify strongly as an American citizen but only weakly as a North American. Many Europeans, however, give a much greater emphasis to their identity as such, for a variety of reasons but also as a result of the active efforts by the European Union to foster that identity. It is possible to imagine a European nationalism emerging through these processes. Given the ubiquity of nations and nation-centered discourse, it is interesting to note that there is very little agreement about how nations came to be. There are, however, three approaches to theorizing nations and how they come into being—each focused on a particular scale of time. In this section these three approaches will be introduced, with more attention paid to the last formulation as it is the most closely linked to narratives and narrativity.

Primordial Theories of the Nation

Primordial theories of the nation were briefly mentioned in chapter 1, but here we will give more space to these views. Primordialists view the nation as a preexisting category, one that is essentially an extension of kinship units. Thus, the nation has existed since human society began (or shortly thereafter). The links between people in Primordial nations are either genetic or cultural (or both). These links reflect a fundamental connection that is perceived by the nation's members themselves as key to their commonality (Geertz 1973). These could be a language, religion, lifestyle, or even a physical trait. The latter of these indicates how nations exist in our imagination at the nexus of biology and culture, much like an extended family—with members of the nation seen as having common ancestors, even if only mythological. This idea of nation as extended family is conveniently ignored when some nations discourage ethnic mixing and promote reproduction within the national group.

Because in this formulation your national identity is rooted in where and to whom you were born, your national identity is essentially fixed in stone (van den Berghe 1981). While there is some usefulness to be found in being part of a grouping like this (like protection for the weak, etc.), it is argued by advocates of Primordialism that this kind of nationalism fills a deep-seated need for collective belonging, often to the material detriment of the national subject (consider, for example, the soldier who dies in war for his nation). Thus, Primordialists argue that trying to ignore these identities is a mistake because they are simply too fundamental to human existence. This kind of perspective is well-suited to explaining the situation in postcolonial Africa, where a common explanation for geopolitical turmoil is that states were created that encompass tens or hundreds of nations within them. Efforts to create a nationalism based on these new states have often struggled precisely because people still think of themselves as Yoruba, Ibo, Tswana, or other national identities.

The strength of Primordialism as a framework is that it highlights the role of cultural factors (and sometimes the biological ones that are deemed culturally important) in the determination of the nation. An important weakness, however, is that Primordialism has no real account for change within nations. If nations are defined by certain characteristics, and appeared long ago out of the kinship traditions of early humans, then how do we account for change, which even a cursory view of history can reveal?

Modernist Theories of the Nation

Modernist approaches are even more diverse than the Primordial ones. They do, however, have two related elements in common (Smith 2000). First, Modernists believe that nationalism is a fairly recent phenomenon—usually dating to the end of the eighteenth century. Second, the nation and nationalism result from trends associated with modernity and modernization: especially industrialization, capitalism, secularism, and urbanization.

> **Modernity** Time period associated with rapid political, cultural, and economic change, generally beginning in the seventeenth century

> **Modernization** Processes associated with industrialization, growth of capitalism, and subsequent social reorganization

Most formulations of Modern nationalism in the Euro-American world begin with the shift in Europe from an agricultural to an industrial society. The agricultural society was spread out over large geographic areas, with very particularistic and local cultural and food production systems. The feudal elites that ruled over these maintained in many ways a completely separate existence. However, with the rise of industrialism these family networks were disrupted as workers moved to cities to make their living from factories rather than from the land. This massive shift of population left many adrift—having understood their "place" in the world through their family connections and local roots, they found themselves now without either—just one of thousands (or millions) of new immigrants in tightly packed, urban tenements. Thus, a new form of collective identity needed to be constructed, and in particular one that united national citizens (no longer feudal vassals) and state leaders (Gellner 1983).

Here is where various Modernist theorists begin to differ amongst themselves. Some, like Eric Hobsbawm (1990), argue that nationalism is a way for elites to gain social control over the increasingly mobile and democratically minded population. However, he argues that this will become increasingly impossible in a globalizing world, when people, goods, and information flow across borders with increasing regularity. As an example, some have argued that the heartland of modernity, Western

Europe, has become postnationalist (Ignatieff 2003), embracing a new state-building in the European Union that is not dependent on (and arguably in contradiction to) traditional notions of nationalism. Just as nationalism was invented in Western Europe and spread throughout the world, postnationalism may do the same.

However, other Modernist scholars disagree with this notion. For instance, Benedict Anderson (1991), whose ideas were introduced in chapter 1, agrees with Hobsbawm that nations provide a new source of identity for those uprooted from their ancestral homes. However, he added the importance of print capitalism, in which vernacular languages became standardized through the uniformity of the printing press, giving readers a sense of being part of a larger community. Although the printing press is in the process of giving way to other, more contemporary, technologies (such as broadband and cable TV) for the dissemination of news, the importance of language in formulating community remains. Thus, Anderson is far less pessimistic about the future of nationalism. Indeed, a second look at the European Union provides just as much evidence of nationalism as of Hobsbawm's postnationalism—politics within the EU often revolves around national leaders opting out of EU directives or trying to gather as many EU resources as they can within their own borders.

What all these perspectives have in common though is an opposition to the Primordialists' notion of nations as categories that exist in their own right. They argue that our belief in nations *now* has led us to interpret the past using our present categories. This can lead to fundamental historical inaccuracies (like believing today's Germans to be fundamentally the same people as the Germanic tribes that began invading the Roman Empire two thousand years ago). The Modernists direct our attention to the processes that produced nations at a specific moment in time and in a specific place.

Poststructuralist Theories of the Nation

While Anderson introduces language as a critical part of understanding nationalism, more recently scholars have begun to wonder about the ways in which language, and popular culture more broadly, are constitutive of nations and nationalism—that is to say, they are the same thing, or constitute each other. While Primordial theories emphasized the distant past and Modernist theories emphasized the relatively recent past, poststructuralist approaches emphasize the present as the site of national (re) constitution.

It is here that narratives and narration reenter our discussion. The Modernist scholars acknowledged the importance of national mythology—

agreed upon conventions of national history that define the national history (Hobsbawm and Ranger 1983). They nevertheless thought about
nations as groups of people, whereas poststructuralist scholars focus on
the mythology as what actually constitutes the nation and views the
people as following from that point. As an example, virtually every high
school and university in the United States teaches a course (or many) on
American history. This course takes as its basis the existence of a nation
whose history is to be told. Thus, before the class is even taught there is a
lesson being given—that there is a United States, and that its story is
worth learning. Further, there is an act of exclusion—other people will
only enter the story as they become relevant to the United States, most
likely as enemies or sources of conflict. This class, once it begins, is traditionally taught as a battle against various external "others"—the British,
the American Indians, the Germans, the Communists—and against various internal "others"—British loyalists, slavery-proponents, and the like.
Thus, American history (and identity) is portrayed as the antithesis of all
these opponents. What we can see is the construction of an American narrative that is dependent on a variety of other non-American things to help
us learn what it means to be a member of the American nation. This is
fundamentally an open-ended narrative, stretching into the past and into
the future (Bhabha 1990, quoted selectively from 1–7, emphasis added):

> *Nations, like narrative, lose their origins in the myths of time and only fully realize
> their horizons in the mind's eye.* Such an image of the nation—or narration—
> might seem impossibly romantic and excessively metaphorical, but it is from
> those traditions of political thought and literary language that the nation
> emerges as a powerful historical idea in the west. . . . *To encounter the nation
> as it is written* displays a temporality of culture and social consciousness more
> in tune with the partial, overdetermined process by which textual meaning
> is produced. . . . These approaches are valuable in drawing our attention to
> those easily obscured, but highly significant, recesses of the national culture
> from which alternative constituencies of peoples and oppositional analytic
> capacities may emerge.

But how do we actually *encounter* this narrative? In the above example,
it was through a textbook, which often comes in many editions as it is
revised and updated. Yet we know from Michael Billig's concept of banal
nationalism (again, see chapter 1) that nationalism is ubiquitous—that we
learn and relearn what it means to be national all the time. This implies
that we encounter our "nationalization" more often than just in our formal education. Indeed, how is this national narrative continued? Episodes
of the narrative appear around us all the time, taking the form of news
programs, movies, television shows (like *Star Trek*, discussed in the preface), end-of-year retrospectives, and so on. The daily news provides epi-

sodic updates of the national story, with other forms of popular culture shifting to reflect the current communal understanding of who "we" are and who "they" (nonmembers of the nation) are as well.

Of course, there is no singular version of American history, identity, or narrative. There is a multitude, all in competition for hegemony because some forms of history, identity, and narrative advantage some groups over others by providing discursive justification for certain policies and actions. This is the case in the example, given at the beginning of the chapter, of Black History Month. Similarly, debates in the United States about whether or not the "Founding Fathers" (itself an interesting term in regards to the role of gender in nationalism) envisioned a Christian country have ensconced themselves in contemporary political debates about the proper role of religion in public spaces.

So, now that we know how we might encounter these narratives, how do particular narratives emerge as hegemonic or not? That has a great deal to do with how individuals perform these narratives. Performativity refers to a repetitive act that either seeks to change social norms or reinforce them (Butler 1990). To extend the example just given, if you decide that the United States is fundamentally a Christian country, you might act out that belief by erecting a nativity scene at Christmas on the grounds of a public school or courthouse. Another way to

> **Performativity** Everyday behavior based on social norms that reproduce those norms

perform identities is through consumption choices—an idea that underwrites boycotting, a very popular form of protest. For instance, in the 1980s many people, and even whole countries, performed their antiracist identities through the boycotting of goods from South Africa, which at the time had Apartheid policies of racial segregation and oppression in place. However, consuming popular culture can be seen as a positive affirmation of identity and narrative as well. As a simple example, the *New York Times* and the *Wall Street Journal* are often characterized as representing two different perspectives on what America is (or should be). The *New York Times* and the *Wall Street Journal* are generally thought of as liberal and conservative, respectively. Which newspaper a New Yorker decides to read then can be seen as a performance of a particular American narrative, a claim that it resonates with the lived experiences of the reader.

All together then, popular culture can be understood as one of the main avenues through which narratives of the nation are produced, and national subjects perform those narratives through their repeated consumption of that popular culture. While these narratives may be quite different from each other, what they share is their association with a particular nation. This is one of the most interesting features of the poststructuralist view of the nation—that there are a multitude of narrations, each claiming to be the truthful narrative of the nation. People then affiliate themselves with these various narrations, and, though they (mostly) all disagree about which narrative is "correct," they all believe themselves to be members of the same nation. Having looked at the concept of narrativity and connected it to the latest theorizations of nations and nationalism, it is now time to examine how these ideas all interact in a specific example from popular culture.

CASE STUDY: THE NARRATIVE OF AMERICA

In this section, we will examine how the comic book superhero Captain America has worked as a public narrative of the United States. Created in 1940 and published continuously since 1964, Captain America's tales provide an ongoing archive of some of the changing meanings associated with America. This case study will first briefly illustrate how the character of Captain America serves as a representation of the United States (à la chapter 3) before discussing the characteristics of serial narratives and delving into a particular narrative of this hero that spans four decades and provides particular insight into how national narratives work.

Representing America

As we saw in the previous chapter, places can be represented in a variety of ways, some subtle (the absence, or nonrepresentation, of the Caribbean in Jane Austen's novels) and some blatant (the exotic Orient found in James Bond movies). Captain America decidedly falls into the blatant category. Given his origin as a jingoistic wartime crusader against Nazi Germany and imperial Japan, this should not be too surprising. In fact, Captain America predates the American entry into World War II, but he nevertheless punches Adolf Hitler in the face on the cover of *Captain America Comics* #1 (see figure 4.1). This was because the early comic book industry was dominated by Jewish artists and writers who were far more aware of Hitler's treatment of German, Polish, and Czechoslovak Jews than most Americans were (Jones 2004). Hoping to push America off the bench and into the fight, Joe Simon and Jack Kirby (writer and artist, respectively) created Captain America and located him in an America that was rife with German spies and subversives. American munitions factories were being preemptively bombed by these "fifth columnists," who sought to weaken America in advance of a future German conquest. Thus, in the world represented by Simon and Kirby the moral geographies are clear—America is freedom-loving and peaceful, while Germany is aggressive and underhanded. As these facts are given, political positions are also imbued with a moral dimension. Any American who opposes U.S. intervention in Europe is weak-minded or corrupt, and those in favor of preparing for war are noble and purposeful. This comes through in a variety of early stories, such as 1941's "Trapped in the Stronghold," in which an American financier supporting the British war effort is kidnapped from the United States by Hitler's agents and sent to a concentration camp while an impersonator of the financier tries to recruit neutral countries for the Axis. Captain America, of course, is wise to these tricks, and rescues the original financier from Germany (Dittmer 2007a).

Captain America himself can be seen as the embodiment of a particular narrative of the United States. Steve Rogers was a New Yorker who volunteered for the army but was rejected because he was too scrawny. Overheard griping because he was so committed to serving the United States but had been turned away, he was brought in to serve as a test subject for the super-soldier serum, a U.S. military project that would give him peak human strength and stamina. Although the experiment was a success and Steve Rogers instantly transformed into the ultimate soldier, the project was shut down after the scientist in charge was killed by a Nazi spy. With only one super-soldier instead of thousands, the U.S. government decided to deploy him as a morale-boosting symbol of America. So, they outfitted him in a star-spangled red, white, and blue uniform and gave him an indestructible shield. While the colorful uniform is somewhat self-explanatory, it is worth considering the symbolism of the shield, as it constructs a narrative of America as fundamentally innocent and the victim of foreign aggression (much like the name of the U.S. Department of Defense—formerly known as the Department of War—does). Further, while Captain America is at the peak of human strength and athleticism, he is not super-strong like Superman or invulnerable to injury like the Incredible Hulk. Instead, he gets by in a world of super-powered villains through his dauntless courage and commitment to continual training.

In retrospect, the Captain America episodes from World War II can seem pretty hokey and unsophisticated. Characterization was minimal and storylines were mostly excuses for the action scenes. Most egregiously, the deployment of blonde-haired, blue-eyed Steve Rogers as a propaganda device *against* the racist Nazi ideology seems perverse. Still, there was a huge market for these stories, both among domestic populations and servicemen serving overseas. *Captain America Comics* was one of the best-selling wartime comic books, selling over one million copies per month (Wright 2001). There was a great deal of pleasure to be had in watching the Nazis be made fools of by a man draped in the American flag, especially in the early part of the war when things were not looking

Figure 4.1.   Cover of *Captain America Comics #1*, which predates Pearl Harbor by ten months (Copyright 2009 Marvel Characters, Inc. Used with permission)

good for the Allies (most of Western Europe was occupied and the United Kingdom was enduring the Blitz).

Thus, Captain America can be seen as embodying a patriotic, innocent representation of the United States. One of his greatest appeals was that he was not entirely a fantasy figure, like Superman. If Superman fought the Nazis, it would be a very one-sided affair. The war would be over in a few scant issues of the comic book, and then what? It would be depressing to read a comic book in which the war was over and live in a world where it was not. Captain America, then, was just right—strong enough to win every battle he was in, but certainly not able to fight the entire war himself. Thus, the world Captain America lived in (especially once the United States was in the war) could continue to be analogous to the one the reader lived in—a symmetry of narratives that made the episodes that much more enjoyable.

When World War II ended, however, interest in these kind of jingoistic tales waned. Without Germans or Japanese to fight, a nationalist figure such as Captain America seemed out of place and purposeless. Further, reader interests began to change, and the golden age of superheroes ended as horror and crime-related comic books became the real growth engine in the industry. *Captain America Comics* struggled to maintain its audience, even briefly becoming *Captain America's Weird Tales* (a horror comic) before being cancelled in 1949 as the Cold War was beginning.

Shortly thereafter, the United States became involved in the Korean War (1950–1953), and the comic's publishers decided to try to tap into the patriotic market again, resurrecting Captain America and telling new tales of the hero (subtitled "Captain America . . . Commie-Smasher!") in which the hero again fought against saboteurs and spies, but this time instead of Nazis they were Communists from the Soviet Union. However, this did not sell either—both because the stories were again thin and the characters one-dimensional, but also because the war-weary American public were not interested in that jingoistic narrative (Wright 2001). The comic book was again cancelled after a short run (1953–1954).

Narrating America

In the above mini-history of *Captain America Comics* from 1940–1954 it should be obvious that the long-term failure of the comic book came about as a result of its divergence from its audience expectations. In 1940, *Captain America Comics* clearly meshed with some element of the audience's public narratives, as illustrated by its enormous sales figures. It was that connection that allowed Simon and Kirby to introduce their desired geopolitical representation to the audience—illustrating Nazis as everything that is un-American. However, after World War II the Captain America narrative no longer seemed to fit the mood of the audience, and the type of America that was represented no longer connected. This relationship between the world portrayed within popular culture and the "real" world is critical. As we saw in the example of Superman in World

War II above, the world as portrayed in popular culture must resemble in some way the readers' world. Even the genres of science fiction and fantasy (in which superhero comics surely must be included) are only interesting to readers because these stories comment, often in dystopian ways, on the world in which the readers live. Think of, for example, the successful film *Minority Report* (2002), which was taken by many as an allegory of President George W. Bush's policies of extraordinary rendition and preemptive war even though the short story the movie was based upon was written well before Bush came into office.

> **Extraordinary rendition**
> Illegal transfer of people across state boundaries; since 9/11 used to refer to U.S. practices of sending suspected terrorists to other countries for torture

This need for continued connection between the narrative of the text and the narrative of the "real" world is particularly problematic for serial narratives. Serial narratives are narratives that unfold in a particular order, like episodes of the Kiefer Sutherland TV show *24*. It is very difficult to understand what is happening in *24* if you have missed any episodes. You can compare this to, for example, an episodic TV show like *Law and Order* or *CSI*, which generally has a self-contained story. In practice, most TV shows have elements of each (e.g., on *Friends*, which was in many ways a traditional episodic show, there were longer story arcs like the relationship of Ross and Rachel). Comic books like *Captain America* are serial narratives, with issues released (usually) monthly and building on previous events that cannot simply be ignored (this principle is referred to in cultural studies as continuity). If each issue must:

> **Serial narratives**
> Narratives that have no preset length or ending

> **Continuity** In serial narratives, the body of knowledge associated with what has happened prior

- Start with the fictional world resembling the reader's world,
- Have conflict (to hold the reader's interest), and
- Conclude with the fictional world still fundamentally resembling the reader's world,

then the narrative woven through the comic books must ultimately be a conservative one in which conflicts are decided in favor of the status quo. Indeed, if you think about superheroes, they are ultimately defenders of the world *as it is*, not as it might be. Villains are, by definition, those who want to change the world (albeit usually to better suit themselves). To illustrate the truth of this, why has Superman not used his powers to solve global hunger by ensuring the equitable distribution of food? Because, as with the World War II example above, once he did so the world would be fundamentally different than the one we live in (Dittmer 2007c).

So, continuity in serial narratives ensures that they must remain parallel in some way to the readers' world. But for long-running serial narratives the world is apt to change in fundamental ways *during* the narrative's unfolding. Thus, while superheroes defend the national status quo, the specifics of that status quo can change. As we saw earlier, this is what happened to *Captain America* in 1954. Creative staff (whether in comics, TV, etc.) must recognize these societal shifts if they are going to remain influential—because, remember, a fundamental premise of this book (and the recent narrative turn of the social sciences, described above) is that narratives (and hence popular culture) are key to our understandings of our own identity. The tension here between cultural elites, who produce narratives, and popular culture audiences, who decide if those narratives "work" with their own ontological narratives, is more fully discussed in chapter 6. For now, we will remain focused on the narrative produced when Captain America returned to newsstands in 1964.

Captain America's decade-long absence from the world of publishing came to an end when he was found frozen in an iceberg in the North Atlantic by a band of superheroes called the Avengers. Captain America had fallen into the ocean in 1945 while trying (and failing) to save his teen partner Bucky from an exploding rocket plane. This kind of event among fans is called a retcon ("retroactive change in continuity") because it contradicts the narrative as it has generally been understood. Caught in suspended animation for twenty years, the World War II veteran woke up to face an America that had turned on itself, questioning its own identity. The

> **Retcon** Retroactive continuity; a rewriting of what has happened prior

1960s were a time of revolution—the civil rights movement, the sexual revolution, the war in Vietnam—all of these made the United States almost unrecognizable to someone from the previous generation. Playing the venerable science fiction role of the "man out of his time" (like Buck Rogers, etc.), Captain America was able to sympathetically comment on these events from an outsider's perspective.

However, Captain America was not the same man he was in his previous incarnation. Having learned the lesson of 1954 (when the hero was last cancelled), Captain America was no longer the sometimes-racist xenophobe and red-baiting hero of the 1940s and 1950s. His role as soldier was downplayed, and a new role as symbol of the American ideal was emphasized. Indeed, Captain America only goes to the controversial war in Vietnam twice, and then only to rescue American soldiers, not to try to fight the war there. In fact, Communism is rarely mentioned, probably because the young audience of the comic book was increasingly dubious of Cold War binaries and skeptical of what they saw as an imperial war in Vietnam.

Captain America was no radical, however, and he straddled political debates by seeming to be a New Deal Democrat (then a fairly centrist position in which to be). With Communism unavailable for Captain America to battle, he instead continued his old rivalry with, of all people, Nazis such as the Red Skull and the Prussian aristocrats Baron Zemo and Baron Strucker. While this seems bizarre given the lack of real-world threat posed by Nazis in the 1960s, it makes sense if you consider the ideological value of Nazis as still to this day being seen as inimical to the mythological values of America. By pitting Captain America against Nazi plots to bring tyranny and social hierarchy to America's shores, the creative staff constructed an opposing idea of America as home to individual freedom and equality. Indeed, Nazis feature in the pages of *Captain America* to this day because they are deemed incontrovertibly un-American.

There was, however, one major problem with this rewriting of the Captain's narrative. If he was frozen in an iceberg in 1945, who was starring in all those comic books from 1945 to 1949 and 1953 to 1954? This violation of continuity was ignored for a time, as it conveniently erased the by-now embarrassing episodes in which Captain America had sought out Communist sympathizers in the United States, much like the publicly censured Wisconsin senator Joe McCarthy. But fans of comic books are notoriously particular about maintaining continuity. The problem was finally addressed in 1972, when it was revealed that, when Captain America fell into the ocean in 1945, the U.S. government assumed he died. A fan of Captain America's discovered a Nazi version of the super-soldier serum that created the original Captain America and blackmailed the U.S. government with it until they made him the new Captain America, even giving him plastic surgery to make him indistinguishable from the original. This narrative, while fantastical and utterly implausible, nevertheless explained the hole in continuity created by the earlier retcon—it was *this* Captain America who featured in those later comic books. Beyond "fixing" the narrative, it actually advanced it. The 1950s Captain America never received the proper medical treatment, causing him to slowly become mentally unbalanced and paranoid. Thus, the red-baiting Captain America was not the "real" Captain America, but instead a pale

Joe McCarthy American senator; anti-Communist crusader famous for unsubstantiated accusations against individuals inside and outside government

imitation suffering from the original sin of blackmailing his own country. This effectively relocates the paranoia and backstabbing of the McCarthyite era outside the "real" America. In fact, the 1954 disappearance of Captain America is explained as being the result of the U.S. government imprisoning him as a danger to society (Dittmer 2007b).

However, in 1972 he escapes, ostensibly the result of a disgruntled government worker upset about Richard Nixon's opening of relations with Communist China. When he appears in the pages of the comic book, the 1950s Captain America says things like "Don't worry, pal. The Coloreds never bother anybody" (Englehart and Buscema 1972a, 6), which the "real" Captain America would never say (see figure 4.2). Naturally, the two Captains America encounter one another and the dialogue emphasizes their ideological differences (Englehart and Buscema 1972b, 22–23):

> *'Real' Captain America:* "You think I'm a traitor? Grow up, fella—times have changed! America's in danger from within as well as without! There's organized crime, injustice, and fascism—or wouldn't you recognize that?"
> *1950s Captain America:* "Are you calling me—a fascist? You mealy-mouthed rat! You're scared to face up to the commies in a war, like a real man! I'm a real man! And I'll kill you to prove it!"

In this exchange the 1950s Captain America is framed effectively as no different than the Nazi villains that the "real" Captain America is used to fighting. American identity in *Captain America* is locked into a "Freedom vs. Fascism" binary that must fit all times. Nevertheless, the history of the United States in the 1950s as commonly understood is difficult to fit into that binary (see the 1998 film *Pleasantville* for a popular representation of the era as repressive). Of course, following superhero convention, the two Captains America battle, with the "real" Captain America emerging triumphant. Thus, this retcon excises that uncomfortable period from the serial narrative of America and leaves behind a morally pure American identity.

While this battle between Captains America from different eras enabled a discursive link to be made between Nazism and red-baiting, with both being categorized as un-American, a 1979 storyline added racism to that category. In this story, Captain America's girlfriend, secret agent Sharon Carter, has been investigating the National Force, an organization opposed to racial integration. Wearing Ku Klux Klan hoods and Nazi swastikas, they hold rallies in Central Park in which they burn crosses that seemingly convert to their cause white people who were protesting against them in the crowd. Sharon had been in the crowd and is thus converted into a National Front supporter. Captain America, looking for her, finds that the National Front is run by someone named the Grand Director (Mackenzie, Buscema, and Perlin 1979, 26): [M]y fellow Americans, I

Figure 4.2.   The 1950s Captain America returns in the 1970s as a proxy for intolerance and bigotry in America (Copyright 2009 Marvel Characters, Inc. Used with permission)

say to you that we must act now— and act swiftly—to make our beloved country strong once more! The only way to insure [sic] America's strength is to make her pure! Because a white America is a strong America!" Captain America himself makes the initial connection to the Nazis (Mackenzie, Buscema and Perlin 1979, 31): "This is my fight. It's been my fight since the days of Auschwitz and Treblinka" [Nazi concentration camps].

As the storyline progresses, a "rumble" is set to occur between the National Front and the African Americans of Harlem, where the National Front has decided to demonstrate. The Grand Director begins to have doubts as to the course of action, but his partner Dr. Faustus (a mind control expert) urges him on. Captain America manages to forestall the race war until the authorities arrive, and then he chases after the Grand Director and Dr. Faustus. When he catches them, he discovers that the Grand Director is, under his robes, actually the 1950s Captain America. Thus, the connection is made between the McCarthyite crusades of the 1950s and the fight against racial equality and integration (and, by extension, the Nazis)—all lumped together as America's opposite in the "Freedom vs. Fascism" frame that was established earlier. However, when Dr. Faustus orders the 1950s Captain America to attack the "real" Captain America, he hesitates and ends up committing suicide rather than bear arms against the representative of the American ideal.

The narrative thread of the 1950s Captain America makes important claims about the larger serial narrative of America itself. Most importantly, it locates racism as outside the "real" America, which is committed to multiculturalism. This is done through Captain America's references to the racism of the National Front as being the same as the racist policies of the Third Reich. Although Nazism and racism are not identical, for the purposes of the American narrative they are indistinguishable. Further, in both the 1972 story and the 1979 story, corruption is seen as external to the "real" America: the 1950s Captain America's paranoia was drug-induced, and the racism of the National Front was the result of Dr. Faustus's mind control gases (indeed, it is unclear if anyone in the National Front was there voluntarily, even the paranoid Grand Director). Despite the messy realities of the civil rights struggle, the American narrative is left morally clean and flawless.

CONCLUSION

Summary

In this chapter we began by outlining what narrativity is, and how it differs from purely rational thought. Of particular importance is this notion that not only are narratives important for our understandings of the world but also that they are key to our understanding of ourselves. As stated earlier, everyone has a role to play in the plots of narratives that they invest in. For example someone who thinks the world is steadily getting worse because of declining morals might consider himself or herself to be someone who "holds the line" by refusing to stand for immorality. In the case of Captain America, we saw how his role changed from someone who "holds the line" against Nazi aggression to someone who serves as a stable point from which to examine the rapidly changing United States of the 1960s and 1970s.

In any event, the narration of nation emphasizes our role in the grand scheme of things—both as narrators and as individuals who perform particular narratives through our actions and consumption patterns. From the poststructuralist perspective, nations are continually being renarrated and reinterpreted. The "national life" is produced through the serialized mediation of these narratives through television, the Internet, comic books, and other webs of connection, as well as our performance of consumption. The nightly news, the monthly comic book, the summertime blockbuster action film—these are all episodes of the national life, which bind together a variety of people without much in common except for their popular culture. Popular culture provides a vast array of resources for people to discuss and debate their collective identity. In so many ways, popular culture and national life are coconstitutive.

Extensions in Your Life

A larger point to be made about the Captain America narrative described above is that narration is often not only just about telling a story, but also about what is not told. National history is not an amalgamation of everything that ever happened; it is a construction that purports to tell the national story. But every history that is written is also a process of ignoring and forgetting. The narrative of the 1950s Captain America shows how uncomfortable truths can be treated within a historical narrative—with various characteristics or actions attributed to outsiders that absolve the main characters of guilt.

- What "outsiders" feature in your nation's or community's narrative past or present?
- What periods in your nation's or community's narrative past are simply not spoken about?
- What do these displacements or gaps in the narrative tell you about the identity this group is fostering?

5

Affect, Embodiment,
and Military Video Games

THE CONCEPT: AFFECT

Ideas

The previous two chapters dealt with discursive relationships between popular culture and geopolitics. That is to say, we were concerned with the relationship between language and place—knowing that how places are represented and narrated has a lot to do with the ways in which they are imagined by people all over the world. However, as said in chapter 3, there has recently been a challenge to the overwhelming focus on discourse and representation in critical geopolitics. This challenge comes from an emergent field sometimes referred to as nonrepresentational theory. While there are a great many possibilities for nonrepresentational geographies, much of the work in this area has focused on the notion of affect.

Affect is a word used in an everyday colloquial sense, which is a good starting point in regards to defining it. According to the Oxford English Dictionary, to affect something is "To have an effect on [it], either materially or otherwise." In the loosest sense then, "affect" means, in an academic sense, sensation that is linked to your environment. However, this is taken in two different directions by theorists.

> **Affect** Sensation linked to your environment; can be both biological and relational

The first formulation of affect is as the connection between the social/ cultural world and the biological realm of our bodies. In the last two chapters we have been very concerned with how people think and talk about places and people—both of which are very much concerned with the intellect. Affect turns our attention to the ways in which places and people trigger neurological/biological responses that have more to do with the biology of nervous systems and chemical-producing glands (Connolly 2002). Indeed, considering daily routines and the thousands of decisions that are made every day most people find that they do not remember making most of the decisions that they nevertheless seem to have made—like pulling a hand away from a hot stove at the last moment. Thus, many of our decisions are made at a precognitive level; they are "gut" decisions that do not have to be thought about, allowing us to save our cognitive power for just a few key decisions at any given moment. These "gut" decisions are nevertheless inflected by culture and society— think about intensely visceral reactions to socially taboo notions, like eating insects or committing incest. Decision making of this sort is thus neither wholly cognitive nor wholly instinctive, but instead exists at the nexus of not only psychology and sociology, but also less metaphorically between the body and the environment.

The second form of affect that exists in the literature is less focused on the biological/environmental interface and instead focuses on relationships between people, or people and objects. This, like the other version of affect just described, is precognitive, or existing prior to active decision making. Just like the Earth moves through outer space, being pulled in various directions by other objects in space and likewise acting on them gravitationally, we exist in reciprocal relationships with the people and things in our environment. What those relationships are is not obvious, even to ourselves, most of the time. But affect serves as "a sense of push in the world," influencing our collective behavior. "Affect, defined as . . . the active outcome of an encounter, takes the form of an increase or decrease in the ability of the body and mind alike to act" (this quote and previous, Thrift 2004, 64).

Both the more neurological form of affect and the more social/relational form have in common a general sense that emotions and other dispositions to our environment are not predetermined, but certainly highly influenced by a myriad of environmental factors. Thus, environmental factors can contribute to affective attachments to place—subconscious attractions and aversions to different geographic locations. Consider the feeling of walking into a cathedral (see figure 5.1). The building is designed to inspire religious thought by lifting our eyes up through the high vaulted ceiling, vertical stained glass windows, high columns, as well as the spire or dome itself. While none of this guarantees we will actually feel that way when we walk in, entering a cathedral clearly has that affective response for many (and even provokes quiet, thoughtfulness, and reflection in many nonbelievers). Affect is not reducible to "emotions" though—it is both biological and social in a way that emotions are not. The body's experience of affect comes in the form of feelings

Figure 5.1.　The interior of this cathedral in Reims, France, is designed to inspire a religious affect through its soaring heights. (Photo: author)

and sensations prior to their being labeled as particular emotions by the mind. This will be explored in greater detail in the next subsection.

Affect can be understood to work in several ways. The first is contagion, which refers to the social nature of affect. Affect is more than an individual's

Contagion Affect's ability to circulate among populations

Amplification Affect's intensification of individual experiences

Resonance Synchronicity between two or more affects to produce a much larger affect than would normally occur

experience—it is something that circulates among people, through body language and the mutual experience of environments. It may be differently experienced by different people, but it will rely on similar environmental cues. Amplification refers to the intensification of experiences, especially through the use of popular culture and the media. The media can take a local experience and amplify it so that it becomes a national one. Amplification can also drag an experience out over greater lengths of time than it would "normally" take. Finally, there is resonance in which amplified affects sync with each other to have a much greater affective impact than they would individually, as they reinforce each other like tuning forks vibrating at the same frequency.

Sean Carter and Derek McCormack (2010) argue that the attacks of 11 September 2001 on New York City and Washington have heightened our awareness of affectivity and its role in geopolitical thinking. In particular, they highlight five ways in which affect has become central to debates. First, they note that the notion of terrorism itself, and a subsequent "War on Terror," requires a heightened understanding of terror, emotion, and, thus, affectivity. In particular it highlights the ways in which affect can be shaped by governments and other political actors. Related to that is con-

Somatic marker Key experience that serves as the basis for "gut" decision making in the future

cern with the role that the 11 September attacks played as an affective reservoir that has provided tremendous justification for military intervention by the United States and its allies. This has been the subject of research by Gearóid Ó Tuathail (2003), who focused on the concept of somatic markers.

Somatic markers draw on the first, more neurological, version of affect described above (Connolly 2002). Ó Tuathail (2003, 858) describes somatic markers as "an organizing and categorizing capacity that sets the ground for higher-order 'deliberative thinking.' Operating below the threshold of reflection and structured by affect-saturated memory and 'gut feelings,' it simplifies and speeds the process of calculative reasoning so that every decision is relatively instantaneous, rather than a rational-choice marathon." He argues that 9/11 made a powerful impression on many, especially Americans, through the avenues of popular culture that mediated it: "dramatic visual footage, poignant still photography, eyewitness experiences, spectacles of catastrophe, 'portraits of grief,' and endless television programs, newspapers articles, movies, documentaries, theatrical plays, and, of course, songs and music" (859).

The third way in which affect has emerged in geopolitical research is in studies of violence and the media. Violence is obviously something that elicits powerful emotions from those involved, but remember that affect is more than just emotions. Violence increasingly functions at great distance and involves more than those immediately in conflict: "The point here is not just that we see more and more images of violence acted out on screens of various kinds. Rather, the point is that the very nature of violence, and the manner in which it is conducted, is organized at least in part to work through the affective logics of mediated spaces, whether this is through tactics of 'shock and awe' [the blitzing of Baghdad in 2003] or suicide bombing" (Carter and McCormack, forthcoming).

The fourth way in which affect has emerged in geopolitical research is through the emergence of research in critical security studies. This is a different field of study from those who research how to make people feel secure (i.e., criminology, terrorism studies, etc.), but rather is the study of how feelings of insecurity are often generated by efforts to secure something. This paradox of security has been highlighted as one of the critiques of the "War on Terror": efforts to find gaps in national security inevitably find them, which makes citizens feel increasingly upset and insecure, which was arguably the goal of the terrorists in the first place. "In a world of virtual threats, the fears and anxieties of which potential futures are generative become crucial to understanding how the logics of intervention are reorganized in the present around efforts to engage with threats that have not yet materialized" (Carter and McCormack, forthcoming). The final point about the intersection of affect and geopolitics is in research on geopolitical decision making. The very idea of affect problematizes the study of elites' and everyday citizens' geopolitical decision making because it reminds us that there is a vast background noise of influence through which conscious decisions are filtered in subconscious ways.

> **Critical security studies**
> Academic movement to question the basis of traditional security studies, especially state-centrism and militarism

Debates

Affect and, more broadly, nonrepresentational theory have emerged as one of the most dynamic, and hotly contested, areas within geography. There are three debates about affect that are of particular interest to popular geopolitics. The first debate is over the way that affect and nonrepresentational theory are often seen as in opposition to the studies of discourse, representation, and narrative that have traditionally dominated popular geopolitics. The second and third debates are narrower, about the advantages and disadvantages of studying affect vis-à-vis studying emotions, and about the way in which media are theorized in studies of affect. Each of these will be discussed here in turn.

Affect has been controversial in the same way that representation and narrative were when they were introduced in the 1980s, and this controversy has been heightened in part because of the way in which these ideas have been framed as "nonrepresentational theory." That phrase may sound pretty straightforward to an outsider, but for a discipline like geography which has always had a major focus on representation (remember geography's origins as "earth-writing" from chapter 1—geography has long been about actively representing or, later, studying representations), the notion of a nonrepresentational geography is anathema to many practitioners within the discipline. The framing of nonrepresentational theory was explicitly intended to distance the project from previous, comfortable ways of studying geography. However, the exclusionary tone of the term led many geographers to feel like their research agenda was now being cast into the disciplinary past, as something retrograde (Castree and Macmillan 2004). This was, as is now apparent, never the intention of those advancing the ideas of nonrepresentational theory; they simply felt that to get affect taken seriously it would have to be isolated from other intellectual currents. One attempt to blunt this effect is the introduction of the term "more-than-representational theory," which is awkward but differently states the premise of the project—that understanding the human experience requires more attention to the senses, the body, and the precognitive moment because the human experience exceeds attempts by discourse to abstract it (Lorimer 2005). Further, there has been other opposition to the study of affect because it often centers on everyday, banal experiences, which are deemed not important enough to merit scholarly attention. As described earlier however, it is the everydayness of affect (and popular culture as well) that makes it so relevant.

> **More-than-representational theory** More inclusive name for nonrepresentational theory

The second debate of note for scholars of popular geopolitics is between proponents of the study of affect and those that instead promote an investment in emotional geographies. Recall from earlier in the chapter that affect is not reducible to the individual's experience of emotions. Rather, affect is centered on a more social sensory experience of the environment and our relationship with it. Not everyone is in favor of this formulation (Thien 2005, 450): "This model of affect discourages an engagement with everyday emotional subjectivities, falling into a familiar pattern of distancing emotion from 'reasonable' scholarship and simultaneously implying that the emotion of the individual, that is, the realm of 'personal' feelings, is distinct from wider (public) agendas and desirably so." This criticism essentially means that, while affect claims to get at a more embodied, experiential type of geography (and geopolitics), it does so by refusing to actually look at individuals' bodies and experiences, and instead focuses on the transhuman relationships. This criticism builds on feminist critiques that argue that the social sciences have long rejected the personal/emotional/feminine in favor of the universal/rational/masculine.

These critics argue that a shift to considering people as "emotional subjects" is a path away from the mechanistic, technocratic understandings of geography that affect promotes. "Considering the production and reproduction of an 'emotional subject' informs our understanding of the relationship between the self and the places of our (en)actions" (Thien 2005, 453). Proponents of emotional geographies also argue that affect has an impoverished notion of power; with affect power resides with whomever can set in place the environmental infrastructure to affect populations, and everyone else is subject to them. However, the perspective of emotional geographies is that individuals exist with varying and complex relationships to power: "The figures of the 'terrorist,' the 'slave' and the 'camp' remind us of the need to challenge universalizing imperatives in social and cultural theories which ultimately represent [a false] illusion of 'choice' for all and a partial theoretical amnesia" (Tolia-Kelly 2006, 216).

The shift in focus from the social to the individual when we shift attention from affect to emotional geographies is, however, seen by proponents of affect as a matter for concern. While the proponents of emotional geographies seek to get as close as possible to the human and personal, scholars of affect worry about the ethics of doing research on such an intimate level. Further, the overriding focus on emotions conjures up a vision of:

> emotional authenticity (veering towards emotional fundamentalism) . . . but this only makes sense if we continue to think of lived experience as emphatically and authentically human, and oppose it to such things as abstraction. My sense is that we will never get near this kind of experience. . . . The affective authenticity of an emphatically human experience will always remain asymptotic—or a matter of faith. (McCormack 2006, 331)

The third debate that is of interest to popular geopolitics regards the role of the media in affective geographies. Much like affect can be seen to have an undertheorized understanding of power, its understanding of the media is very slight and largely relies on understandings of the environment (of which media are a part) conveying messages: "the discovery of new means of practicing affect is also the discovery of a whole new means of manipulation by the powerful" (Thrift 2004, 58). In other words, we live in environments that mediate the intentions of the powerful into our precognitive selves. An example suitable to this argument could be the use of chemicals to make the air on casino floors smell "fresher," thus boosting people's spending at the slot machines by an average of 45 percent. This would seem to be pretty strong evidence that the powerful (in this case, casino owners) can shape our environments such that we no longer can make our own decisions. However, consider this notion for a moment—the implication is that we are all dupes of the environment that we live in. There is no room for resistance, no room for alternative affects, because the "real" work is done before we are even aware of anything (recall that affect is prior even to feeling).

> Classical media-effects research is often criticized for assuming a hypodermic model of media power, ascribing to "the media" the ability to inject their preferred messages into the minds of their audiences. [Scholar of affect] Connolly goes one better than this: his account of media-*affects* is meant almost literally as a hypodermic model of influence, with media technologies ascribed remarkable determinative power in infusing affective dispositions under the skin of their audiences. (Barnett 2008, 193, emphasis in original)

Just as we noted in chapter 2, the cultural studies tradition has long been wary of imputing particular effects to mediated culture, because the ways in which audiences make sense of popular culture can be incredibly varied. Similarly, it could be said that it is very difficult to know what effect popular culture has on us in a precognitive sense. Proponents of affect would argue that consumers are predisposed to a very few interpretations by precognitive affect, but there is no way to verify what they are, and from what range of interpretations we were predisposed. "This allows the critic to substitute their own analysis of the imputed effects/affects of Film or campaign advertisements for any substantive analysis of the practices in which these sound-images are embedded" (Barnett 2008, 193). This is a critique that will be taken up in more detail in chapter 6, when we address audience-based research.

Now, however, we will turn our attention to one of the "powerful" groups that are hypothesized to be behind our affective mediascapes: the Military-Industrial-Media-Entertainment (MIME) complex. The media and entertainment elements of this complex are often criticized as contributing to an affective mediascape that promotes militaristic responses via American popular culture. We will thus discuss the rise of the MIME complex before looking at this chapter's case study: first-person shooter video games (a product of the MIME complex) and their intersection with the concept of affect.

INTRODUCTION TO THE MILITARY-INDUSTRIAL-MEDIA-ENTERTAINMENT COMPLEX

In his 1961 farewell address to the American people, President Eisenhower gave what is probably his most famous speech. In it, he coined a term that has remained with us ever since. The term is military-industrial complex, and it refers to an emerging assemblage of campaigning politicians, military elites, arms companies, and their lobbyists, that came into existence as the United States was, for the first time, creating a peacetime military intended to have a global presence. Here is the relevant quote from his speech:

> **Military-industrial complex** President Eisenhower's wary term for the institutional relationships of militarism emerging during his term in office

> This conjunction of an immense military establishment and a large arms industry is new in the American experience. The total influence—economic, political, even spiritual—is felt in every city, every State house, every office of the Federal government. We recognize the imperative need for this development. Yet we must not fail to comprehend its grave implications. Our toil, resources and livelihood are all involved; so is the very structure of our society. In the councils of government, we must guard against the acquisition of unwarranted influence, whether sought or unsought, by the military-industrial complex. . . . Down the long lane of the history yet to be written America knows that this world of ours, ever growing smaller, must avoid becoming a community of dreadful fear and hate, and be instead, a proud confederation of mutual trust and respect.

The speech is generally viewed as incredibly prescient, and is all the more interesting given Eisenhower's previous career as a five-star general in the U.S. Army during World War II.

EXPANSION OF THE COMPLEX

Since 1961 most of Eisenhower's concerns have emerged as reality, with the Department of Defense trumping the Department of State as the major governmental organ of foreign policy in the United States and military budgets escalating in both wartime and peacetime. Policy has increasingly been made by a group of professionals that include military officials, retired military officials who now lobby on behalf of arms manufacturers, and academics in think tanks that are funded by the military and arms manufacturers. Threats are found as a reason to justify ever-higher spending on new weapons systems. As political scientist Chalmers Johnson has argued (2004, 61–62):

> The result [of the professionalization of the military following Vietnam] was the development of a kind of military opportunism at the very heart of government, with military men paying court to the pet schemes of inexperienced politicians and preparing for lucrative postretirement positions in the arms industry or military think tanks. . . . The military establishment increasingly became a gigantic cartel, operated to benefit the four principle services—the army, navy, Marine Corps, and air force—much the way the Organization of Petroleum Exporting Countries (OPEC) functions to maintain the profits of each of its members.

To keep congressional support intact, manufacturing of military equipment has been distributed across the nation, so that any politician trying to cut military spending threatens job cuts in hundreds of other legislators' districts. This coalition of military leaders, politicians, and arms industry representatives has produced the largest military establishment the world has ever seen.

In 2009, the U.S. budget called for $713.1 billion to be spent on the military (this also includes the bill for the U.S. nuclear weapons stockpile, which is run by the Department of Energy, as well as the wars in Iraq and Afghanistan). Even without the expenditures on those wars, the United States spends about as much on its military as the rest of the world combined and about ten times as much as China, the country most often cited as a potential rival in conventional forces. The military-industrial complex has naturalized this state of affairs so that it is a taken-for-granted facet of American life. Both political parties broadly support this and even call for the expansion of the U.S. military. Most Americans support the notion of a "strong military," but the actual level of the strength is not really a topic of political debate.

James Der Derian (2001) has argued that the discursive absence of this debate is part of an ongoing revolution in politico-military affairs that seeks to mask the costs of militarism from domestic populations. He refers to this as "virtuous war." "At the heart of virtuous war is the technical capability and ethical imperative to threaten and, if necessary, actualize violence from a distance—*with no or minimal casualties*" (Der Derian 2001, xv, emphasis in original). The part of this that concerns popular geopolitics is less the technical capability (by and large the product of the weapons procurement described above as the military-industrial complex) than the *ethical imperative* for military action. Der Derian argues that in order to achieve the ethical imperative the military-industrial complex has adapted to include elements of the media and the entertainment industries (hence, the longer title: MIME complex).

> **Military-industrial-media-entertainment complex** Extension of Eisenhower's term to reflect the complex's attempts to shore up ethical support for militarism

Beyond absenting the debate about the military budget from the public sphere, the media play key roles by promoting the low casualty rates of recent U.S. engagements (for example: an amazing zero, excluding accidents, in the Kosovo bombing campaign) while never mentioning casualty rates for the other side, and by providing the government's perspective to the war narratives (through phenomena such as embedded reporting, which was used to much government satisfaction in the 2003 invasion of Iraq). The entertainment industries provide a similar boon to the U.S. engagement in "virtuous war" by producing movies, video games, etc., that are broadly supportive of U.S. goals and contribute to the masking of other peoples' perspectives, death counts,

> **Embedded reporting** Phenomenon of sending reporters in alongside troops during the 2003 invasion of Iraq; criticized as undermining reporters' independence

and humanity. While counter-examples surely can be found (recent Hollywood films such as 2007's *Rendition* and *Redacted* leap to mind, and antiwar films have been a staple since the Vietnam War), they are notable as such. These militarized media serve to provide ethical cover for the operations of a global American military, which has bases in over fifty countries around the world. Although much of this ethical cover is accomplished through strategies of representation and narrative, increasingly attention is being paid to the affective strategies in play.

History of the Military-Entertainment Alliance

The interconnection between military technology and entertainment technology is nothing new. As Paul Virilio (1989) has documented, the ability to see the enemy and kill them has developed in parallel to the ability to take moving pictures—both seeing innovation in the late 1800s as both the Gatling gun and the motion picture camera required the rotation of a drum or reel to rapidly move bullets or film through a chamber quickly. Typically, the flow of technology has been from military to more lighthearted uses, but this is not always true as we shall later see.

Cinema in particular has typically been supportive of the military. Cecil B. DeMille used to lead parades of actors carrying prop weapons down Hollywood Boulevard during World War I. War movies emerged as a distinct genre shortly after the creation of the industry and the Treaty of Versailles that ended the First World War in Western Europe. Shortly after the end of the war, movies were being made that dramatized the soldier heading off to war, facing adversity, struggling with the moral implications of war, and returning home to find moral absolution in his girlfriend or wife. The United States took the lead in the industry

> *Birth of a Nation* 1915 silent film set during the Civil War that promoted white supremacy; biggest Hollywood money-maker until 1937

as a result of the lack of rebuilding necessary in the United States after the war, but the political use of film in Europe quickly eclipsed what was being done in the United States (D. W. Griffith's *The Birth of a Nation* [1915] notwithstanding). There, political movements seized on film as a way of bringing legitimacy to their goals and methods (Virilio 1989, 54):

> In 1934 Hitler called on Leni Riefenstahl to make *Triumph of the Will*, offering the young director an unlimited budget, a hundred and thirty technicians and ninety cameramen (to be placed on specially built lifts, turrets and platforms). All this to film the week-long congress of the National-Socialist Party in Nuremberg, and to spread the Nazi myth around the world with a film of unprecedented magnificence.

However, the primary purpose of the Nazi Party meeting in Nuremberg was to be the subject of the film. This is an example of the conspicuous doubling that takes place with war and the media. Much like the "shock and awe" tactics that were used to launch the 2003 invasion of Iraq, it is difficult to know whether so many bombs were dropped because they were tactically necessary, or because they were necessary for the mediated images of American power they would provide.

After the Second World War began, most participating countries became involved in the use of cinema for propaganda purposes, with Hollywood directors like John Huston and Frank Capra leading the American effort. Capra's *Why We Fight* series (seven movies, released 1942–1945) is perhaps the most famous, and was planned by Capra as a direct response to *Triumph of the Will*. Intended to counteract the strong isolationist impulses of many Americans, the first hour-long episodes of *Why We Fight* were meant to shore up the will to fight among servicemen, but later lapsed into historical narrative of the war and its antecedents. British propaganda films were abundant as well, such as *In Which We Serve* (1942) and *The Next of Kin* (1942), the first about the importance of doing your duty in combat and the second about the ever-popular wartime truism, "loose lips sink ships."

Nazi propaganda is of course well known, and in fact the analysis of Nazi propaganda marked the beginnings of modern social science's engagement with the media. Germany had a Ministry for Public Enlightenment and Propaganda that was responsible for maintaining the moral support of the German people for government activities. The most infamous cinematic foray for Nazi Germany (outside of the aforementioned *Triumph of the Will*) is *The Eternal Jew* (1940), which portrays in documentary style Hitler's vision of the Jews as an unhygienic and lazy race, especially when contrasted to the healthy German race. The movie is now banned in Germany from public viewing. Similar to Nazi Germany, Fascist Italy had established a Ministry of Press and Propaganda by 1935, and it was subsequently renamed the Ministry of Popular Culture in 1937 (Caprotti 2005). The ministry was in charge of the production of propagandistic newsreels that presented the news from a Fascist perspective, to be viewed at the beginning of feature films in theaters. Documentaries and feature films were also produced through collaboration with the government.

Today's world of high-profile cinema, stars, and paparazzi seems a million miles from the heavy-handed propaganda of the Second World War. Nevertheless, there is a great deal of interplay between the military and Hollywood still today. The U.S. Army has actively been involved with Hollywood since 1927's *Wings* (Barnes 2008). Filmmakers with military assistance get access to ships, planes, and tanks, but they also get military input on scripts—with the understanding that if they do not accept that advice they will lose access to millions of dollars worth of military equipment that they need to make a realistic-looking movie. This is not a problem for some movies—such as *Iron Man* (2008), a movie supported by the U.S. Air Force about a superhero whose alter ego is a patriotic munitions producer. However, movies critical of the war in Iraq have had a more difficult time getting military approval. While this is a long way from censorship (after all, the movies can be, and are, made anyway) the military support for pro-military movies amounts to a government subsidy for private, commercial enterprise that dovetails with the vision of virtuous war described above.

The entertainment industry is, of course, far broader than simply Hollywood. Der Derian gives us an example from the world of video games of more synergy between the military and entertainment. Unusually, this is an example of the entertainment industry providing technology to the military (as stated earlier, usually it has occurred in the other direction, as in the case of the Gatling gun and the motion picture camera). Der Derian narrates (2001, 88):

On a tight budget, and always looking for off-the-shelf technology, the Marine Corps Modeling and Simulation Office had decided to appropriate rather than innovate, to simulate what marines do best: to fight independently in squads with small arms. There wasn't a smart weapon in sight, just a computer-generated four-man fire team in a retooled game of *Doom*. The monsters had been replaced by distant, barely visible forces that kept popping out of foxholes and from around bunker walls to lay down some lethal fire.

Simulating combat has long been one of the most difficult things for armed forces to do, simply because the affective environment of warfare is so difficult to reproduce. Reprogramming the classic video game *Doom* is not the first time the military has had to import expertise in simulation from the entertainment industry (Der Derian 2001, 89):

> In 1931 the navy purchased the first aircraft simulator from its designer, Edward Link. By 1932, the military still had only one Link Trainer; the amusement parks had bought close to fifty. Now the developmental lag between the real thing and its simulation has just about disappeared. From the F-16 to the F-117A, the M1A2 tank to the Bradley armored vehicle, the Aegis cruiser to the latest nuclear aircraft carrier, the video-game version arrives on the shelves almost as soon as the weapon system first appears.

As we shall see below, however, the development of the MIME complex has graduated to another level since Der Derian's research, with the U.S. military actually producing its own video game *for the market*. The need to understand and simulate the role of affect, feeling, and emotion in foreign policy and in combat has long been an imperative for political and military leaders who want to ensure that soldiers and sailors continue to be an effective fighting force, but as we saw above there is also an increasing interest in sustaining the moral underpinnings of militarism among democratic populations. In the next section we will see how video games have been used to contribute to both these goals simultaneously through the immersion of citizens and potential soldiers in their affect-laden virtual environments.

CASE STUDY: FIRST-PERSON SHOOTERS AND *AMERICA'S ARMY*

Having heard about affect and its influence on the geopolitical literature, and then about the construction of the MIME complex, it is now time to look at a concrete example of the way in which the concept of affect is deployed in the United States and around the world in ways that produce a militarized culture. It could be said that, in the context of popular culture and the military, representations and narratives show us *why we fight*, and affect is the key to understanding *how it is to fight*—and that by shifting the terms of discussion it limits the debate to technical questions rather than ethico-political ones. To demonstrate this, our case study will look at the genre of popular culture that is perhaps most associated with affect: video games.

Video games are a relatively recent object of study in the social sciences, even more recent than the rest of popular culture, and are closely wrapped up in what has been referred to as the visual turn in social theory. As Rachel Hughes puts it (2007, 3), "The term 'visuality' is used to denote vision as something that is always culturally mediated. 'Visuality' encompasses things that are visible to us as well as the visual technologies and viewing positions that enable us to see things in the ways that we do." In other words, seeing is more than just looking at something—it is culturally mediated in that we often look in particular ways and from particular places. Controlling what is

> **Visual turn**   Shift in social theory toward the importance of the visual, including different ways in which looking and seeing can be theorized

seen, and by whom, is critical to anyone engaged in international relations. Consider briefly the controversial photos of prisoner abuse by American soldiers in Abu Ghraib, Iraq. Fraser MacDonald (2006) has argued similarly that nuclear deterrence relies simultaneously on the obvious visuality of nuclear testing (so that potential adversaries know you have nuclear weapons) and on highly secretive technological development (preventing spies from seeing your progress).

Thus, the visual turn can be understood within the nonrepresentational theory described at the beginning of this chapter. Neither viewing the Abu Ghraib photos nor spying on government secrets can be understood as the transmission of an ideological message like in representation or narration. Visuality also relates to affect in that it is both biological (the function of the eye as an interface between the body and the social world) and social or relational (a way in which the body's environment is understood and also in which the subject understands itself in relation to that environment).

Adding a layer of complexity to the study of other forms of popular culture, video games incorporate another affective dimension: the active, relational engagement of the player with the game environment. This alone marks video games as one of the most interesting fields in popular geopolitics. As video gaming technology has become more sophisticated, it has be-

> **Immersion**   State of being in which full interaction is possible with an environment, either real or virtual

come common for games to implement a three-dimensional visualization in an attempt to make players feel immersed in the virtual environment.

Immersion has been described by humanities and technology professor Janet Murray (1997, 98–99) as:

> a metaphorical term derived from the physical experience of being submerged in water. We seek the same feeling from a psychologically immersive experience that we do from a plunge in the ocean or swimming pool: the sensation of being surrounded by a completely other reality, as different as water is from air, that takes over all of our attention, our whole perceptual apparatus . . . In a participatory medium [like video games], immersion implies learning to swim, to do the things that the new environment makes possible . . . the enjoyment of immersion as a participatory activity.

Immersion toys with the human/environment affective experience, attempting to get players to forget the "reality" in which they sit and instead substitute the sounds, sights, and perspectives associated with the game. Indeed, Murray hints that this feeling accounts for much of the pleasure associated with video games.

Because of this feeling of affective immersion, video games have emerged as one of the most controversial forms of popular culture among parents and commentators because of moral panics over their effect on children (such as in the now-nefarious *Grand Theft Auto* series, which has been lambasted for supposedly inspiring crime and antisocial behavior). However, it is that same hope that video games can desensitize/train players to the performance of violence that has made them so popular with the American military.

> **First-person shooter**
> Video game in which the visual experience is of immersion in the body of a virtual combatant

While war games have long been part of the state's planning for war, the video game genre of the first-person shooter has emerged at the nexus of the MIME complex. The first-person shooter puts the player in the position (literally, inside the head and looking out through the eyes) of a soldier in combat (see figure 5.2).

> It is the perspective of the combatant that is given preference here: gamers are given the illusion of inhabiting the same space as the avatar and see what they see. [While playing a first-person shooter] there are no panning or aerial shots, no cuts to close ups or reverse shots from the perspective of the enemy. Instead, the view remains solidly first-person. This never-changing perspective heightens the sense of "being there" and immersion in the gaming narrative. (Bryce and Rutter 2002, 72)

The breakthrough first-person shooter was the aforementioned *Doom*, which distinguished itself from its predecessors through its affective im-

Figure 5.2. The perspective of first-person shooters is intended to replicate that of a soldier in combat. Here, a young woman plays *America's Army* at the U.S. Army booth at the Bell Helicopter Armed Forces Bowl college football game in December 2008. (Photo: Annette Crawford, courtesy of U.S. Department of Defense)

pact on players—building tension and anxiety among players as they wander creepy deserted hallways.

> With its atmospheric rumblings and the slow build up of tension in the music by Bobby Prince, Doom was effectively the first major computer game to have a film-like soundtrack. This soundtrack was integral to the accumulation of tension for players traveling the eerie mazes of the game, constantly awaiting attack. As well as music, the game featured low breathing sounds, suggesting that enemies waited around every corner. (Bryce and Rutter 2002, 73)

Later games have emphasized real world combat as much as, or more than, the science fiction alien encounter featured in *Doom*. First-person shooters can "provide a real world hook by offering privileged glimpses from the front lines, and some of the backgrounds in these games are lifted directly from video footage of landscapes in which the U.S. military has recently been engaged" (Power 2007, 272). The collapse of time and space that enables the player to participate in the D-Day invasion or the 1991 Gulf War is part of the magic that attracts players to the games. As Marcus Power (2007) has pointed out, however, since the 9/11 attacks games have increasingly moved from a concern with historical warfare into contemporary conflicts, especially those in Afghanistan and Iraq. Further problematizing the genre is that first-person shooters are often paradoxically so dedicated to realism in combat that they neglect the circumstances of the conflict. Enemy soldiers are largely interchangeable, and the difference between fighting in a historical war or a contemporary one is largely a function of the style of uniform you wear and the weapons with which you are equipped.

Marcus Power (2007) and Robertson Allen (2007) have paid particular attention to one game, *America's Army*, which has been produced by the U.S. Army as a recruiting technique. The intention behind this is to identify talented individuals through their performance in the game, which points to the purported level of affective "realism" in the game—the army believes that those who perform well in the game will perform well in the army. Indeed, the game is structured to resemble a soldier's progress in a military career, beginning with basic training, on to deployment, and then finally participating in conflicts that resemble those faced by the U.S. military in the post-9/11 era. The game has a built-in advantage over other first-person shooters on the market in that it is absolutely free—its development funded by the U.S. Department of Defense and the game subsequently distributed through an array of Internet mirror sites. Another advantage that the game has is access to the army's combat veterans, who are attached to the development of the game (which is updated several times a year) as advisors.

Game play is focused on teamwork, with players teaming up virtually as squads to undertake missions, often dealing with prisoners (either capturing or defending) and set in a landscape that could be (but is not identified as) Afghanistan. Violence in the game is fairly abstract and bloodless, a departure from the realism that is the hallmark of the game, but an obviously purposeful modification of the affective reality of combat when you consider the goal of the game is soldier recruitment. Power (2007) reports that there is concern about the affective consequences of combat simulation of this sort, as the quick-twitch reflexes that video games foster become amplified by adrenaline-pumping combat conditions, potentially resulting in a lack of awareness of consequences among actual soldiers and a subsequent "kill 'em all" reaction by soldiers in the field, such as that demonstrated in the Haditha massacre of 2005 when U.S. Marines killed at least fifteen noncombatants in retaliation for a roadside bombing. Indeed, research has indicated that play of first-person shooters boosts aggression and physiological arousal in the short-term (Barlett, Harris and Boldassaro 2007). The ability of first-person shooters to be used as training devices and for the desensitization of soldiers to violence has also been utilized by resistance movements throughout the Middle East, who have modified ("modded") various first-person shooters so that the main character is an insurgent fighting against Western oppressors, effectively inverting the tacit narrative that is associated with the affect-saturated game play.

In either case, the teamwork associated with game play is performative (see chapter 4). All of the players, experiencing the same gaming scenarios, fighting the same enemies, and experiencing the same affects, bring into existence a community that is linked by the immersive virtual forum in which it takes place. Further, gaming's emphasis on reflexes and adrenaline pushes it more into the realm of visceral affect than cognitive representation—dissolving the boundaries between the human and the nonhuman (or machine). As Robertson Allen (2007) notes, this immersion is important for the U.S. Army as it is going through a process of transforming its units to be more networked and interconnected, but with smaller "footprints" on the ground. By operating in small squads of highly technological soldiers (dubbed the "Future Objective Force Warrior"), the U.S. Army's hope is to replace large, intrusive troop movements with quick intrusions of cyber-warriors, each equipped with the latest in war-fighting and communications technologies. Thus, the model of game play serves as an explicit training ground for a future army career, embracing the hybridity of the human and the virtual.

This real/virtual hybridity is encouraged by the army in many ways, not only in the actual immersion of game play. For instance, the avatars in the game are real soldiers, with real military records and biographies on display. To see their records, the player goes to a "virtual recruiting station," where they receive "honor points" (the currency of the game) just for showing up. Further exploding the categories of the virtual and the real, the U.S. Army is known for conducting military maneuvers at video game conventions that exactly mirror scenarios in the game, or alternatively parachuting into the parking lot. This certainly serves to amplify the affects of later game play.

The affective role of first-person shooters is not limited to contagion or amplification. Rather, these games can resonate with affective predispositions among many players. Many players replay historical engagements, especially those known as American defeats or shames, such as the Vietnam War or the Battle of Mogadishu (the battle portrayed in *Black Hawk Down*), seeking an affect of redemption or vengeance. "Games also offer a (cinematic) romanticization of war that is both seductive and powerful, and they can provide a (heroic) experience of winning a war single-handedly" (Power 2007, 286). More than anything though, they give players the affective experience of combat, but one stripped of danger, political context, and consequences. The focus on affective "realism" in video games contributes to a militarized medium that emphasizes military culture (honor, teamwork, professionalism) while deemphasizing what is outside that culture.

As one soldier in the film *Black Hawk Down* remarks, "Once the first bullet flies past you, all the politics goes out the window."

CONCLUSIONS

Summary

The conceptual part of this chapter began by outlining the various strands of thought that are united in the concept of affect, both the more neurological and the more relational. It then covered several criticisms of affect, including opposition from more discursively minded scholars and also criticism from those who want studies of affect to pay more attention to individuals and the ways in which they experience affects. The growth of scholarly attention to affect can be partly attributed to the attacks of 11 September 2001, which brought concepts like "terror" more fully into the realm of geopolitical thought.

In the case study portion of this chapter the idea of the MIME complex was introduced. The MIME complex produces a culture of militarism in the United States, perhaps best emblematized by the fact that the United States spends more than the rest of the world combined on its military. The military-industrial complex has long been recognized as a machine for procuring funding for the U.S. military, but recently attention has turned to the ways in which the media and entertainment industries work to procure ethical cover for U.S. interventions around the globe. In particular this chapter focused on the affectivity of first-person video games, which can be seen to predispose viewers and players to a culture of militarism. However, affect itself is not a militaristic or antirational form of relating to the world; it is instead pliable and can be put to any end, of any political persuasion.

Extensions in Your Life

On the one hand, affect is a difficult concept to consider applying in everyday life, given its precognitive basis. However, a fruitful place to start is to consider our living spaces.

- What kind of architecture surrounds you on an average day?
- What other kinds of affective influences might be predisposing you to certain engagements with the world?
- How can we have an affect that will cultivate a disposition in the world that reflects a preferred geopolitical imagination?

6

The Active Audience and Evangelical Geopolitics

THE CONCEPT: THE ACTIVE AUDIENCE

Ideas

In chapter 2 of this book, we introduced several different ways of theorizing popular culture. The work of the Frankfurt School, Antonio Gramsci, and Michel Foucault were introduced as theorizations of popular culture that saw it as a way to subvert class-based or other identities by introducing ideological content to popular culture's consumers. While there were differences among these theorists, they were linked in their view of popular culture as something produced by elites and consumed by everyday people. Michel de Certeau, however, was also introduced as providing a different kind of perspective, one that focused on how audiences manage to subvert the popular culture that is available and use it in ways never intended by the original producers. Up until now, the case studies in this book have drawn primarily from the first tradition (especially from Gramsci and Foucault) but in this chapter we will instead be drawing more from the perspective that de Certeau embodies—the active audience.

> **Active audience** Notion of audiences not simply as passive recipients of messages, but also as creators of meaning

To a certain extent, this shift itself embodies a criticism of the work found in previous case studies. These analyses, of comic books, movies, literature, video games, etc., are presented as authoritative understandings of the meanings found in these forms of popular culture. However, they are most definitely not—they are readings of those media by academics who have their own geographies and histories that they bring to the consumption process. While there is a role and a purpose for this (as hopefully the preceding case studies have shown), it is nevertheless important to think more critically about popular culture's meanings and how they are created through the process of consumption. In other words, we are shifting from an understanding of meaning as *inherent* to a text ("text" referring to any kind of popular culture) to an understanding of it as *attributed* to a text by its consumers.

This is an appealing perspective for a variety of reasons, but perhaps most obviously because it seems to reflect our own self-perception as something more than just victims of elite cultural producers. We do not simply think what they want us to think, and we do not simply go out and consume things because they tell us to. We exercise choice and restraint, often resisting especially ham-handed attempts to colonize our consciousnesses by doing the exact opposite. Even in the case of pop music, an industry that is often criticized for its assembly line production of radio-friendly acts like the Pussycat Dolls, Miley Cyrus, and 3 Doors Down, it has been estimated that only 10 percent of albums that are released are commercially successful. This reflects the power and unpredictability of audiences' practices of consumption.

Of course, producers of popular culture, like Island Records or Warner Brothers Studios, have tremendous power to shape their products. The example of pop music should not lead us to believe that producers are powerless—the efforts of cultural producers to create demand for their products through advertising surround us all the time. For example, following the 11 September 2001 attacks, SUV (sport-utility vehicle) sales sky-rocketed in the United States as these trucks became retooled to have aggressive styling that made them look more like mobile fortresses. The Nissan Pathfinder was rebranded as the Nissan Pathfinder Armada, and now is simply the Nissan Armada. The new-look SUVs caught the public's imagination as a defensive measure to provide security for children during a time of geopolitical uncertainty (Bradsher 2004; Lauer 2005). Nevertheless, many Americans opted not to buy SUVs. Clearly marketing has limits. How can we reconcile these disparate experiences—the inculcation of an idea via advertising and our frequent rejection of such messages?

It is perhaps best to think of these two perspectives as extremes, and instead think of a text (like a car commercial, or a magazine article, or a movie) as a cultural resource that may be utilized by consumers to create meaning that is attributed to the text. Each text has certain attributes that might predispose audiences to a particular meaning. This is because the very fundamental purpose of language is communication—conveying meaning. Life is full of misunderstandings and cultural dissonance, but it would be a mistake to think that effective communication is not possible at all.

Now, the question of conveying meaning is of course separate from the question of convincing an audience that a meaning is true and important to them. Conveying the idea to people that an SUV is safe is much simpler than making them want to part with $28,000. What made the SUV marketing so successful? There are many answers to that, some of which have to do with the marketing materials and some of which have to do with identity. SUV advertisements often show images of families experiencing the outdoors, driving to exotic places, and successfully surmounting physical obstacles. The SUV, both in commercials and through its visual design (during this period), was intended to symbolize freedom, which resonates with American notions of the good life. Further, the SUV represents an independence from the need for good road infrastructure (regardless of actual off-road ability, which is often quite poor) and hence an ability to evacuate from an area should there be danger. To the extent that individuals felt vulnerable in the time after 11 September 2001, they likely felt a desire for SUVs and were thus open to the marketing efforts of companies like GM and Nissan. Thus, our understandings of, and openness to, textual meanings is as linked to our identities as they are to the texts themselves.

Geographer David Livingstone (2005) has theorized the act of textual interpretation as occurring through two types of geography. The first type he terms cartographies of textual reception. This term refers loosely to the imagined communities described in chapter 1. These communities, as you may remember, are groups of people who, because of their common linguistic and other connections, think of themselves as a collective unity. This is a connection that links people across potentially vast distances. The implications of these cartographies might seem obvious to you—for example that people from Japan will make different sense of a film like *Pearl Harbor* (2001) than an American audience would. The second type of geography through which textual interpretation occurs has been termed by Livingstone as the cultural geographies of reading. This refers to the more complicated social networks in which every textual consumer is embedded. Every consumer of popular culture is embedded in many different so-

> **Cartographies of textual reception** Fault lines among audiences that primarily reflect linguistic and other macroscale cultural differences

> **Cultural geographies of reading** Microscale differences among readers that reflect different social identities and networks

cial networks that provide the frameworks for his or her interpretations of the text.

Once popular culture is thought of in this way, it is very difficult to go back to the previous, more ideological view. For example, consider the film *X-Men* (2000). This film features a group of mutants (genetically gifted people) who have banded together to form a team, the X-Men, for mutual protection and to create a safe-haven for young mutants who are persecuted by "normal" humans. One of the mutants in the movie, Magneto, unlike the X-Men, argues for a strategy of confrontation that will see mutants in the ascendancy on Earth. Professor X, the leader of the X-Men, instead argues for a policy of accommodation that will see prejudice decline over time as mutants and humans become accustomed to each other. This conflict (and the longer storylines available in the original comic book series) has been read in many ways by its audiences. Some readers saw the story as an allegory for American race relations, with Professor X standing in for Martin Luther King, Jr. and Magneto standing in for the more confrontational Malcolm X (Trushell 2004). This reading makes especial sense in the comic book, which was first published in 1963. The revelation at the beginning of the movie that Magneto is a Jewish Holocaust survivor heightens the probability of the movie being read as a tale of ethnic conflict.

> **Martin Luther King, Jr.**
> African-American Baptist minister who promoted nonviolent struggle in the American civil rights campaign

> **Malcolm X**   African American civil rights advocate who rejected nonviolent struggle as inadequate in the face of continued white oppression

However, to many audiences the franchise's tale of the oppressed genetic minority has equally often seemed to be that of homosexuals (Earnest 2007), especially in the last two X-Men movies. In X2 (2003) the plot remains focused on ethnic conflict (the plot is driven by a new law requiring mutants to register with the government) but there is a scene in which mutant Bobby Drake (Iceman) "comes out of the closet" to his parents by demonstrating his power to them. His mother's response—"Have you tried *not* being a mutant?"—is something of an in-joke with homosexual viewers as the clichéd response of many parents of homosexuals over time. The third film, *X-Men: The Last Stand* (2006), is driven by a medical cure for mutanthood, intersecting with political debates in the United States about homosexual marriage and whether or not homosexuality is a choice or a genetic trait. The movies, and the comic books before them, provide cultural resources which will be interpreted and used by audiences in a variety of ways.

Debates

So, while once geographers and other cultural theorists could safely marginalize the audience in studies of meaning, it is no longer possible to do so. However, that does not mean that there is no controversy surrounding the active audience. The question still remains: how do you research audience interpretive processes?

There are a number of problems with conducting research on audience interpretations. These problems can be summed up as falling into two categories—the theoretical and the practical. Theoretically, audience research is difficult because it is inspired by the idea that these interpretations are diverse and hard to pin down. So, how do you uncover this complexity and then generalize about it to draw conclusions? Some scholars (e.g., Radway 1988) even argue that it is impossible for two people to have the exact same experience with a cultural text, both because these hypothetical people bring different geographies and histories to the experience and because the actual experience with the text is always unique (for example, sitting with a book on a beach, perhaps drinking a Corona, versus reading it on a crowded subway next to a snoring drunk; or reading a newspaper in print versus online). Therefore, it is a mistake to compare people's interpretations at all. Further, it may be a mistake to believe that there is an audience at all; instead there is only a variety of individual experiences.

This perspective undoubtedly has some theoretical merit, and is certainly a stronger argument than the traditional Frankfurt School perspective that treats audiences as monolithically passive. However, this perspective perhaps is overreliant on a narrow understanding of cultural consumption as limited to reading. While there is a longstanding tradition of thinking of reading as a solitary act, the consumption of other forms of media are often quite overtly social—like going to the movies and watching television (think of how many dread going to the movies alone). In fact, even reading is more social than usually given credit for, as discussing reading material (the news, the latest in Oprah's book club, etc.) is one of the classic forms of small talk. Finally, remember from the discussion earlier in this chapter that David Livingstone argued that there are at least two scales at which we can understand cultural consumption as a profoundly social experience. Even if you read something all alone and never tell anyone about it, your experience and interpretation of the book is connected to your social networks and identity. Again, the actual situation is somewhere in between the radical perspectives of "everyone consumes culture similarly" and "there is nothing social about cultural consumption." What this means practically, then, is that scholars have to be very circumspect in the kinds of conclusions that they draw about audience research.

Another theoretical problem with audience research is hinted at in the above. If researchers are going to ask people what they think of a cultural text, like a movie, what exactly are they hoping to discover? Consider a hypothetical research project in which researchers want to know the impact of the movie *Hotel Rwanda* (2004) —an Oscar-nominated film about the genocide in Rwanda ten years prior. If researchers surveyed people leaving the theater about what they thought the movie was about, how they felt about the genocide in Rwanda, and whether they felt fundamentally changed by the movie-going experience, a high proportion would probably respond in ways that reflect the movie's powerful moral and geopolitical undertones. However, if the same people were surveyed a year later, it is likely that most (if not all) would report that they remembered the movie but had not changed their level of political engagement at all (despite an ongoing conflict in Darfur that resembles that found in Rwanda and Burundi). This is because we are deluged by mediated messages, and it is in the aggregate that they have an impact. It is a fruitless task to identify one cultural artifact as having an effect on people in all but the most unusual circumstances.

Practically, then, audience research is complex and daunting. There are many potential problems—who is the audience for the particular popular culture? People who are likely to volunteer to participate in a study are also more likely to be fans of that particular form of popular culture, and will have a different understanding and emotional connection to the material than someone consuming it for the first time. That might be fine, but makes it difficult to generalize about the research's conclusions to the entire audience. Also, the act of asking someone about popular culture itself might change the processes of meaning-making used by the audience member. If someone watches a Jerry Bruckheimer film because they love explosions, and a researcher asks about the geopolitical implications of the film, then that viewer is likely to reinterpret the movie in a way that they would not have in their normal consumption of the film. A final problem can be the vast geographic and temporal scope of people consuming popular culture—how can we study the audience of a book, which is consumed in private and anonymously over the several years in which a book is print?

Researchers have attempted to address these concerns, both theoretical and practical, in a variety of ways. Early research on pop culture consumption centered on subcultures (Storey 1996). Subcultures are groups within a larger culture that differ in some fundamental way from the rest of the culture in which they are immersed. Subcultures have been popular in cultural studies for a vari-

> **Subcultures** Groups distinct within the larger culture in which they exist

ety of reasons. First, and most practically, remember that cultural studies emerged in the 1970s in the United Kingdom, a time of youth rebellion against Cold War nuclear confrontation and the conservative social policies of Margaret Thatcher, when subcultures were out front and center in British life (especially so in London). Second, given that the theory and politics of cultural studies celebrate the active subversion of popular culture, youth subcultures were very attractive:

> Through a process of "bricolage", subcultures appropriate for their own purposes and meanings the commodities commercially provided. Products are combined or transformed in ways not intended by their producers; commodities are rearticulated to produce oppositional meanings. Examples include teddy boys wearing Savile Row Edwardian jackets, mods wearing Italian suits, punks using bin-liners and safety pins. In this way (and through patterns of behavior, ways of speaking, taste in music, and so on), youth subcultures engage in symbolic forms of resistance to both dominant and parent cultures. (Storey 1996, 135–136)

Bricolage Something creatively produced from whatever materials are at hand

A further reason research into subcultures became dominant is because it narrows down the scope of cultural consumption to a select group that is capable of being studied by a single researcher.

However, these subcultural studies were subsequently criticized because they focused on the spectacular and exceptional, ignoring the everyday and the common. The assumption is that subcultures are where resistance occurs, and therefore there is some "normal" culture out there that is passive and dominated. The elitism of older theorizations of popular culture (as an inferior form of culture to high culture) had effectively been taken up by the scholars of cultural studies, who by celebrating overt resistance missed out on the everyday resistance that is practiced by everyone.

The altering of popular culture texts by audiences has been most pronounced with fan subcultures, which have been a focal point for much of this work in cultural studies. Fandom refers to the most ardent supporters of a popular culture franchise, such as *Star Wars*, or, increasingly, to supporters of someone who is involved in popular culture across multiple media, such as TV/movie scriptwriter and producer Joss Whedon, or movie director/comic book author Kevin Smith. Fandom is significant because, like the subcultures associated with earlier research in cultural studies (punks, etc.), fandom overtly takes popular culture seriously in ways that "regular" audiences do not (at

Fandom Social networks composed of fans of particular elements of popular culture

least publicly). This leads to derision by outsiders, found most obviously in stereotypes of *Star Trek* and *Lord of the Rings* fandom as basement-dwellers trapped in a permanent state of adolescence. Ethnography of fandom, however, is often very revealing—both for the demographic diversity of fandom and also for the variety of meanings that the popular culture has across this spectrum of individuals (Brooker 2002).

Fandom is viewed by cultural studies scholars as an overt site of performative consumption (Hills 2002). Performative consumption is a term that tries to describe popular culture's openness of meaning—reminding us that culture is forever in a process of reinterpretation by people who are themselves performing their own identity. This perpetual reinterpretation prevents the closure of meaning, a truth of which we need to continually remind ourselves. Fandom literally produces its own cultural artifacts based on popular culture—some of which have even become incorporated by the original producers, such as the growth of Mulder and Scully's romantic relationship, which developed slowly over the last several seasons of the *X-Files*. This romance first appeared many years earlier in fanfic (fan fiction), stories written by fans that often vary greatly from the intentions of the original producers. The most salaciously studied topic in cultural studies has been "slash" fiction, so called because of the shorthand used to denote these stories of homosexual relationships among characters who are not portrayed as homosexual in the canonical stories (i.e., Kirk/Spock, Frodo/Samwise, etc.). Interestingly, these stories are usually written by heterosexual women—another example of how fandom and performative consumption often defy expectations.

> **Performative consumption**
> Creation of new culture through the consumption of mass-produced culture; reflects view of culture as always in process

> **Fanfic** Fan fiction; new stories written by fans about characters from popular culture

INTRODUCTION TO EVANGELICAL GEOPOLITICS

The next section of the chapter will outline evangelical Christian approaches to geopolitics, which will be fused with this discussion of the active audience and performative consumption in the case study of this chapter, which involves the *Left Behind* book series. Evangelicalism is a broad term for a subset of Protestant Christianity that is often used quite imprecisely. In the context of this book it will be used in a way that is common in North America, that is, to describe a constellation of conservative

Protestant groups (often eschewing denominational labels) that have in common a belief in salvation through a personal relationship with Jesus Christ (often referred to as being "born again") and in the literal interpretation of the Bible. It is useful to look at evangelical geopolitics when discussing the active audience because of this laser-like focus on the Bible as a source of understanding about the world. This is an incredibly diverse group, and the term evangelical should be sparingly used (in most circumstances) because its imprecision is often a mechanism for stereotyping (especially in politics). Theological and other differences split this group into many different subgroups. One of the dominant strands of theology within the evangelical fold is known as premillennial dispensationalism.

> **Evangelicalism** Broad category of Protestant Christianity; adherents usually emphasize the authority of the Scriptures and a personal relationship with Jesus

> **Premillennial dispensationalism** Belief that this is the last era prior to the establishment of Jesus's promised kingdom; Jesus will save true Christians from painful transition between eras

Dispensationalism refers to the belief that human history is divided into seven different dispensations, or eras. These dispensations are all characterized by a new agreement between God and mankind, each of which is eventually broken by a flawed humanity. Dispensationalists typically believe that we are living in the sixth dispensation, commonly referred to as the church age. The final dispensation, the millennium, will be defined by one thousand years of peace. The exact nature of the millennium, and the transition from the church age to the millennium, is a source of debate among dispensationalists, as we will see in a moment.

Cyrus Scofield was key to the spread of the "premillennial" brand of dispensationalism through his successful efforts to convince the prestigious Oxford University Press to include premillennial dispensationalist notes in the margins of their Bibles (a great example of the role of mass media in spreading discourse). Premillennialism is the belief that Jesus will return to take away all true-believing Christians in an event called the Rapture. Shortly thereafter will begin a seven-year period known as the Tribulation, which will be marked by the rise of a figure, popularly known as the Antichrist, to world domination, as well as

> **Rapture** Event in which many believe Jesus will lift all believers into heaven, only to return for his forthcoming rule on Earth

> **Tribulation** Seven years of war, natural disaster, and disease that many believe will serve as a last warning to convert to Christianity before Jesus's final return

> **Armageddon** Final
> battle that many believe
> will occur between the
> forces of the Antichrist
> and Jesus, in the Valley of
> Megiddo of today's Israel

a series of wars and natural disasters. The end of the Tribulation will see the return of Jesus to overturn the rule of the Antichrist in a massive battle (usually called Armageddon, after its prophesied location in Meggido—see figure 6.1), judge the nations of the world, and establish a Christian kingdom based in Israel, which Jesus will rule for a thousand peaceful years. At the end of the millennium, time will literally come to an end, with the Jews and Christians being taken up to heaven for eternity (Weber 2004).

Figure 6.1.   Map locating Megiddo in modern Israel (UCL Drawing Office)

As stated before, this is but one strand of eschatology found within evangelical thought. For instance, postmillennialism believes that there will be no Rapture and no Tribulation, and that Jesus only returns once, at the end of the millennium of peace. This millennium is not begun by the "birthing pangs" of the Tribulation and the warfare of Armageddon, but rather by steadily improving world conditions that are linked to the spread of Christianity around the world. It is here that we can see the connection between these eschatologies and geopolitics. While postmillennialism is decid-

> **Eschatology** Theology and philosophy of the end of the world

> **Postmillennialism** Eschatology that argues there will be no Rapture or Tribulation, only a peaceful segue into Jesus's heavenly kingdom

edly optimistic about the future of the world, premillennialism is quite the opposite—sure that disaster and war are inevitable.

In fact, for premillennialists, the more dangerous the world becomes, the closer they believe the world is to the return of Jesus. While nobody is supposed to know when the Rapture will occur, it is widely believed that the moral decay of the world as well as an increase in warfare and natural disaster will presage the beginning of the Tribulation, and, since premillennialists desire the return of Jesus, an increase in warfare and disaster is, in principle, a good thing. Now, what I am saying is only logical inference based on the theology and eschatology of premillennial dispensationalism; in reality premillennial dispensationalists have quite complex and contradictory views on the fate of the world, as we shall see in the case study.

It is important to note the source of these beliefs about the future, as they likely seem pretty far-out to nonbelieving readers of this book. Most of this eschatology comes from the prophetic books of the Bible, which include Daniel, Ezekiel, Revelation, and a few others. These texts, written in different places and times, have been interpreted by many as being the word of God given through human mouthpieces (the ancient Jews had a tradition of a court prophet who would provide God's guidance on moral and political affairs). While many have sought to determine the exact date and events associated with the end of the world by studying the prophetic books of the Bible, this is mostly a history of embarrassment as "date-setters" have often claimed to know the date of the end of the world, only to be found wrong. However, prophecy-minded individuals have had their hopes rise steadily over the last half of the twentieth century and the beginning of the current century as geopolitical events seem to be lining up. Pivotal in this regard was the founding of the modern state of Israel, which is thought to signal the last generation before Jesus's return. Further, some prophecies required Israel to exist for other events to occur. Other events that have caught prophecy-watchers' eyes include the creation of the European Union, which can be seen to fill in for the Roman Empire in passages that refer to that ancient empire (which played the part of villain in many biblical prophecies), as not only does the EU increasingly include the former territories of the Roman Empire, but it was founded by the Treaty of *Rome* in 1957.

From a nonreligious perspective, this can seem genuinely worrying for several different reasons that are important to note. In a country like the United States that has global power and influence, the notion that a vast segment of the electorate is actively wishing for disaster and warfare is certainly troubling. At a very minimum, the belief that future events are preordained can lead to a geopolitical apathy among the electorate (or the opposite—in the 2008 presidential campaign many grassroots evangelicals openly worried about Barack Obama potentially being the Antichrist, who is supposed to be charmingly seductive and promise peace to a war-weary, gullible public). However, it is important to note that evangelicals thinking in these terms differ from the rest of the population only in the specifics of their geopolitical logic. As the preceding chapters have shown, we all use different logics to make geopolitical decisions, finding some kinds of evidence more important than others and generally basing decisions on sketchy geopolitical imaginations and gut feelings.

This does not mean that all geopolitical perspectives are equal, and that they should therefore be spared critique. It does mean, however, that criticism of premillennial dispensationalism's geopolitics should focus on the probable outcomes of these geopolitical practices versus others, and not on the often-personal attacks which people can resort to when different worldviews collide. In fact, the reason evangelical geopolitics is useful to study is because it offers a prism through which to study everyday geopolitical processes of meaning making across a spectrum of differing worldviews. In more "mainstream" geopolitical reasoning it is difficult to see whether a geopolitical imagination stems from popular culture, education in public schools, or from other sources because they are so overlapping and similar in message. However, an expression of evangelical geopolitics is fairly obvious in origin when viewed alongside other knowledges.

In the next section we will begin by describing the plot of the *Left Behind* books, which are a fictionalization of the Rapture, Tribulation, and return of Jesus Christ, before discussing the ways in which that story has been received and reinterpreted by its active audience. Through this we will not only discover the specifics of a premillennial dispensationalist geopolitical imagination but more generally draw conclusions about how everyone (evangelical or otherwise) makes sense of the world that is mediated to them through the news, popular culture, and other sources of knowledge.

CASE STUDY: *LEFT BEHIND* AND THE *LEFT BEHIND PROPHECY CLUB*

Introduction to *Left Behind*

The publication of *Left Behind* in 1995 by evangelical publisher Tyndale House marked the beginning of a resurgence in "born again" publishing. It was the first of a twelve-book series of *New York Times* bestsellers that, despite its runaway success, remained off the radar of many literature buffs because of its very specific appeal (and marketing) to evangelical readers. Written by Tim LaHaye (theologian) and Jerry Jenkins (evangelical novelist), *Left Behind* began with the startling scene of people mysteriously disappearing from an airliner in flight. Similar scenes had occurred all over the world, leaving disaster and chaos in the wake—this was the Rapture, described in the previous section. The pilot of the plane from this opening scene soon realizes that his evangelical wife was right when he discovers that she and their son are among the missing, leaving him to convince their sceptical secularist college student daughter the error of their ways. Converted now to evangelicalism but "left behind," they are condemned to live through the Tribulation—their souls now safe but their lives in steadily escalating jeopardy. They become the core of the Tribulation Force, a highly skilled group dedicated to saving as many souls as possible during the Tribulation and being as much of a pest as possible to the Antichrist (whom they quickly identify as Nicolae Carpathia, a charismatic politician from Romania who becomes leader of the United Nations in the chaotic aftermath of the Rapture). The twelve books of the original story (which concludes with the victorious return of Jesus) were followed by three prequels, an epilogue (together these books have sold over sixty-five million copies), a video game, a graphic novel, and another book series narrating the Tribulation as seen through children's eyes (which have sold an additional ten million copies). Simply put, *Left Behind* has been a multimedia phenomenon.

Nevertheless, *Left Behind* is not a definitive statement of Christian eschatology; it is in fact quite controversial, with many pastors disliking the series because its teachings are at variance with their own and they find themselves in competition with the books among their own church members. As contemporary as the *Left Behind* phenomenon appears, "this apocalyptic reading of the Christian Bible, based on giving the Christ of Revelation a substantial precedence over the Jesus of Luke, has long been characteristic of the Christian millenarianism that has periodically re-emerged during times of radical change in European and American society" (Agnew 2006, 184).

Geopolitical Summary of *Left Behind*

Given the first section of this chapter, you should be wary of anyone like myself telling you what *Left Behind* means in a grand sense. Instead, what follows is an attempt to summarize for you the geopolitical events of the books, a very partial reading that ignores other possible (but equally valid) readings of the books, such as those rooted in morality and theology (for more analysis of the books see Dittmer and Spears 2009).

Following the Rapture and ensuing chaos described above, the books flash back to tell us of the events that led up to the Rapture (of obvious interest to evangelical readers looking forward to their own Rapture). An Israeli scientist had created a formula that would allow the deserts to bloom and thus had the potential to feed the entire world and end hunger on a global scale. However, Russia attacked Israel in order to get the formula, only to have their invading forces devastated by seemingly divine intervention (not a single Israeli was hurt). Then the Rapture occurs, and Nicolae Carpathia rises from being a Romanian legislator to president of Romania, and then finally to secretary-general of the United Nations. This is accomplished through a supernatural charisma that even incorporates mind control. He begins to turn the United Nations into a world government, renaming it the Global Community, shifting the entire world onto one currency, and abolishing all national militaries (retaining 10 percent of the world's weapons for the Global Community). He also moves the Global Community's headquarters from New York City to New Babylon, a new city built on the site of the ancient Babylon of prophecy (in Iraq), and creates an ecumenical world religion that the whole world joins, except for Orthodox Jews and evangelical Christians. The American militia movement, lamenting the loss of American sovereignty to the newly powerful Global Community, launches a rebellion at the behest of the American president, only to be crushed by ruthless nuclear strikes, leaving the Tribulation Force as the only organized opposition to the new world order.

Carpathia, in his new role as the supreme potentate of the Global Community, moves to consolidate his power by taking control of the world's media and distributing the benefits of the Israeli formula to the people of the world. The Tribulation Force, however, knows through their study of prophecy that disaster will soon occur, and they make that information available on their website. A global earthquake soon devastates the world's infrastructure, causing a hitch in Carpathia's plans and calling attention to the website of the Tribulation Force. More disaster strikes, including an asteroid that causes a tsunami and the poisoning of the world's oceans. The successful prediction of these events by the Tribulation Force, combined with Israel's divine immunity from disaster, leads to mass conversions to evangelical Christianity, especially by Israeli Jews. All non-Christians are then afflicted by a plague of metallic locusts that sting, causing months of agony.

The Tribulation Force, knowing full well that the Antichrist's control of the economy will soon be used to demand loyalty to his regime, begins to set up an alternative economy based on cooperative bartering. Indeed, Carpathia soon compels the population to get a tattoo and subdermal microchip in order to trade. The Tribulation Force recognizes this as the mark of the Beast which, if taken, marks the bearer as bound forever to the Antichrist (and therefore hell-bound). The next blow to the Antichrist's regime comes in the form of two hundred million invisible horsemen who slaughter nonbelievers for months, killing one-third of the Earth's remaining population.

After being assassinated Carpathia rises from the dead, now indwelt by Satan himself. He turns the one world religion into a personal cult (dubbing it Carpathianism), and the Tribulation Force becomes more overt—using the twin distractions of a plague of boils sent to nonbelievers and the turning of the world's oceans into blood as an opportunity to hold a mass conversion of Jews in Israel and lead them to the ancient fortress of Petra (see figure 6.2). The furious Antichrist launches a nuclear strike on Petra only to find that it is divinely protected, with food and water appearing supernaturally inside and a force field protecting it from any assault.

> **Petra**   Nabataean capital city in today's Jordan, hewn out of stone and only known by Westerners since 1812

Carpathia in his fury turns on those not in Petra, ordering that unconverted Jews be taken to concentration camps and Gentiles not bearing the mark of the Beast be shot on sight. Further, he gathers his armies at Megiddo for a final assault on Petra. However, asteroids begin to rain down on the earth and a burning cross appears in the sky. Jesus himself appears in the air, and as he speaks the bodies of Carpathia's army split open horrifyingly and are swallowed by the earth. The battle over, Jesus condemns Carpathia and his supporters to the Lake of Fire to burn for eternity and resurrects all of the Tribulation Force members who died in the confrontation.

Left Behind Fandom and the *Left Behind Prophecy Club*

Amy Frykholm (2004) has conducted interviews with fans of *Left Behind* to see what meanings they find in the books, visiting homes and churches

Figure 6.2.   Image of Petra, in Jordan (Photo: David Bjorgen)

to see the fans in a variety of environments. She found that the books served a variety of purposes and took on many meanings. Reading the books was most definitely a social event, as each book was passed around church communities as a ritual of reassurance; in a world perceived secular and threatening to the church community, being able to read the books and discuss them helped to seal the bonds of community. The narrative of the book seems to reflect the readers' own sense of vulnerability:

> The world progresses in a way decidedly hostile to the interest of these Christians, and within the narrative, true Christianity must become increasingly isolated and marginalized. Christians must face discrimination and persecution, the world must become increasingly dominated by evil, and true believers must seem increasingly scarce. (Frykholm 2004, 106–107)

However, the books are also rejected as a specific narrative of the Tribulation—with readers recognizing the difference between biblical scripture (which is deemed inerrant) and biblically inspired texts, which serve another purpose. Indeed, the *Left Behind* books were used as a disciplinary tactic—reminding readers that the Rapture could occur any time and it is best to be prepared. While the books were intended as a way to convert people to the evangelical perspective, they thus are just as useful at keeping current adherents strong in their faith.

While not strictly believing the narrative of *Left Behind*, most readers seemed to use it as an intermediary between the Bible and current events. This was critical because the prophetic books of the Bible are often quite opaque to the novice reader, and the evangelical tradition emphasizes the importance of a personal relationship with God, in part through scriptural study. Consider this quote from the book of Ezekiel:

> And thou shalt come from thy place out of the north parts, thou, and many people with thee, all of them riding upon horses, a great company, and a mighty army: And thou shalt come up against my people of Israel, as a cloud to cover the land; it shall be in the latter days, and I will bring thee against my land, that the heathen may know me, when I shall be sanctified in thee, O Gog, before their eyes (Ezekiel 38:15–16 [KJV])

This quote is generally taken by prophecy-watchers to refer to a key prerequisite of the Tribulation, an attack by other nations on Israel. However, as can be seen, that is not an obvious "literal interpretation" of the passage. Thus, *Left Behind*'s fictional take on the Bible:

> provides evidence for the Gnostic view toward which readers already tend to that there is indeed an alternative plot behind the seeming chaos of the world that is driving it toward a particular end. The script of history that *Left*

Behind illuminates and the Bible confirms also provides a script for believers and advocates for specific modes of behavior and configurations of social life. (Frykholm 2004, 110)

Indeed, the passage from the book of Ezekiel given above is translated into the Russian invasion of Israel that occurs in flashback at the beginning of *Left Behind*. The details of the divine intervention are provided by a major character who serves as a reporter during the war. Thus, *Left Behind* helps fans by transforming the prophecies of the Bible into more digestible narrative.

As described in the first section of this chapter, however, readers are not just consumers, digesting narratives; they also engage in performative consumption—producing their own versions of texts. This is especially true of evangelicals, as they are supposed to read the Scriptures and determine their meaning without the mediation of a priest. As *Left Behind* has gotten older the geopolitical narrative described above has begun to date and seem less plausible. Since the first book's publication Russia (imagined by evangelicals in particular as a godless country as a result of seventy years of Marxist ideology) has declined as a threat from its Cold War peak of confrontation with the West (only to reemerge in the press as a threat following its intervention in South Ossetia and Abkhazia in 2008) and Islamic terrorism has become a more obvious source of geopolitical danger. In short, evangelicals seek to make sense of current events via their biblical scripts. As *Left Behind* dates, it becomes less and less helpful. What kinds of narratives of the Tribulation are being created by fans of *Left Behind* in this kind of situation? The answer lies on a website called the *Left Behind Prophecy Club*, which is run by the publishers of the books as a web community for fans of the books. On the website is a discussion board for current events, in which fans discuss geopolitical events that might be of biblical significance.

Here, new narratives of the "End Times" are spun and debated. However, not every opinion is deemed equal by evangelicals. While the Internet is often imagined to be inherently democratizing (see chapter 7) it nevertheless reflects social inequalities as much as the "real world" does. Matt Hills (2002) identified three different types of assets that increase fans' ability to create new, hegemonic meanings. The first, social capital, refers to a fan's connectivity within a social group—how well known is he or she? The second, cultural capital, refers to the fan's knowledge of the popular culture in question (in this case this might mean the Bible or *Left Behind*). The final form is symbolic capital, which is the ability to convert other forms of capital into actual prestige or power—in the case of the web forum that might mean the ability to write well or something similar.

On the *Left Behind Prophecy Club* website, all three types of capital were on display as posters debated the meanings of various events and arrived at consensus about a variety of topics during the period from April 2005 to January 2007 (Dittmer 2008). The first topic of general agreement among the posters was about the special role of Israel in the beginning of the millennium. Virtually every poster to the forum supported Israel and was opposed to a two-state solution with Palestinians. Further, some posters had gone to great effort to label modern-day maps with places mentioned in the Bible as being within Israel to show how far Israel has to expand in order to fulfill prophecy and allow the return of Jesus (see figure 6.3). This featured role for Israel is entirely consistent with the *Left Behind* books and is a long-standing element of the premillennial dispensationalist eschatology.

A second consensus on the web forum was about Iran. The period during which these posts were made was a time of escalating nuclear tension between the United States (where most posters lived), Israel, and Iran. This fit into the eschatological script well, because Persia (Iran's former name) is mentioned in the book of Ezekiel as one of the nations that attacks Israel. To help connect news stories about a nuclear Iran with the biblical Persia, Revelation 9:18 (KJV) has been interpreted as referring to nuclear war: "By these three was the third part of men killed, by the fire, and by the smoke, and by the brimstone, which issued out of their mouths." While other countries, like Libya and Ethiopia, are lumped in with Persia in the book of Ezekiel, they received a fraction of the web forum attention that Iran did. This shows the ability of the fans to rescript the End Times in ways that seemed more plausible in regard to current events.

The third consensus achieved on the website was the role of Islam. Islam served for most (not quite all) of the posters as the opposition to not only Christianity but also to the United States. This was not only linked to the ongoing American "war" against Islamist terrorism (which the posters considered God's will, regardless of secular American motives) but also the nuclear tension with Iran. Beyond the geopolitical motives, there was something more personal in the posts as well—occasionally the word "Muslim" would be used as a slur, when one poster was arguing with another. The slur was used as a stand-in for "stupid," probably because Muslims believe in Jesus but do not acknowledge him as the Son of God (rather, only a prophet). It should be noted that this use of "Muslim" as a slur was decidedly a minority practice; however, viewing Islam as a geopolitical opponent of the United States was nearly ubiquitous. The role of Islam as a main player in the End Times is not a feature of the *Left Behind* series, which began well before the attacks of 11 September 2001 (but concluded afterwards). It would seem to be, like Iran, an inclusion

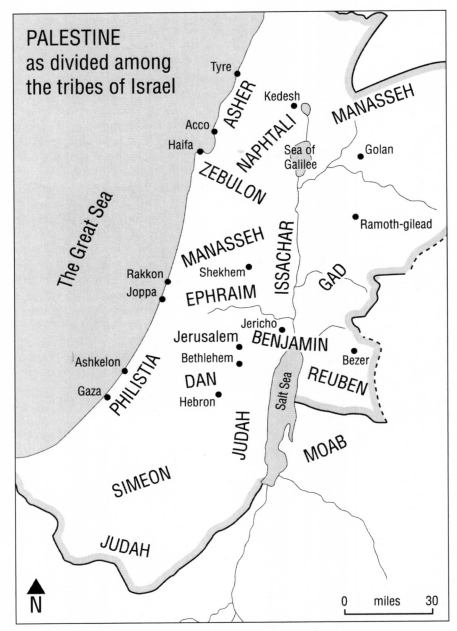

Figure 6.3. One example of a mapping of ancient Israel, intended to argue against a two-state solution to conflict with Palestinians as well as further Israeli expansion (UCL Drawing Office, redrawn from a map found at www.spiritrestoration.org)

made by fans based on the confluence of American geopolitical imaginations with those flowing from an evangelical perspective.

Together, these three points of consensus show that in practice evangelical fans of *Left Behind* draw from a variety of often-contradictory perspectives and knowledges in the construction of their geopolitical imaginations. The doctrine of premillennial dispensationalism has built in enough flexibility to allow it to adapt to changing geopolitical circumstances, giving fans tremendous latitude in their interpretive processes. Sometimes however, the flexibility in ordering and specifying End Times events was not enough in the face of the rigor required by other aspects of the faith. Some posters expressed concern that Jesus would come back too soon, and their loved ones would be left behind. The idea of their loved ones burning in hell was disturbing to them and they felt their faith tested in those moments (Dittmer 2009). The forum thus illustrates the contradictory positions in which our fragmented identities can put us. The geopolitics of the end of the world can be very appealing as an evangelical Christian, but horrifying as a wife or husband of an unsaved spouse. Again, this is not unique to premillennial dispensationalists, but something true of all of us—the same contradiction can be found in a secular parent who feels the nationalist pull of war but also worries about a son or daughter in the military.

CONCLUSIONS

Summary

In this chapter we provided an alternative approach to representations and narratives by focusing on the processes of meaning making that are embedded in the consumption of popular culture. Rather than being passive consumers of ideological messages produced by cultural elites, consumers are active and powerful agents, using cultural resources tactically to provide meaning, entertainment, and structure to their lives. Nevertheless, they are not entirely liberated—rather processes of meaning making are embedded in Livingstone's cartographies of textual reception and cultural geographies of reading. Fans provide a powerful example of not only the creative use of existent cultural resources but also show us how different kinds of capital influence individuals' ability to project their preferred meanings and have them adopted by others within a fan subculture. Research into cultural consumption and active audiences is theoretically and practically complicated, but nevertheless is a necessary antidote to oppressive readings of popular culture that put those who enjoy popular culture and take great pleasure from it in the role of passive victims. The concept of performative consumption offers a succinct way of expressing the role of consumption not as an endpoint for cultural processes, but as a jumping off point for more social engagement between consumers. Popular culture is not a static, dead thing, but instead an open-ended social process that we all partake in and that helps animate our social lives.

The case study for this chapter built on the introductory material on different evangelical theologies and their associated eschatologies. The connection between religious narratives of the end of the world and contemporary geopolitical concerns of nuclear war and terrorism become apparent when premillennial dispensationalism's period of Tribulation is cast as just another geopolitical imagination. It then becomes possible to look at the *Left Behind* books in ways similar to our earlier discussions of Captain America and James Bond. This chapter differs though by moving through and past a discussion of narrative and representation to see how fans of *Left Behind* have renarrated the End Times to connect them with an always-in-flux set of current geopolitical Others. In this case study we saw how fans of *Left Behind*, through filters of social, cultural, and symbolic capital, arrived at new points of agreement about the likely sources of geopolitical danger for their dual identities as citizens of the United States and subjects of the Kingdom of God.

Extensions in Your Life

Often in (geo)political debate today we hear about Islam and it is characterized as *being* something, whether violent, peaceful, harsh toward women, or whatever. Often debate is then focused on the end of the sentence—on whether or not Islam *is* violent, whether or not Islam *is* respectful of women's human rights. As this chapter illustrates, however, we perhaps ought to be directing our attention to the middle of those sentences—to the *being* and the *is*. These are the words that attempt to fix culture—to make it static and dead. By rendering Islam (or evangelicalism, or any culture) into an object it becomes impossible to imagine change from within; it only becomes possible to manipulate from outside the object. However, in this chapter we saw how cultural change can occur, for good or for ill, in just the span of a few years—driven from within by active agents.

- How are "outside" cultures described on the news shows you watch?
- Are they described as static and imprisoned by their own culture, or are they portrayed as dynamic and in flux, active agents in their own future?
- In what ways do you see yourself as an active participant in popular culture?

7

+

Hegemony, Subaltern Identities, and New Media

THE CONCEPT: SUBALTERN IDENTITIES

Ideas

In chapter 2 we focused briefly on the concept of hegemony, which was about convincing others that your culture was also theirs, thus disarming any sense of difference. In Gramsci's formulation, this was a way of explaining how capitalism had staved off a long-expected workers' revolution, but subsequently the notion has been adopted for a variety of divisions other than economic class. The weaker party in these divisions is often referred to as *subaltern*, or outside the hegemonic power structure. In this chapter we are going to revisit hegemony, considering it this time not in the national context but instead at the global scale and from the perspective of the subaltern.

If we look back on all the popular culture we've discussed in case studies thus far, whether they are James Bond movies, *Captain America* comics, *America's Army*, Jane Austen novels, the *Left Behind* novels, political cartoons, etc., you might note that they are all produced in the United States and the United Kingdom. This is partly to match the language of this book with that of its examples. However, it also reflects the global reach of English-language, and especially American, culture (often subtitled or otherwise made available to global audiences). While in many places this popular culture is loved for its (often) high production values, in others it is disdained for its geopolitical connotations. A 1994 *New York Times* survey of American popular culture exports connected American domination to geopolitics:

Is America's dominance due to intrinsic strengths of its culture—its sheer flair and energy, its incarnation of democracy itself as marketable entertainment, its forging of a new international language? Or, as foreign critics lament, is it merely a function of American military and economic domination? Or capitalism run amok, a "pure monopoly in the worst sense," as Jacques Toubon, the French Minister of Culture, put it in the recent debate over world trade barriers? (Rockwell 1994)

It is perhaps understandable then that some peoples around the world might chafe under a deluge of American popular culture: the Americanization of popular culture around the world not only occupies space that other, more indigenous, forms of popular culture might occupy, but also makes the rest of the world feel peripheral and threatened by American cultural hegemony. However, there are two powerful intellectual counterweights to this Americanization thesis that are available. The first is termed "anti-geopolitics," while the second is rooted in postcolonialism.

> **Americanization**
> Process by which American culture replaces a local culture

Anti-geopolitics refers to attempts to produce geopolitical knowledges that challenge and even contradict the hegemonic discourses produced by traditional elites. Practitioners of anti-geopolitics deny the hegemonic notion that the interests of elites are the same as the interests of everyone else, and are resisting that cultural domination from above. "Anti-geopolitics represents an assertion of permanent independence from the state *whomever is in power*, and articulates two interrelated forms of counter-hegemonic struggle. First, it challenges the *material* (economic and military) geopolitical power of states and global institutions; and second, it challenges the *representations* imposed by political and economic elites upon the world and its different peoples, that are deployed to serve their geopolitical interests" (Routledge 2003, 236–237, emphasis in original). In the realms of formal and practical geopolitics, this resistance can most often be seen in the realm of dissident intellectuals, but only because of the generally high visibility of their dissent.

> **Anti-geopolitics** Strategy of the subaltern that entails reversing values associated with categories

> **Zapatistas** Revolutionary group in Chiapas, Mexico, that has eschewed combat in favor of bringing international pressure to bear via Internet organizing

More common, but less visible to metropolitan populations, is the resistance of large populations, such as the Zapatistas of southern Mexico. Originally the Zapatistas were a guerrilla movement that fought for

Mayan Indian rights in the geographically and politically peripheral Yucatan Peninsula (see figure 7.1), upset by the social changes that they associated with the rise of state-backed commercial agriculture. The Mayans were forced off their land in favor of large farms on which they then had no choice but to serve as peasant labor. This shift was part of a plan by Mexico to increase the state's economic power by backing the export of cash crops—a classic example of the state pursuing a "national interest" that was not necessarily good for everyone.

However, traditional guerrilla resistance soon gave way to a very media-savvy form of anti-geopolitics, which took advantage of the 1994 entry by Mexico into the North American Free Trade Agreement to highlight the inequalities that free trade and neoliberal economics were creating in southern Mexico and beyond. Their press releases and Internet activism have

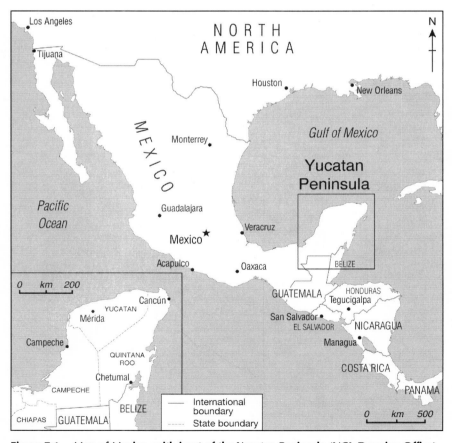

Figure 7.1. Map of Mexico, with inset of the Yucatan Peninsula (UCL Drawing Office)

been very effective in projecting an antigeopolitical discourse into the public sphere, one that emphasizes the local and indigenous in opposition to the hegemonic state and international institutions of free trade. Their model has been replicated around the globe, and organizations with similar goals to the Zapatistas have networked to share information and strategy. This media-centric strategy has been so successful that the Zapatistas have abandoned traditional guerrilla tactics entirely—in 2001 they even marched through Mexico City unmolested to meet with Mexican legislators.

In regards to the Americanization thesis and popular geopolitics, antigeopolitics can be seen in popular culture that is produced locally and focuses on local values in opposition to those of the state and/or international elites. Therefore, the Americanization thesis can be criticized simply for ignoring the large amounts of popular culture that never break out of the subaltern national context into an international realm where theorists might take note of it. For example, 2007's war movie *Valley of the Wolves* (see figure 7.2) tells the true story of Turkish special forces troops in northern Iraq who were captured by American troops, hooded, and later released with an apology. The real-life national humiliation of Turkey (a U.S. ally) subsequently bore fruit in the Rambo-esque revenge narrative of *Valley of the Wolves*, the most expensive movie ever made in Turkey and one of its most popular. American troops are portrayed burning mosques during prayers, spraying bullets into a wedding party, and executing prisoners without trial, and a Jewish doctor (Gary Busey) even takes organs from prisoners and sends them to be transplanted in the United States, the United Kingdom, and Israel. The primary narrative is of a Turkish intelligence agent who avenges his friend's suicide (he was shamed via the hooding) by hunting down and killing the American officer responsible for the Turkish humiliation. If this narrative seems objectionable, imagine most American war films you have seen and you will see it is basically the inversion of a very familiar formula. This is classic anti-geopolitics in that it offers discursive resistance to the traditional narratives of American war films, in which American troops are icons of morality and fairness and almost always win (Dodds 2008; Yanik 2009). It would be unlikely to be taken into account by those alleging the domination of American culture because it had a very limited release in Europe (although it was quite successful among Turks living in Germany) and was seemingly not shown in the United States.

Postcolonialism is a complex body of thought, an intellectual critique that tries to break down the categories and spatial boundaries into which conventional hegemonic knowledges put people and places. This is in contradistinction to the confrontational reversals of anti-geopolitics, which leave categories and boundaries largely intact. Consider the example, from chapter 1, of "the Orient." As Edward Said (1978) reminded

Figure 7.2.   Poster of *Valley of the Wolves* (in Turkish, 2007, courtesy of Pana Films)

> **Postcolonialism** Strategy
> of the subaltern that
> refuses the categories
> imposed by the hegemon

us, the Orient was created as a mirror to the Occident (or West). By representing the Orient in particular ways, the West was implicitly constructed as the Orient's opposite—a positive beacon of civilization and order. Thus, a class of people and places, the "Oriental," was created as a way to bring order to the messiness of reality. The postcolonial perspective looks at the ways in which geopolitical knowledge such as this has been constructed, and asks for whom it is beneficial.

This is important because knowledge, in the Western tradition, is often seen as a way of shutting down debates, by proclaiming what is, and what is not, available for disputation. Knowledge is generally seen as universal (i.e., the same everywhere), with rational thought contributing to progress, itself defined as the expansion of human knowledge. This is a very powerful and attractive way of thinking, especially in the West, which sees such rapidly changing technologies, all owed to scientific advances. However, when we apply the insights of physical science to the social world we can often overreach. While gravity may be a constant wherever you go, people's social experiences are not constant in all places. For example, in the United States the meaning of "the police" is often contested, with white Americans generally seeing the police as a protective force whom you would ask for help in any situation. However, African Americans, with collective memories of the police beating protestors still relatively fresh from the Civil Rights era and more recent police beatings such as that of Rodney King (1991) and Abner Louima (1997), sometimes formulate a different meaning for the police: as protectors of white privilege. Both of these formulations are rooted in actual experiences, but one has emerged as hegemonic in popular culture—the notion of the police as a force for good certainly dominates television shows like *CHiPs*, *CSI*, and *Law and Order* (the occasional "corrupt cop" or "a few bad apples" story, like 2001's *Training Day*, notwithstanding). These shows and movies always have a specifically multicultural cast in an effort to portray the police as anything but a defender of traditional privileges. In this way, we can see popular culture as serving those who have a vested interest in viewing the police as a legitimate user of force. Postcolonial approaches shake up those foundations and ask questions about the power inherent to those who construct "valid" knowledges.

Postcolonial theorists argue that knowledge itself has been so dominated by European and North American scholars that knowledge based on experiences from other parts of the world is delegitimized. Joanne Sharp (2003) argues that there are several ways in which postcolonial thought challenges the boundaries that Western knowledge has imposed on its various "others." First, postcolonial thought is highly suspicious of geopolitical binaries such as the aforementioned Oriental/Occidental, as well as others such as civilization/barbarity, developed/underdeveloped, and land power/sea power. Having exposed these as being more about those creating the categories than about those being unwillingly categorized, postcolonial theorists have abandoned binaries as useful ways of analyzing the world. These binaries are more notable for how they have legitimated the exercise of geopolitical power time and time again, with the reputed laziness, barbarism, and immorality of non-Europeans legitimating the colonization of resource-rich lands by reputedly hard-working, civilized, and moral Europeans (or European-descendents) in Africa, the Middle East, North America, Latin America, Southeast Asia, and across the Pacific. Remember that for hegemony to take root these structures of knowledge must permeate colonized peoples; in this way they can be prevented from rising up against their colonial masters.

A second impact that Sharp identifies in postcolonial thought is a heightened role for ambiguity in our understandings of people and places. Often it is easy to feel trapped between the modern, universalist claim that people are the same everywhere, which erases cultural difference, and the opposing view that people's culture is entirely determinative of who and what they are. Both notions are objectionable—the first because it leads to the assumption that everyone would want what we want if only they had the chance, the second because it limits people to static, unchanging categories (often defined through binaries). Thus, postcolonial thought often rejects labels at all.

Postcolonial thought's third impact, Sharp argues, is in its recognition of hybrid identities. Here I will refer back to the *New York Times* article quoted above (Rockwell 1994):

> Then again, maybe "Hollywood" is itself no longer all that American, and its success abroad may be a testimony to its cosmopolitanism. When our supposedly national film industry boasts an Austrian named Schwarzenegger as its biggest star, a Belgian named Van Damme close behind in action films and a Chinese, Bruce Lee, as an honorable ancestor, when the French and the Japanese own studios or invest heavily in "American" films, when Hollywood gets half its profits from outside the U.S., when the new star of the Chicago Bulls is a Croatian named Toni Kukoc, then just how parochially American is our entertainment industry, anyway?

Although suffering a little from its mid-1990s popular culture references, this quote hints at the notions of hybridity that postcoloniality offers. The blending of diverse values and conceits begins to undermine any kind of geographic categories that we might try to impose on people or things. An example of the traditional way of thinking about hybridity would be the nationalist movements that fought for national independence from the empires of Britain, France, the United States, and others. These groups fought for their own state, on the model of those founded in Europe. So, while they generally achieved these material outcomes they remained prisoners of the geopolitical imagination spread from Europe—that of nation-states, with borders, a capital, and all the trappings of power that their former colonizers had. Often, the new national elites became just as corrupt and aloof as the old colonial elites had been—a performance that has been called mimicry. The choices then are either European rule, or rule in the European style.

Mimicry   Adoption of the behaviors and attitudes of colonizers

The postcolonial take on this is quite different however, seeking liberation of the prevailing geopolitical imagination. Hybridity refers to the possible flexibilities of identity that become visible once we abandon the idea of mutually exclusive categories of identity. In other words, the citizens of relatively new postcolonial states ought to feel free to adopt European cultural elements that are useful but also do not have to turn their back on precolonial traditions (which are not necessarily better for being such). An example of this might be in the style of governance: postcolonial countries can adopt the democratic ideals of their colonizers but adapt them to traditional forms of government which were previously authoritarian. For instance, many African democracies have two spheres of governance, with the state in charge of some aspects of government and traditional customary law (and its associated leaders) taking place alongside, but separate from, the state. This can be seen as another rejection of the either/or binary system of thinking, and is particularly useful given the increasing interconnection of people, goods, and ideas that we see flowing across borders, commonly referred to as globalization. Sharp pinpoints the role of hybridity in postcolonial thinking (2003, 63–64):

Hybridity   Flexibilities of identity that are possible once identity is seen as fluid and not predetermined

> The challenge is not only to processes of power within particular spaces, but also the definition of these spaces—about where the center and margins are located (the colonial center and colonized margins)—but also who decides on these locations: who has the power to draw these maps of political geography and to define one place as center, one as margin, and to define individuals as subjects and as subjugated to the rules of others. This fluid concept celebrates impurity and actively resists the will to power of drawing boundaries and naming.

Of particular importance to hybridity are the geographic spaces in which interaction occurs. Films such as *Bend It Like Beckham* (2002) document the ways in which immigrants do not just assimilate, but rather change the places in which they settle. In this film, a Sikh teenager in London battles both her family's traditional expectations and the difficulty of intercultural relationships to get recruited to play football (soccer) for an American university on a scholarship. Negotiating all these identities is like threading a needle for her. Places where these interactions occur become hybrid themselves, and are often attractive to a large number of people who are drawn to the diverse cultural possibilities.

Debates

The two ways of expressing resistance to hegemonic power described above, through anti-geopolitics and through the postcolonial approach, are mutually contradictory. Anti-geopolitics reverses the values associated with categories as a form of resistance while postcolonial thought tries to dissolve those categories. There has been a lot of debate over the relative merits of each for subaltern peoples. Both tactics are used by subaltern peoples, often depending on their appropriateness for specific contexts.

One example in which both tactics can be identified is the phenomenon of Southern identity in the United States. In the United States there is a common representation of the American South as backward, ignorant, and racist. For example, in popular culture a Southern accent is often a comedic code for a stupid character. Dave Jansson (2003) has

> **Internal Orientalism**
> Use of an internal population group as a contrast to demonstrate the superiority of a national whole

argued that this form of internal Orientalism portrays the American South as the "other" for a putatively progressive, intelligent, and unprejudiced rest of the United States in the same way that the notion of the Orient makes the Occident look good by unspoken comparison.

While there is not room to do justice to the topic of Southern identity here, a brief overview is possible in regards to anti-geopolitics and postcolonial thought. One group that has utilized the tactics of anti-geopolitics to resist this negative representation is the League of the South. Founded in 1994, the League of the South is a neo-Confederate group that envisions the white South as a distinct nation descended from "Anglo-Celtic stock." They practice anti-geopolitics by inverting the values associated with the South, seeing it in positive terms as Christian as well as devoted to family and freedom. Thus, the rest of the United States is tacitly condemned as irreligious, antifamily, and pro–government meddling.

This reinscription of old categories can be contrasted with the efforts of some to rewrite the geographies of the U.S. South in a postcolonial style. For instance, some scholars have reinterpreted the South as not just part of the United States, but as a region that has numerous relationships with parts of the United States but also with the Caribbean, Latin America, and sub-Saharan Africa (see for instance Gilroy 1993; Smith and Cohn 2004). This strategy dissolves the South/non-South binary, freeing the American South from having to be understood only in relation to hegemonic understandings of the United States. Instead, Southernness is seen as a hybrid culture resulting from the role of the South as a meeting ground between different peoples from all around the Atlantic rim. Needless to say, this hybridity is anathema to the League of the South's conception of an ethnically pure nation, but both tactics seek to overturn the hegemonic representation of the South as inferior to the rest of the United States.

Despite the use of the racist League of the South as an example of anti-geopolitics, it is important to see the power of its tactic. In contrast to the postcolonial approach, anti-geopolitics provides a strong position from which to argue. It is easy to see that, when subaltern peoples are dominated, it is not enough to try to dissolve the identity that is associated with oppression. The political weakness of the postcolonial approach is evident in this situation, and this has been the cause of much debate. One solution to this problem has attempted to blend anti-geopolitics and postcolonial theory. This solution has become known as strategic essentialism (Spivak 1988), or the adoption of a particular identity for a period of time, as it is useful, and then the dissolution of that identity. This is a flexible form of politics that prevents individuals from having to occupy, and justify, a specific identity all the time. For example, while all the various identities associated with the American South (Cajuns, whites, African Americans, Hispanics, lowlanders, highlanders, city-dwellers, rural residents, etc.) may not feel connected to each other most of the time as "Southerners," they can come together to resist negative, hegemonic representations by the rest of the nation when needed and then go back to their everyday, fragmented lives. Thus, the debate between anti-geopolitics and postcolonial theory is resolved through the synthesis of the two—itself a form of hybridity.

> **Strategic essentialism**
> Temporary adoption of an identity for the purposes of creating a political coalition

INTRODUCTION TO THE NEW MEDIA AND WEB 2.0

Over the past two decades we have seen the emergence of what are collectively known as the new media, an array of generally digital, computer-based forms of communication such as traditional websites, email, blogs, and networked computer games such as Second Life. What makes these media "new" is their higher level of interaction among consumers and their rootedness in relatively accessible production methods. For instance, consider web publishing in relation to traditional publishing. For most people, publishing even a small book is beyond their capability, requiring the hiring of a publisher to print the book and lots of money to get a large print run. Thus, the sources of books in the traditional publishing world were relatively limited. This model has often been referred to as the "one-to-many" model of mass communication. However, with web publishing there is relatively little cost to putting a good-looking website on line. The smaller cost associated with web publishing means that many more voices are able to be heard. This is sometimes referred to as the "many-to-many" model of the new media.

> **New media** Media that rely on digital technologies for distribution; marked by higher levels of interactivity and easier production than prior media

The new media were initially seen as a boon for subaltern voices. Recall that one of the criticisms inherent to the Americanization thesis was that popular culture is dominated by the products of Hollywood and other entertainment industries that are in turn dominated by large corporations. Thus, the new media offered the possibility of many more voices being heard at the global scale. As an example, we have already mentioned the Zapatista movement of Mexico, which served as a model of this kind of rallying and organization. The earliest groups to take advantage of these possibilities were leftist groups opposed to the neoliberal form of economics that they saw as the root of American empire (see chapter 3):

> [In the late 1990s an] international protest movement surfaced in resistance to neo-liberal institutions and their related globalization policies, while democracy, social justice, and a better world were championed. Since then, broad-based populist political spectacles have become the norm, thanks to an evolving sense of the way in which the internet may be deployed in a democratic and emancipatory manner by a growing planetary citizenry that is using the new media to become informed, to inform others, and to construct new social and political relations. (Kahn and Kellner 2004, 87–88)

This protest movement perhaps reached its apogee on February 15, 2003, when between six and ten million people around the world protested the possible invasion of Iraq on the same day as the result of Internet organizing. The world had simply never had a protest on this scale before. However, the ability of the Internet to confront hegemony, even with the incredible success of the global protests, is clearly visible in that the invasion of Iraq began just over a month later.

Governmental attempts to monitor Internet and email content have been enhanced since the onset of terrorist attacks on the United States post-2001 and on the United Kingdom post-2005, ostensibly to prevent terrorist organizing but with the added capacity of monitoring domestic dissent. The Federal Bureau of Investigation (FBI) deployed a computer package called Carnivore, which sifted through information packets sent from suspects' computers and saved their email on a portable memory device. This system was abandoned by 2005 in favor of software that simply could be bought off-the-shelf by the U.S. government. The U.S. government has also exerted its power to shut down specific websites that it has found objectionable. For example, Alneda.com was an Al-Qaeda–affiliated website registered in Malaysia. It was deregistered by the Malaysian government after American pressure in 2002, after which the domain name was immediately nabbed by a patriotic American Internet pornography "entrepreneur," who used the website to track which Islamist websites its visitors were coming from, allowing him to map out the Internet infrastructure used at the time by Al-Qaeda and provide his information to the FBI (Di Justo 2002).

> **Carnivore** Software used by the FBI to read private emails until 2001, when it was replaced by another program

In another example, China extracted from Google the concession that the government could block certain websites from appearing in search results. Thus, hegemonic power can be seen to still be of use even in a decentered, seemingly naturally leveling environment like the Internet. The excitement with which the new media were greeted by political theorists and futurologists has been dampened despite some notable successes by Internet activists trying to create a social movement. Stephen Marmura (2008, 251) describes why some geopolitical issues, like American policy in Israel/Palestine, are harder for Internet activists to intervene in: "Significantly, the importance with which the US-Israeli strategic relationship holds to both dominant political elites and competing segments of the American public sets this issue apart from less contentious ones, such as homeless shelters or home schooling [which are classic case studies of local Internet organizing]." Thus, the new media can serve as a platform from which to organize, but it does not circumvent the usual circuits of national and transnational power.

Indeed, one of the most powerful ideas associated with the Internet is its use as a platform for what would otherwise be considered fringe ideas, if they were considered at all. As stated before, the low cost of entry onto the World Wide Web makes it attractive as a venue for getting a message to a wide audience. Having said that, this notion has generally been proven to be more mythic than real. Stephen Marmura (2008) has argued that a distinction must be made between the Internet's ability to serve as a forum for the representation of geopolitical issues in ways that serve the subaltern, and the Internet's ability to broadcast that representation to large numbers of people. The Internet is good at the former, but poor at the latter. "Fringe" sources of information are likely to sit unnoticed on the web for very long periods of time because the Internet generally requires an active search to find something. It is always possible to stumble upon something inadvertently, or while looking for a "mainstream" source of information on a geopolitical topic, but that is relatively rare. Users of the Internet tend to group themselves into cliques with similar reading and viewing habits.

Are web-surfers more likely to find out about the war in Iraq from Fox News[1] or eIraq?[2] Are they more likely to find out about the war in Afghanistan from CNN[3] or from the Revolutionary Association of the Women of Afghanistan?[4] If they wanted to know what was happening in Israel, would they be more likely to land on the website of the BBC[5] or on the website of the Christian Broadcasting Network?[6] They are far more likely to go with the first one of each pair, if only because it comes up sooner when you type "Iraq," "Afghanistan," or "Israel" into a search engine. Also, the Internet's proliferation of information does much to provide alternative sources, but does little to help users sort through it. Journalistic standards associated with major news organizations, as well as the power of their brands, will generally lead wary and confused readers to the sources of information on which they are already accustomed to relying (the impact of Internet "bookmarks" is also found here). This is not to say that mainstream sources of information are not ideological, simply that users

> **Digital divide** Term used to describe the gap in Internet accessibility, usually between wealthy and poor

are generally comfortable with that ideology or are at least used to it and feel they can see through it as savvy consumers. Of course, there is also the issue of Internet access, sometimes referred to as the digital divide. While Internet access is far from universal in the West, it is a rarity in much of the rest of the world, where traditional media such as radio, print, and television remain dominant among most of the population.

---

1 www.foxnews.com/world/iraq/index.html
2 www.electroniciraq.com
3 topics.edition.cnn.com/topics/afghanistan
4 www.rawa.org/temp/runews/
5 news.bbc.co.uk/1/hi/in_depth/middle_east/2001/israel_and_the_palestinians/default.stm
6 www.cbn.com/cbnnews/world/Israel/index.aspx

We can see then that subaltern peoples' media strategies are limited, even with the new media as a possibility. The Internet and similar media allow subaltern voices to bypass the corporate, hegemonic mainstream media and either engage in anti-geopolitics or in postcolonial discourse that dissolves the hegemonic framing of an issue. However, the use of new media is unlikely to be widely influential unless it somehow piggybacks on some form of broadcast media, or is part of some sort of viral marketing campaign. It seems substantially evident then that it is not the technology of the new media that provides success for subaltern voices contesting hegemonic representations and narratives—it is the manner in which the new media are utilized in their particular contexts to build new social movements. This necessarily involves more than just "getting a message out," it requires people's identities to be changed as a result of their engagement with new media. As Natalie Fenton (2008, 236) has argued, "The internet . . . has the potential to change the practice of democracy radically because of its participatory and interactive attributes. It allows all citizens to alter their relationship to the public sphere, to become creators and primary subjects, to become engaged in social production. In this sense the internet is ascribed the powers of democratization."

Fenton's theory of the Internet and political identity dovetails nicely with relatively recent technological innovations that have been dubbed Web 2.0. Web 2.0 refers to the generation of Internet sites that utilize user-made content, harnessing the creativity and teamwork of the Internet users themselves to create a constant stream of new information and exchange. Examples of this include the streaming video website YouTube, social networking websites like Twitter and Facebook, the online database of knowledge Wikipedia, and the ever-more-ubiquitous blog. These websites

> **Web 2.0** Term used to describe Internet content that is produced by users

have expanded the circle of "cultural producers" even further than the "original" Internet did, as now only minimal skills are required to web-publish a profile of yourself, a video of your drunken exploits, your views on politics, fashion, or whatever. An exuberant *Time Magazine* even broke with tradition in 2006 and declared its Person of the Year "You" (Grossman 2006). Here is the breathless, exultant prose:

> The new Web is a very different thing. It's a tool for bringing together the small contributions of millions of people and making them matter. Silicon Valley consultants call it Web 2.0, as if it were a new version of some old software. But it's really a revolution. And we are so ready for it. We're ready to balance our diet of predigested news with raw feeds from Baghdad and Boston and Beijing. . . . And we didn't just watch, we also worked. Like crazy. We made Face-

book profiles and Second Life avatars and reviewed books at Amazon and recorded podcasts. We blogged about our candidates losing and wrote songs about getting dumped. We camcordered bombing runs and built open-source software. . . . We're looking at an explosion of productivity and innovation, and it's just getting started, as millions of minds that would otherwise have drowned in obscurity get backhauled into the global intellectual economy.

As we have seen above, the Internet, even Web 2.0, is not a technological fix for the social injustices associated with our contemporary geopolitics. However, the performance of new identities available through the more advanced interactivity of Web 2.0 does offer potential for the development of locally produced popular culture that will support subaltern geopolitical perspectives that are distinct from those of the United States or Europe.

But under what circumstances can this subaltern popular culture become global, potentially influencing Western hegemonic views in ways that the "democratic properties" of the Internet promise? In the case study for this chapter we will examine the element of Web 2.0 that is perhaps most often cited as the most politically subversive: blogs. In particular, we will be looking at blogs in the Arab world, a region often criticized for its lack of free press, and thus an area where, despite its geopolitical prominence, subaltern perspectives are rarely given voice in Western media. Thus, the case study will be combining the concepts of anti-geopolitics and postcolonial thought with the political potential often seen to exist within Web 2.0 and the new media more broadly.

CASE STUDY: SALAM PAX AND THE MUSLIM BLOGOSPHERE

One of the great hopes of the new media, as we saw above, was that it would lead to a new, more inclusive form of politics. The most exciting arena for this kind of politics is perhaps the blog. Blogs are important avenues of pseudo-journalism, with political activists providing commentary on both mainstream news and also on issues that are raised exclusively in the blogosphere. The blogosphere is the social world of blogs, which are bound together by the hyperlinks with which they reference each other. Blogging is a highly referential form of media; a regularly updated blog requires

> **Blogosphere** Term used to describe the social network of blogs, connected by the hyperlinks with which they reference each other

material on which to comment, and so blogs tend to feed on each other (and on other websites). This hyperlinked nature of the blogosphere has made it ripe for political subversion.

Because Google, the widely used search engine, ranks websites on its search results page in part because of how many other sites link to them, many bloggers would get their blogger compatriots to link to websites that would help them make a political point. This would cause that website to rise to the #1 search result for a major search keyword. This practice is referred to as a Google bomb (Kahn and Kellner 2004). For instance, in 2003 a group of leftist bloggers got together and linked to President George W. Bush's official White House biography with the keywords "miserable failure," so that if you Googled "miserable failure" Bush's biography would be the #1 result. Google has since retooled its search engine criteria to avoid Google bombs, but the next method of subversion is surely only a couple of clicks away.

> **Google bomb**
> Subversive attempt to make a certain website the #1 result when certain keywords are put into an Internet search engine

More conventionally, however, blogs have been seen as a potential reinvigoration of democracy, or even the harbinger of democracy in places where there is none. Eugenia Siapera (2008, 2009) has conducted research on the role of blogs in the Muslim world. In the idealized vision of blogs, people are freed from reliance on corporate or otherwise corruptible sources of news by an open marketplace of ideas, a new public space in which information can be exchanged and debate may produce new, ever more rational policies. The ease with which anyone can create and maintain a blog ensures that the limitations of "traditional" media will not apply and the powerful can be circumvented. In fact, it is bloggers themselves who control (increasingly) every facet of their blog's appearance, modifying their old posts, accepting (or not) readers' comments, etc. Blogs provide the possibility to give subaltern voices, like Muslims who live in countries with no tradition of press freedom, a venue to represent themselves and their ideas, values, and desires.

The idea of Muslim bloggers is itself somewhat subversive of hegemonic imaginary geographies, as the West has long been connected (in Westerners' minds) with modernity and technology and Islam has been connected with traditionalism. Muslim bloggers can be doubly subversive as they contest the universalizing perspective that Western bloggers often have. The idea of a "rational marketplace of ideas" as described in the previous paragraph is something of a myth—it assumes that some people have no personal agendas that they are pursuing, that everyone is seeking a policy that is the best of everyone as a whole. This is simply not the case, but, as we said at the beginning of the chapter, hegemony involves convincing subaltern populations that their interests are the same as those of the powerful. In the "rational marketplace," "Muslim people cannot participate in the public sphere as Muslim, but as 'human beings' in the abstract sense. But this abstract sense is in fact quite concrete, as it refers to a specific kind of person: an educated, secular, middle-class man, able and willing to use his reason in a specific manner ostensibly for the 'common good'" (Siapera 2009, 33). Thus, the mere existence of Muslim bloggers linked to Western voices through the blogosphere calls into question the claims to universality of those Western voices (at least when they differ strongly from Muslim voices).

Salam Pax is the pseudonym of an Iraqi blogger (the name means "peace" in Arabic and Latin, respectively) who became famous in the run-up (and aftermath) of the 2003 invasion of Iraq by the United States, United Kingdom, and other partners (Katz 2003). His blog, entitled "Where is Raed?," defied most Westerners' preconceptions about Iraq and Iraqis. Originally intended simply as a way to stay in touch with his friend (Raed) who had moved to Jordan, the blog turned into an international sensation and a symbol of the way the new media were creating new potentialities in geopolitics. Salam's disdain for the Saddam Hussein regime was matched by his sadness over the fate of Baghdad. Further, his English was flawless and his knowledge of Western culture (he had studied architecture in Vienna) made him feel accessible by the Western blogging masses. Perhaps Salam was close enough to Siapera's "educated, secular, middle-class man" to make himself heard in the blogosphere.

Still, to focus on the lack of traditional Iraqi voices in the blogosphere is to lose sight of the unique voice that Salam was able to bring to the online world of heated debate and discussion prior to, and during, the invasion of Iraq. His mother, a former sociologist with the Iraqi Ministry of Education, quit when told she could not get promoted without becoming a Ba'athist. His father did the same, giving up a successful career as an economist. Their fiercely independent stance is reflected in their son, who blogged anonymously, knowing that if the Hussein

> **Ba'athist** Originally an Arab nationalist party, now largely associated with the former regime of Saddam Hussein in Iraq

regime (or the postinvasion militias) discovered who he was he would be in grave danger. His ambivalence toward both the regime and the invading armies led Western readers to conclude alternately that he was either a CIA agent or an Iraqi secret agent. His blog, then, provides a fascinating window into what life was like in Baghdad both before and during the invasion.

As early as September 2002 (the actual invasion was in late March 2003) Salam was preparing a shopping list for supplies to get himself through the bombing he foresaw. Life though was not dominated by the run-up to war, at least not for Salam. He seems more concerned early on with his favorite band (Massive Attack), the inconstant flow of money from his job, and—as many bloggers are—which other bloggers have linked to his blog (i.e., "linkylove"). However, the upcoming war was a major topic in the blogosphere, and Salam was quick to skewer those who argued that an American invasion of Iraq was altruistic and would lead to a new era of peace and prosperity. In response to a *New York Times* article about postwar planning (still six months prior to war), Salam wrote (Pax 2003, 14):

> Excuse me. But don't expect me to buy little American flags to welcome the new colonists. . . .
>   Yeah, go ahead. Just flush all the efforts of people who were sincere in their fight for an independent Iraq down the drain. People fought, demonstrated and died so that my generation gets to see all their dreams turned upside down [during the 1991 and 2003 invasions]. . . .
>   God, I feel sorry for anyone who has ever had an ideal and fought for it. . . . If they'd only known that this was going to happen—that it would all just end up being another colony—they wouldn't have bothered. It's much better to spend your time on sex, drugs and belly dancers. Uncle Sam is going to come and tell you how to run a country properly and how to spend your money on weapons from him—"Don't go buying useless Chinese technology, habibi."

However, he had no illusions of life under Saddam Hussein and UN sanctions (Pax 2003, 12):

> For how much would you sell your kidney?
>   Salah sold his for $250. His fiancée sold hers as well, for the same price. They've been engaged for a while and they needed the $500 (that's equivalent to a million Iraqi dinars) to build two extra rooms in parents' house for them, to live in. I know this because a relative of mine was the buyer.
>   Breathe in. Change the subject.

In the last few months of 2002 Salam mixed his usual irony and sarcasm ("Bomb us already. Stop pussyfooting." Pax 2003, 23) with an increasing engagement in debates within the blogosphere about his authenticity and identity. As always, Salam is refreshingly up front about his own inability to speak for the Iraqi people (Pax 2003, 27):

> I have spent half of my life out of this country and had to be taught how to re-grow my roots by someone who isn't even Iraqi by nationality, he just loves the place (thank you, Raed). We both have a mistrust of religion and have read the *Tao Te Ching* with more interest than the Koran. And we both have mouths which have gotten us into trouble. The regular joe would be more inclined to beat the shit out of us infidels.

Nevertheless, Salam continued to pick apart Western media narratives of the build-up to war (Pax 2003, 35): "My favourite headline until now is from Reuters: WORLD SEES CHANCE FOR PEACE, IRAQ MUM ON UN VOTE. Funny, the world sees peace, while I have to prepare a bomb shelter in my house." Perhaps most critically however, Salam engaged in open discussions with other bloggers (Pax 2003, 38):

> I know the war is inevitable and I know nothing you said was meant as an attack on me personally—and I know Saddam is a nutcase with a finger on the trigger. But this is my country and I love its people. There is no way you can convince me that a war is OK. I worry about what will happen during the attacks and I worry more about what will happen afterwards. I take walks in parts of the old city and I can't stop thinking "Will this be still there this time next year?" You are right; on an emotional level I cannot and will not accept a war on Iraq. But on the other hand . . .
>
> Look, there is no way I am going to say it, mainly because I do not trust the intentions of the American government.

Other exchanges were more heated, as the war neared. In December there was a scare as heightened press coverage (old media) raised the awareness of Salam's blog. He attempted to delete the blog but was talked out of it by Raed. He also documented everyday life in Baghdad, such as the increase in rolling blackouts (one of which occurred during the Christmas concert of the Iraqi National Symphony Orchestra).

As the new year (2003) began, Salam set about organizing his emergency supplies while the Iraqi government dug wells in urban areas, in anticipation of a breakdown in infrastructure during wartime. In the realm of the Internet Salam documented the lunacy of online polls speculating about when the invasion of Iraq might begin as well as spam email sent by U.S. intelligence services to all Iraqi email accounts urging them to not fight in the event of an invasion. Similarly, the Iraqi Internet service began slowly excluding more and more sites from visitation as censorship increased. Salam worried, consequently, about his own blog being cut off.

As January became February, Salam noted trenches being dug in Baghdad in anticipation of urban warfare, not by the army but by Ba'athist insurgents ("I am either angry or scared. I can't make up my mind." Pax 2003, 85) and told of his family gathering to watch Colin Powell's dramatic PowerPoint presentation to the United Nations in which he laid out the case for war (they had to use an illegal satellite dish to do so). March, however, brought even more preparation for war, with the Iraqi army digging massive ditches in which they planned to burn oil as a smokescreen, and human shields from the United States and United Kingdom poured into Baghdad and then poured out again when they found they were not to be fed at the Iraqi government's expense. Salam was incensed (Pax 2003, 109): "Did you take enough pictures of children begging in the streets to show your friends back home how much you care about the plight of the poor in the Third World?"

On March 20, Salam reported that soldiers were in trenches and that night the American ultimatum expired (Pax 2003, 125): "The worst is seeing and feeling the city come to a halt. Nothing. No buying, no selling, no people running after buses. We drove home quickly. At least inside it did not feel so sad." He then virtually live-blogged the beginning few days of the war, updating the blog every few hours as the bombs alternately dropped or did not. Warned by international media of the take-offs of B-52 bombers from Great Britain, Salam could anticipate when the bombs should drop, if they were aimed at Baghdad (Pax 2003, 131): "The attacks on Baghdad were much less than two days ago. We found out today in the news that the city of Tikrit got the hell bombed out of it. Today the B52s took off at 3pm—in half an hour we will know whether it is Baghdad tonight or another city. Karbala was also hit last night."

However, as the days rolled on the war became another (albeit extraordinary) part of everyday life (Pax 2003, 137): "Dishes are fun to do while you think about the possibility of the big window in front of you being smashed by the falling tons of explosives and so on." On March 24, day five of the war, the Internet went down entirely in Iraq. Salam began a regular diary, however, which he emailed to a friend when email became available on May 7. They were then published in his name. During this initial period, Salam's readers and commenters worried that something horrible had happened to Salam—either discovery by Saddam Hussein loyalists or an American bomb fallen into his neighborhood, causing "collateral damage."

After the war, Salam remained an internationally known figure, even writing articles for the British newspaper *The Guardian* until late 2004. He has subsequently been involved in a series of journalistic jobs and outreach projects. Most importantly however, during the invasion of Iraq, Salam Pax served as a subaltern voice, providing antihegemonic narrative from the city most talked about, but never heard—Baghdad. Denying himself the proscribed role of "Iraqi on the street," he problematized outsiders' preconceptions of what Iraqis "are" by being different—secular, Western in cultural outlook, and homosexual—than expected. He nevertheless was willing to "strategically essentialize" the Iraqi people to provide an antigeopolitical perspective (Pax 2003, 138): "One more word by Americans on TV about 'humanitarian aid' will make me kill my television. They have the audacity to turn us to beggars, while we will have to pay for the research and development of the weapons they are field-testing on us *and* they will do it as if they are helping us with their 'humanitarian aid.'" Salam effectively breaks down the categories of Western/Iraqi by making himself relatable to the Western audience of his blog; he then nevertheless provided an Iraqi perspective as the bombs fell on his city and the tanks rolled in. This kind of dialogue would have been unthinkable prior to the era of the new media; however, clearly the new media did not prevent the war though the exchange of ideas. The impacts of the new media and Web 2.0 are as yet unknown, as new uses and practices continue to emerge.

CONCLUSIONS

Summary

In this chapter we began by discussing the flipside of hegemony, which is the subaltern. The role of hegemonic knowledge in geopolitics was discussed, as were two subaltern strategies for contesting that knowledge. The first, anti-geopolitics, attempted to invert the categories created by hegemons. Whereas in Orientalist thought the Orient is bad (oppressive, stagnant) while the Occident is good (democratic, progressive), an anti-geopolitical perspective might revalue the Orient as good (traditional, focused on values) and the Occident as bad (imperialist, corrupt). This kind of simplistic strategy can be quite effective but perpetuates the categories of the hegemon. An alternative strategy is offered by postcolonial thought, which aims to dissolve those categories and free up subaltern peoples to pick and choose from various knowledges. This, however, may be intellectually satisfying but can be politically weak. Therefore the idea of strategic essentialism, or the use of temporary coalitions built around identities, was introduced as a possible way to blend these strategies.

In this chapter we also discussed the emergence of the new media and Web 2.0, both of which introduced users of technology as producers of popular culture. Technology like the Internet, blogging, YouTube, and the like offer opportunities for the subaltern to bypass traditional media, which are often criticized for being too congruent with hegemonic knowledges (see for example Salam Pax's criticism of the Western media, even as he relies on it for information the Hussein regime was not releasing). The potential for the new media to reinvent democracy and even geopolitical imaginations by opening up new public spaces (such as through blogging) is there, but it remains to be seen to what purpose these technologies will be put.

The chapter concluded with the case study of Salam Pax, an Iraqi blogger who provided a subaltern voice during the run-up to Iraq's 2003 invasion. As such, he engaged in both postcolonial discourse (Iraq was a British mandate after 1920) and also antigeopolitical discourse as he found necessary in his interactions with the larger, mostly Western, blogosphere.

Nevertheless, the establishment of the blogosphere between the First and Second Gulf Wars did not end up preventing the 2003 invasion.

Extensions in Your Life

If, as is likely, Stephen Marmura's argument about people seeking media perspectives that are rooted in their own culture is true for many of us, we might want to consider branching out and engaging with other sources. Of course, there is no reason to accept other media uncritically any more than we should adopt our "own" media uncritically.

- From where do you get most of your daily information about the world?
- How might your sources of information influence what you hear about, and how those places are described?
- What are the advantages of having so many voices at our fingertips via technology like the Internet?
- What are the disadvantages of that deluge of information?

8

Conclusion:
Identity, Subjectivity,
and Going Forward

This chapter is intended to serve (literally) as a bookend, paired with the introductory chapter. In that chapter the subject matter of popular culture and geopolitics was introduced with identity as a thread that connected them and ran through all the chapters of this book. After a brief synopsis of the book this chapter gives a more extended treatment of the social constructionist view of identity and subjectivity, drawing on the collective insights of the rest of the book. Similarly, while the introductory chapter discussed the project of popular geopolitics and how the book was structured, this chapter will speculate about the future of that project and consider ways for the reader to continue an interest in popular geopolitics beyond this book.

BRINGING IT ALL TOGETHER

This book began with a brief introduction to the topic and the book before moving on with two chapters that sought to outline two different bodies of knowledge, those associated with geopolitics and with popular culture. Very briefly the history of each was sketched, illustrating how in the development of both fields of study there had been a long-term shift toward the complication of taken-for-granted ideas by a heightened appreciation for everyday people's ideas and actions. In the case of geopolitics, that involved connecting the inherent politics associated with war and diplomacy with the type of consumption activities usually undertaken in our living rooms, shopping malls, movie theaters, and on the Internet. The case studies of the last five chapters have tried to show how these every-day activities not only reflect prevailing geopolitical trends but also ac-tively construct them. The global scale of geopolitics is inseparable from the everyday scale of our lives.

A fundamental tenet of popular geopolitics that has emerged is that geo-politics is not only about how we see other people, but also how we see ourselves—our identity. The five concepts highlighted in the case study chapters of this book each addressed the processes through which our iden-tities are generated, contested, and sometimes obscured even to ourselves. Representation of place (chapter 3) is how we describe the Other—the peoples and places that are deemed fundamentally different than "us" or "me." Narrative (chapter 4), related to representation, is a method of under-standing how "we" or "I" got to this situation, whatever that might be and wherever it might be going. Affect (chapter 5) attends to the connections between the self and the surrounding environment, geopolitical extensions of the self that are preconscious and usually unaccounted for in the more cognitive elements of geopolitics, like representation and narrative. The ac-tive audience (chapter 6) problematized accounts of representation and narrative that ignored the agency of the bodies that consume popular ac-counts of geopolitics, in some ways arguing the opposite point from schol-ars of affect, who provide little space for consumers to resist their environ-ment, short of changing it. Hegemony and the subaltern (chapter 7), the two inverse sides of any power relationship, relate to the active audience by problematizing the absolute openness of any audience to a discourse—in other words, that chapter tries to reveal the role of structural and other forms of power in shaping even the ways in which we view ourselves (and conversely how people use power to resist hegemony). The cumulative ef-fect of considering all these concepts at once can be extreme disorienta-tion—we are not the absolute decision makers that we often think we are. Our thought processes are preconditioned by cultural (and affective) influ-ences that we have been inundated with since childhood. We still have the incredible capacity for critical thinking, but it is simply not possible to rise above our own subjectivity and consider geopolitics from a completely objective perspective.

SOCIAL CONSTRUCTIONISM AND SUBJECTIVITY

In chapter 2 we briefly mentioned subjectivity, which we then defined as an individual's sense of self, including perspective, thoughts, emotions, and the like. Subjectivity has been a major subject of controversy across the social sciences, even bridging into disciplines such as psychology (e.g., Salgado and Hermans 2005).

For a long time, it never would have occurred to scholars to question how we know who we are. René Descartes' famous Latin dictum *Cogito ergo sum* ("I think, therefore I am") was the first and last word on the subject. The subject as Descartes conceived it was a singular, coherent consciousness that existed through time (indeed, this is how most people conceive of themselves in everyday life). This notion has been subsequently branded the Cartesian subject given its close association with Descartes.

> **René Descartes** French mathematician and scholar, known as the father of modern philosophy

> **Cartesian subject** Notion that the subject is singular and unified throughout time

Sigmund Freud's theories of the subconscious (*id*) as something separate from the conscious, rational self (*ego*) began the process of questioning the notion that there is a core to us that is in control. However, the social constructionist perspective on the subject makes this simple distinction between ego and id seem elementary. Social constructionism is part of a larger postmodern perspective that has animated much of the work in popular geopolitics that is described in this book. Social constructionists have been very critical of the innate value of knowledge (you will recognize this notion from chapter 7, among others). Rather than using language to try and describe a fundamental truth (like who you really are), language and discourse are tools used to make action possible. Note the parallels in the following quote from psychologists João Salgado and Hubert Hermans between the social constructionist notion of the subject and our ideas of representational binaries and Orientalism from chapters 1 and 3.

> **Ego** In Freud's system, our rational/cognitive processes

> **Id** In Freud's system, our unconscious drives

> In this way, the construction of meaning is completely dependent on relationships between people, including self-related meanings. Each context specifies certain social and relational games, by which people try to make themselves intelligible to others and try to make others intelligible to themselves. In other words, meaning is a matter of linguistic and social negotiation. Selfhood, in this matter, is only a particular case of intelligibility: what I am is a matter of how we symbolically and pragmatically negotiate the meanings assigned to my own person. (Salgado and Hermans 2005, 6)

Thus, when considering the role of identity in popular geopolitics the subject is generally considered fragmented or nomadic (Deleuze and

Guattari 1983; Radway 1988). Instead of a monolithic subject, individuals take various subject positions that reflect different roles or identities that the individual recognizes. The popular no-tion of a singular, Cartesian self is consti-tuted through interactions of your biologi-cal self with discourses (Hall 1996). Again, here are Salgado and Hermans (2005, 6); note how their "sense of identity" parallels our discussion of narrative in chapter 4: "The sense of continuity and permanence—the sense of identity—is something that arises from the continuous pro-cesses of creating and granting intelligibility and coherence in the course of relationships with others."

> **Subject positions**   Many different identities from which we select in different social situations

To further complicate matters, as our bodies come into different rela-tions with discourses, different subject positions emerge (Grossberg 1987). Even a relatively young adult can look back on some earlier time (early adolescence is always good for some laughs) and recall an incident where he or she acted entirely differently than he or she would now, such as be-ing embarrassed about a trait you have that you now celebrate (or are at least okay with). Sometimes those memories even take the perspective of the third person—we know we were there, we know what we did, but we remember it all as a story, just like we remember stories that we did not actually take part in (like a plot from television, or a friend's funny story you have heard a few times).

Once we acknowledge that the "self" changes over time (i.e., there is no fundamental "me") it is a smaller step to recognize that the self often changes over very short time spans, flipping back and forth between differ-ent subject positions. This should not be surprising when we consider how social life is saturated with multiple (and often competing) discourses. Jan-ice Radway describes it thus (1988, 364, emphasis in original):

> Social subjects can be multiply addressed by discourses that coincide or over-lap, but they can also be addressed by discourses that contest and even con-tradict each other. This possibility for discontinuity highlights the other fea-ture of the larger process of subject formation I want to stress—that is, the fact that social subjects *actively* participate in the process (although by that participation they do not fully control it or its effects) by deliberately articu-lating bits and pieces from several, often competing, discourses themselves.

In other words, we can actively contribute to the changing of our selves by actively engaging with some discourses and institutions over others. When presented with rival discourses that appeal to contradictory ele-ments of our "selves," we can actively intervene to decide how (and who) we want to be in that instance, as we saw in chapter 6 in the example of evangelicals tacking back and forth between their subject positions as both Christian and American. We saw this again in chapter 7 via Salam Pax's harnessing his subject positioning as both Iraqi and as cosmopolitan; we are not prisoners of our subject positions, but we cannot exactly leave them behind either.

The social constructionist perspective of the subject, which as you can see has served as the philosophical underpinning for this book and for much of popular geopolitics, has nevertheless come in for some criticism. One such criticism is that social constructionism, in its disdain for the notion of a core self has left no room for private experiences that are not shared with others through discourse. If all "I" am is a narrative that holds my disparate elements together, who is telling the narrative?

This problem is addressed by Mikhail Bakhtin, who was a scholar of culture who came up with the idea of dialogism (1982). Dialogism originally referred to the idea that texts are always in dialogue with each other (see chapter 2 for our discussion of intertextuality). However, this is more than simply authors (or musicians, filmmakers, or whatever) being influenced by one another. Instead of a unidirectional influence (forward though time, with prior works influencing new ones), dialogism argues that older works are influenced by new works—always capable of being reinterpreted and thus changing in meaning. The implications of this for subjectivity can be seen by replacing the "works" in the previous sentence

> **Mikhail Bakhtin**   Russian philosopher; famous for his contributions to literary theory and rhetoric

> **Dialogism**   Notion that texts are always in correspondence with each other, forwards and backwards through time

with narrators. "The self cannot be understood . . . except in relation to an audience whose real and imagined responses shape the way in which we define ourselves" (Kelly 1992, 44).

Thus, Bakhtin holds out the possibility of an essential self, one that can only be glimpsed from outside ourselves; that is, as we said regarding popular culture in chapter 6, the audiences with whom we interact themselves have a role in defining who we are. This is not only true in a literal sense, but also in the sense that our selves are always in dialogue with each other. "If we assume that thought is, in fact, a dialogue with oneself . . . we do not need to assume that self-consciousness is grounded in a kind of internal or homuncular ego or observer. Consequently, it is pos-

> **Polyphony**   Literally "multiple voices"; in literature, the possibility of a novel capturing multiple points of view rather than just the author's; in the study of identity, the constitution of the self through conflicting subject positions

sible to admit that self-consciousness is a matter of communication with oneself . . . , a matter of our ability of relating with ourselves" (Salgado and Hermans 2005, 10). Bakhtin then argues that there is no self without polyphony—they are mutually constitutive. This makes intuitive sense when laid alongside our discussion of geopolitical identity (Self/Other) found in chapters 1 and 3.

This discussion has been a winding, yet too brief, tour around one of the deepest human questions—"who am I?" Subjectivity is a topic of interest to scholars from a multitude of disciplines from geography to psychology to literature. It is impossible to understate its relevance for topics such as geopolitics and popular culture, as can be seen from the way in which our discussion of subjectivity in this chapter has intersected with ideas that we encountered in every other chapter. Therefore it should be clear that the processes by which self-identity is generated are paralleled by the processes by which collective identities (nations, religions, political parties) are constructed. The difference lies in the specifics of the discourses involved and the scale of the media involved. Our personal identities are formed through interaction with others, most often face-to-face but sometimes via technological mediation. Our collective identities are also formed through dialogue, but more often these interchanges take place through popular culture and other mass media. Hopefully this book has provided the grounding to go forth and engage in the world with a more sophisticated understanding of the processes in play and how it is possible to fit into them.

THE FUTURE

Popular geopolitics was described in the introductory chapter as both a subject matter and a project. While these are distinct, their futures are obviously tied together. If anything, the short history of popular geopolitics has been a successful one, with more people getting involved and new perspectives being introduced from both other areas of geography and from other disciplines. However, much like human geography itself, there is so much theoretical foment that it is difficult to foresee the future. For instance, developments in nonrepresentational theory call into question the philosophical underpinnings of popular geopolitics, and a popular geopolitics that was focused on audiences rather than texts would look very different from the popular geopolitics we have today, becoming closer to cultural geography and cultural studies than to the rest of the work done in critical geopolitics. All of these futures are wide open, and in fact the most likely scenario is an as-yet unforeseen development that shakes everything up in new ways.

The end of this book is hopefully not the end of your interest in popular culture and geopolitics. If you are interested in going forward with the topic, it could be a never-ending source of interest and passion. There are two distinct ways in which to carry on.

Continuing Reading

This book has provided the background in ideas and concepts that are necessary to engage with the academic literature that is out there. There are a number of journals that publish material related to popular culture and geopolitics. A sampling of titles is included in table 8.1. Of course, it is not necessary to be reading academic journals to be continuing your education in popular geopolitics. More and more books are becoming available on the topic, both from the traditions of geography and also international relations, such as Joanne Sharp's *Condensing the Cold War: Reader's Digest and American Identity* (2000) and Cynthia Weber's *Imagining America at War: Morality, Politics, and Film* (2005). Poking around in a neighborhood bookstore or online should uncover many others.

Contesting Discourses, Performing Identities

Still, there are many other ways to learn about popular geopolitics than just by reading. In fact, there is something to be said for learning by doing. Of course, we are all "doing" popular geopolitics all the time

Table 8.1:   Journals That Publish Papers about Popular Geopolitics

Political Geography
Geopolitics
Annals of the Association of American Geographers
Transactions of the Institute of British Geographers
Environment and Planning D: Society and Space
Geography Compass
Social and Cultural Geography
Cultural Geographies
Gender, Place, and Culture
Antipode
ACME: An International E-Journal for Critical Geographies
Arab World Geographer
Security Dialogue
Millennium: Journal of International Politics
British Journal of Politics and International Relations

whether we know it or not because, as we saw in this and the preceding chapters, our everyday lives are enmeshed in geopolitics—they are mutually constitutive.

Remember how in the last two chapters we discussed the openness of culture, its fundamental pliability. The opportunity is always present to engage with geopolitical discourses and intervene, not only to reshape our society but also ourselves. The dialogic perspective of identity means that, when we change the discourses we are immersed in, or shift the thinking of the people around us, we by definition change ourselves because it is impossible to know who we are but through social interaction.

So what can you do? One of the strengths of geopolitical discourse is that it makes us feel miniscule and insignificant as individuals. "What can *I* do to change the course of globalization?" "The media representation of Arabs does not match my experience. What can I do?" Nevertheless, our actions and inactions are what generate these discourses, or at least enable them. Therefore, it stands to reason that our actions and inactions can change them, should we so desire. As we saw in chapter 7, there are limits to this because of inequalities in power among various actors, but with good tactics you can often overcome weakness.

The most important thing to have prior to starting out is a definite perspective. This book has outlined concepts and case studies, but it is up to the reader to use those concepts to identify a geopolitical stance. Then, with some tactical thinking it is possible to come up with a plan. Luckily there are numerous ways to intervene in popular geopolitics and impact the processes of identity formation and meaning making that have been outlined in this book. If someone is really into popular culture, and going to make a career out of it, he or she is uniquely placed to influence the representations and narratives that are deployed in public discourse. While the public seems to hate being lectured by heavy-handed celebrities and moralizing movies, that is not necessarily what is needed. What we need is an entertainment industry that is merely socially aware, and does not resort to unsubtle processes of Othering and fear. Instead of this fear and resentment, we could substitute a popular culture that tries to foster more positive relationships between ourselves and our environment (for more on this, see Connolly 2007).

Of course, it is not necessary to make a career out of reworking popular geopolitics. It can begin with a single letter to the editor, entering words and ideas into the public sphere. It can begin with a blog—following the example of Salam Pax, the reluctant international journalistic star. Perhaps someone would like to start a blog that reviews movies, literature, and music from a critical geopolitical perspective. That would simply involve thinking and writing about the popular culture already being consumed and putting those thoughts out on the Internet for public consumption. As Foucault argued, power is constituted through the thousands of daily interactions we all have; therefore we are all implicated in the everyday enactments of geopolitics.

Bibliography

Adorno, T., and M. Horkheimer. 1979. *Dialectic of enlightenment*. London: Verso.

Agnew, J. 2006. "Religion and geopolitics." *Geopolitics* 11, no.2:183–91.

———. 1994. "The territorial trap: The geographical assumptions of international relations theory." *Review of International Political Economy* 1, no.1:53–80.

Allen, J. 2004. "The whereabouts of power: Politics, government and space." *Geografiska Annaler, Series B* 86, no.1:19–32.

Allen, R. 2007. *The unreal enemy of America's army*. Master's thesis in anthropology, University of Washington.

Anderson, B. 1991. *Imagined communities: Reflections on the origin and spread of nationalism*. London: Verso.

Arnold, M. 1869. *Culture and anarchy*. London: Smith, Elder & Co.

Atkinson, D. 2000. "Geopolitical traditions in modern Italy." In *Geopolitical traditions*, ed. K. Dodds and D. Atkinson, 93–117. London: Routledge.

Badley, I. 1996. *Writing horror and the body: The fiction of Stephen King, Clive Barker, and Anne Rice*. Oxford: Greenwood.

Baker, A. 1997. "'The dead don't answer questionnaires': Researching and writing historical geography." *Journal of Geography in Higher Education* 21, no.2:231–43.

Bakhtin, M. 1982. *The dialogic imagination: Four essays*. Austin, TX: University of Texas Press.

Barlett, C., R. Harris, and R. Baldassarro. 2007. "Longer you play, the more hostile you feel: Examination of first person shooter video games and aggression during video game play." *Aggressive Behavior* 33, no.6:486–97.

Barnes, J. 2008. "The Iraq war movie: Military hopes to shape genre." *Los Angeles Times*, 7 July 2008. www.latimes.com/news/nationworld/world/la-na-armyfilms7-2008jul07,0,5966660.story (accessed 15 July 2008).

Barnett, C. 2008. "Political affects in public space: Normative blind-spots in non-representational ontologies." *Transactions of the Institute of British Geographers* 33, no.2:186–200.

Bhabha, H. 1990. "Introduction: Narrating the nation." In *Nation and narration*, ed. by H. Bhabha, 1–7. New York: Routledge.

Billig, M. 1995. *Banal nationalism*. Thousand Oaks, CA: Sage.

Black, I. 2007. "Fear of a Shia full moon." *The Guardian*, 26 January 2007. www.guardian.co.uk/elsewhere/journalist/story/0,,1999399,00.html (accessed 3 Oct 2008).

Black, J. 2004. "The geopolitics of James Bond." *Intelligence and National Security* 19, no.2:290–303.

Bowman, I. 1921. *The new world: Problems in political geography*. Yonkers, NY: World Book.

Bradsher, K. 2004. *High and mighty: The dangerous rise of the SUV*. Cambridge, MA: Public Affairs.

Brooker, W. 2002. *Using the force: Creativity, community and "Star Wars" audiences*. London: Continuum.

Bryce, J., and J. Rutter. 2002. "Spectacle of the deathmatch: Character and narrative in first-person shooters." In *ScreenPlay: Cinema/videogames/interfaces*, ed. by G. King and T. Krzywinska, 66–80. London: Wallflower.

Butler, J. 1990. *Gender trouble: Feminism and the subversion of identity*. New York: Routledge.

Caprotti, F. 2005. "Information management and fascist identity: Newsreels in fascist Italy." *Media History* 11, no.3:177–91.

Carter, S., and D. McCormack. 2006. "Film, geopolitics and the affective logics of intervention." *Political Geography* 25, no.2:228–45.

———. 2010. "Affectivity and geopolitical images." In *Observant states: Geopolitics and visual culture*, ed. by F. McDonald, K. Dodds, and R. Hughes. London: I.B. Taurus.

Castree, N., and T. Macmillan. 2004. "Old news: Representation and academic novelty." *Environment and Planning A* 36, no.3:469–80.

Chang, C. 1986. "Post-Marxism or beyond: Hall and Foucault." *Journal of Communication Inquiry* 10, no.3:71–85.

Chapman, J. 1999. *License to thrill: A cultural history of the James Bond films*. London: I.B. Taurus.

Clifford, N., and Valentine, G. (eds.). 2003. *Key Methods in Geography*. Thousand Oaks, CA: Sage.

Connolly, W. 2002. *Neuropolitics: Thinking, culture, speed*. Minneapolis, MN: University of Minnesota Press.

———. 2007. *Capitalism and Christianity, American style*. Durham, NC: Duke University Press.

Dalby, S. 1991. "Critical geopolitics: Discourse, difference, and dissent." *Environment and Planning D: Society and Space* 9, no.3:261–83.

de Certeau, M. 1984. *The practice of everyday life*. Berkeley, CA: University of California Press.

Deleuze, G., and F. Guattari. 1983. *Anti-Oedipus: Capitalism and schizophrenia*. Minneapolis, MN: University of Minnesota Press.

DeLyser, D., S. Herbert., S. Aitken, M. Crang, and L. McDowell (eds.). 2009. *The SAGE Handbook of Qualitative Geography*. Thousand Oaks, CA: Sage.

Der Derian, J. 2001. *Virtuous war: Mapping the military-industrial-media-entertainment network*. Boulder, CO and Oxford, UK: Westview.

Diamond, J. 1999. *Guns, germs, and steel: The fates of human societies*. New York City: Norton.

Di Justo, P. 2002. "How Al-Qaida site was hijacked." *Wired*, 10 August 2002. www.wired.com/culture/lifestyle/news/2002/08/54455?currentPage=1 (accessed 8 Aug 2008).

Dittmer, J. 2007a. "'America is safe while its boys and girls believe in its creeds!': Captain America and American identity prior to World War 2." *Environment and Planning D, Society & Space* 25, no.3:401–23.

———. 2007b. "Retconning America: Captain America in the Wake of WWII and the McCarthy Hearings." In *The amazing transforming superhero!: Essays on the revision of characters in comic books, film and television*, ed. T. Wandtke, 33–51. Jefferson, NC and London: McFarland.

———. 2007c. "The tyranny of the serial: Popular geopolitics, the nation, and comic book discourse." *Antipode* 39, no.2:247–68.

———. 2008. "The geographical pivot of (the end of) history: Evangelical geopolitical imaginations and audience interpretation of *Left Behind*." *Political Geography* 27, no.3:280–300.

———. 2009. "Maranatha! Premillennial dispensationalism and the counter-intuitive geopolitics of (in)security." In *Spaces of security and insecurity: New geographies of the war on terror*, ed. A. Ingram and K. Dodds, 221–38. Aldershot: Ashgate.

Dittmer, J., and Z. Spears. 2009. "Apocalypse, now? The geopolitics of *Left Behind*." *Geojournal* 74, no.3:183–89.

Dodds, K. 1996. "The 1982 Falklands War and a critical geopolitical eye: Steve Bell and the if... cartoons." *Political Geography* 15, no.6–7:571–92.

———. 2003. "Licensed to stereotype: Geopolitics, James Bond and the spectre of Balkanism." *Geopolitics* 8, no.2:125–56.

———. 2005. "Screening geopolitics: James Bond and the early Cold War films (1962–1967)." *Geopolitics* 10, no.2:266–89.

———. 2006. "Popular geopolitics and audience dispositions: James Bond and the Internet Movie Database (IMDb)." *Transactions of the Institute of British Geographers* 31, no.2:116–30.

———. 2008. "Hollywood and the popular geopolitics of the War on Terror." *Third World Quarterly* 29, no.8:1621–37

Earnest, W. 2007. "Making gay sense of the X-Men." In *Uncovering hidden rhetorics: Social issues in disguise*, ed. B. Brummett, 215–32. Thousand Oaks, CA and London: Sage.

Englehart, S., and S. Buscema. 1972a. "The Falcon fights alone!" In *Captain America and the Falcon #154*, ed. R. Thomas, 1–31. New York: Marvel.

———. 1972b. "Two into one won't go!" In *Captain America and the Falcon #156*, ed. R. Thomas, 1–31. New York: Marvel.

Fenton, N. 2008. "Mediating hope: New media, politics and resistance." *International Journal of Cultural Studies* 11, no.2:230–48.

Fisher, W. 1987. *Human communication as narration: Toward a philosophy of reason, value, and action*. Columbia, SC: University of South Carolina Press.

Flusty, S. 2007. "Empire of the insensate." In *Indefensible space: The architecture of the national insecurity state*, ed. M. Sorkin, 29–50. New York and London: Routledge.

Foer, F. 2004. *How soccer explains the world: An unlikely theory of globalization*. New York: HarperCollins.

Foucault, M. 1974. *The order of things: An archaeology of the human sciences*. London: Routledge.

———. 1977. *Discipline and punish: The birth of the prison*. London: Allen Lane.

———. 1989. *The archaeology of knowledge*. London: Routledge.

Fraiman, Susan. 1995. "Jane Austen and Edward Said: Gender, culture, and imperialism." *Critical Inquiry* 21, no.4:805–21.

Frank, T. 2004. *What's the matter with Kansas? How conservatives won the heart of America*. New York: Metropolitan.

Freud, S. 2000. *Three essays on the theory of sexuality*. New York: Basic.

Frykholm, A. 2004. *Rapture culture: Left behind in evangelical America*. Oxford: Oxford University Press.

Geertz, C. 1973. "The integrative revolution: Primordial sentiments and civil politics in the new states." In *The interpretation of cultures*, ed. C. Geertz, 255–310. New York: Basic.

Gellner, E. 1983. *Nations and nationalism*. Oxford: Blackwell.

Gilmartin, M. 2004. "Geography and representation: Introduction." *Journal of Geography in Higher Education* 28, no.2:281–84.

Gilroy, P. 1993. *The Black Atlantic: Modernity and double consciousness*. London: Verso.

Goss, J. 2004. "*Unforgiven* and the spirit of the laws: Despotism, monarchy and democratic virtue in Clint Eastwood's last western." In *Film and History CD-ROM Annual*. jongoss.info/papers/unforgiven.htm> (8 March 2008).

Gramsci, A. 1992. *Prison notebooks*. New York: Columbia University Press.

Gregory, D. 1994. *Geographical imaginations*. Oxford, UK: Blackwell.

Grossberg, L. 1987. "The In-Difference of Television." *Screen* 28, no.2:28–46.

Grossman, L. 2006. "*Time*'s person of the year: You." *Time*, 25 December 2006. www.time.com/time/magazine/article/0,9171,1569514,00.html (accessed 8 Aug 2008).

Hall, S. 1996. "The problem of ideology: Marxism without guarantees." In *Stuart Hall: Critical dialogues in cultural studies*, ed. D. Morley and K. Chen, 25–46. London and New York: Routledge.

———. 1997. "Introduction." In *Representation: Cultural representations and signifying practices*, ed. S. Hall. London: Sage.

Hills, M. 2002. *Fan cultures*. London: Routledge.

Hobsbawm, E. 1990. *Nations and nationalism since 1780*. Cambridge: Cambridge University Press.

Hobsbawm, E., and Ranger, T. (eds.). 1983. *The Invention of Tradition*. Cambridge: Cambridge University Press.

Hughes, R. 2007. "Through the looking blast: Geopolitics and visual culture." *Geography Compass* 1, no.5:976–94.

Hyndman, J. 2001. "Towards a feminist geopolitics." *The Canadian Geographer* 45, no.2:210–22.

———. 2004. "Mind the gap: Bridging feminist and political geography through geopolitics." *Political Geography* 23, no.3:307–22.

Ignatieff, M. 2003. *Empire Lite*. New York: Vintage.

Jansson, D. 2003. "Internal orientalism in America: W.J. Cash's *The Mind of the South* and the spatial construction of American national identity." *Political Geography* 22, no.3:293–316.

Johnson, B., and Cloonan, M. 2008. *Dark side of the tune: Music and political violence*. Aldershot: Ashgate.

Johnson, C. 2004. *The sorrows of empire: Militarism, secrecy, and the end of the Republic*. London and New York: Verso.

Jones, G. 2004. *Men of tomorrow: Geeks, gangsters, and the birth of the comic book*. New York: Basic.

Kahn, R., and D. Kellner. 2004. "New media and internet activism: From the "Battle of Seattle" to blogging." *New Media & Society* 6, no.1:87–95.

Katz, I. 2003. "Introduction." In *The Baghdad Blog*, ed. I. Katz, ix–xiv. London: Atlantic.

Kelly, A. 1992. "Revealing Bakhtin." *The New York Review of Books* 39, no.15, 24 September 1992, www.nybooks.com / articles / 2815 (accessed 5 Sept 2008).

Kohut, A., and K. Parker. 2007. "Cable and network TV worst offenders: Public blames media for too much celebrity coverage." The Pew Research Center for People and the Press, 2 August 2007. people-press.org / reports / pdf / 346.pdf> (27 Feb 2008).

Lacan, J. 1998. *The four fundamental concepts of psychoanalysis*. London: Vintage.

Lauer, J. 2005. "Driven to extremes: Fear of crime and the rise of the sport utility vehicle in the United States." *Crime, Media, Culture* 1, no.2:149–68.

Leavis, Q. D. 1965. *Fiction and the reading public*. New York: Russell and Russell.

Lees, L. 2004. "Urban geography: Discourse analysis and urban research." *Progress in Human Geography* 28, no.1:101–107.

Leib, J. Forthcoming. "Creating 'facts' on the bumper: Identity, nationalism, geopolitics, contestation and license plates." *Geographical Review*.

Liebes, T., and E. Katz. 1990. *The export of meaning: Cross-cultural readings of "Dallas."* Oxford: Oxford University Press.

Livingstone, D. 2005. "Science, text and space: Thoughts on the geography of reading." *Transactions of the Institute of British Geographers* 30, no.4:391–401.

Lorimer, H. 2005. "Cultural geography: The busyness of being 'more-than-representational'." *Progress in Human Geography* 29, no.1:83–94.

MacDonald, F. 2006. "Geopolitics and 'the vision thing': Regarding Britain and America's first nuclear missile." *Transactions of the Institute of British Geographers* 31, no.1:53–71.

Mackenzie, R., S. Buscema, and D. Perlin. 1979. "Aftermath!" In *Captain America #231*, ed. R. Stern, 1–31. New York: Marvel.

Marmura, S. 2008. "A net advantage? The internet, grassroots activism, and American Middle-Eastern policy." *New Media & Society* 10, no.2:247–71.

McCormack, D. 2006. "For the love of pipes and cables: A response to Deborah Thien." *Area* 38, no.3:330–32.

Megoran, N. 2008. "From presidential podiums to pop music: Everyday discourses of geopolitical danger in Uzbekistan." In *Fear: Critical geopolitics and everyday life*, ed. R. Pain and S. Smith, 25–25. Aldershot: Ashgate.

Murray, J. 1997. *Hamlet on the Holodeck: The future of narrative in cyberspace*. Cambridge, MA: MIT Press.

Myers, G., T. Klak, and T. Koehl. 1996. "The inscription of difference: News coverage of the conflicts in Rwanda and Bosnia." *Political Geography* 15, no.1:21–46.

Nast, H. 2003. "Oedipalizing geopolitics: A commentary on condensing the Cold War." *Geopolitics* 8, no.2:190–96.

Ó Tuathail, G. 1996. *Critical geopolitics: The politics of writing global space.* Minneapolis: University of Minnesota Press.

———. 2003. "'Just out looking for a fight': American affect and the invasion of Iraq." *Antipode* 35, no.5:856–70.

Pax, S. 2003. *The Baghdad Blog.* London: Atlantic.

Pinkerton, A., and K. Dodds. 2009. "Radio geopolitics: Broadcasting, listening and the struggle for acoustic spaces." *Progress in Human Geography* 33, no.1:10–27.

Power, M. 2007. "Digitized virtuosity: Video war games and post-9/11 cyber-deterrence." *Security Dialogue* 38, no.2: 271–88.

Radway, J. 1988. "Reception study: Ethnography and the problems of dispersed audiences and nomadic subjects." *Cultural Studies* 2, no.3:359–76.

Roberts, G. 2006. "History, theory, and the narrative turn in IR." *Review of International Studies* 32, no.4:703–714.

Rockwell, J. 1994. "Pop culture; The new colossus: American culture as power export." *New York Times*, 30 January 1994. query.nytimes.com/gst/fullpage.htm l?res=980CE7DB1E30F933A05752C0A962958260&sec=&spon=&pagewanted=a ll (accessed 25 July 2008).

Rose, G. 2007. *Visual methodologies: An introduction to the interpretation of visual materials.* London: Sage.

Routledge, P. 2003. "Anti-geopolitics." In *A companion to political geography,* ed. J. Agnew, K. Mitchell, and G. Ó Tuathail, 236–48. Oxford: Blackwell.

Said, E. 1978. *Orientalism.* London: Penguin.

———. 1993. *Culture and imperialism.* New York: Knopf.

Salgado, J., and H. Hermans. 2005. "The return of subjectivity: From a multiplicity of selves to the dialogical self." *E-Journal of Applied Psychology* 1, no.1:3–13.

Secor, A. 2001. "Toward a feminist counter-geopolitics: Gender, space and Islamist politics in Istanbul." *Space and Polity* 5, no.3:191–211.

Severin, S., and J. Tankard Jr. 1992. *Communication theories: Origins, methods, and uses in the mass media.* White Plains, NY: Longmans.

Sharp, J. 1996. "Hegemony, popular culture and geopolitics: The Reader's Digest and the construction of danger." *Political Geography* 15, no.6–7:557–70.

———. 2000. *Condensing the Cold War: Reader's Digest and American identity.* Minneapolis: University of Minnesota Press.

———. 2003. "Feminist and postcolonial engagements." In *A companion to political geography,* ed. J. Agnew, K. Mitchell, and G. Ó Tuathail, 58–74. Oxford: Blackwell.

Siapera, E. 2008. "The political subject of blogs." *Information Polity* 13, no.1:97–109.

———. 2009. "Theorizing the Muslim blogosphere: Blogs, rationality, publicness and individuality." In *International Blogging,* ed. A. Russell and N. Echchbai, 29–46. Bern: Peter Lang.

Sidaway, J. 1998. "What is in a gulf? From the 'arc of crisis' to the Gulf War." In *Rethinking Geopolitics,* ed. S. Dalby and G. Ó Tuathail, 224–39. London and New York: Routledge.

Smith, A. 2000. "Theories of nationalism: Alternative models of nation formation." In *Asian Nationalism*, ed. M. Leifer, 1–20. New York: Routledge.

Smith, J., and Cohn, D. 2004. *Look Away! The US South in New World Studies.* Durham: Duke University Press.

Somers, M. 1994. "The narrative constitution of identity: A relational and network approach." *Theory and Society* 23, no.5:605–49.

Spivak, G. 1988. *In other worlds: Essays in cultural politics.* New York & London: Routledge.

Stock, P. 2000. "Dial 'M' for metonym: Universal exports, M's office space and empire." *National Identities* 2, no.1:35–47.

Storey, J. 1996. *Cultural studies and the study of popular culture.* Athens: University of Georgia Press.

Thien, D. 2005. "After or beyond feeling? A consideration of affect and emotion in geography." *Area* 37, no.4:450–56.

Thrift, N. 1996. *Spatial formations.* London: Sage.

———. 2000. "It's the little things." In *Geopolitical traditions: A century of geopolitical thought,* ed. K. Dodds and D. Atkinson, 380–87. London: Routledge.

———. 2004. "Intensities of feeling: Towards a spatial politics of affect." *Geografiska Annaler, Series B* 86, no.1:57–78.

Tolia-Kelly, D. 2006. "Affect—an ethnocentric encounter? Exploring the 'universalist' imperative of emotional/affectual geographies." *Area* 38, no.2:213–17.

Tomlinson, J. 2001. *Cultural imperialism.* London: Continuum.

Trushell, J. 2004. "American dreams of mutants: The X-Men; 'Pulp' fiction, science fiction, and superheroes." *Journal of Popular Culture* 38, no.1:149–68.

U.S. Government. 2005. "Federal Business Opportunity Solicitation H92239-05-T-0026." www1.eps.gov/spg/ODA/USSOCOM/FortBraggNC/H92239%2D05%2DT%2D0026/listing.html (accessed 13 April 2005).

van den Berghe, P. 1981. *The Ethnic phenomenon.* New York: Elsevier.

Virilio, P. 1989. *War and cinema: The logistics of perception.* New York and London: Verso.

Weber, T. 2004. *On the road to Armageddon: How Evangelicals became Israel's best friend.* Ada, MI: Baker Academic.

White, H. 1973. *Metahistory: The historical imagination in nineteenth century Europe.* Baltimore, MD: Johns Hopkins University Press.

Wright, B. 2001. *Comic book nation: The transformation of youth culture in America.* Baltimore, MD: Johns Hopkins University Press.

Yanik, L. 2009. "Valley of the wolves—Iraq: Anti-Geopolitics Alla Turca." *Middle East Journal of Culture and Communication* 2, no.1:153–70.

Zhukov, Y. 1965. "Morality of the bourgeois world: The advocate of the 'Right to Kill'." *Pravda* no. 272.

Index

24 (TV show), 52, 84
300 (movie), 21

Abkhazia, 128
Abu Ghraib, 105
active audience, 111, 113, 115, 117–19,
    121–23, 125, 127, 129, 131
Adorno, Theodor, 28
affect, 43–44, 51, 91–99, 101, 103–10
Afghanistan, 14–5, 18, 29, 60, 100, 108
African Americans, 89, 142. *See also*
    Black History Month
agency, 29, 31, 67
Al-Qaeda, 2, 144
Americanization, 134, 136, 143
America's Army (video game), 104,
    107–8, 133
amplification, 94, 109
Anderson, Benedict, 17–19, 77. *See also*
    imagined communities
Antichrist, 119–20, 122–23, 125
anti-geopolitics, 134–36
arc of crisis, 22
archival research, 38–39
Argentina, 63–64, 66–67
Armageddon, 120–1
Arnold, Matthew, 23

Austen, Jane, 57, 80, 133
axis of evil, 14, 22

Baghdad, 95, 149, 151–52
Bakhtin, Mikhail, 159–60
Balkans, the, 60
banal nationalism, 19–21, 78
Bangladesh, 59
Barbados, 59
BBC (British Broadcasting
    Corporation), xiv, 145
Bell, Steve, 64, 66–68
Benjamin, Walter, 28
Bend It Like Beckham (film), 141
Billig, Michael, 19–20, 78
Bin Laden, Osama, 45. *See also*
    Al-Qaeda
binaries, 86, 139
Birth of a Nation (movie), 102
Black History Month, 73, 79. *See also*
    African Americans
Black Sea, 61
blogs and blogging, 21, 37, 143, 146–53
Bond, James, xiv, 39, 44, 58, 60, 63,
    67–68, 80, 132–33
Borat (movie), xv
Bosnia, x, 41

173

Bowman, Isaiah, 7–8, 48
bricolage, 117
Brookings Institution, 13
Bruckheimer, Jerry, 116
Burundi, 116
Bush, George H. W., 14
Bush, George W., xv, 13–15, 18, 31, 45, 64–65, 84, 148

Cameroon, 59
Canada, 14–15, 18
capitalism, 17, 28, 30, 32, 76–7, 133–34
Capra, Frank, 102
Captain America, 80–90, 132–33
Caribbean Sea region, 57, 80, 142
Carpathia, Nicolae, 123–25. *See also Left Behind*
Cartesian plane, 9
cartographies of textual reception, 113, 131
cartography, 48
Caspian Sea, 61–2
Catholic Church, 24
Central Asia, 2, 5, 7, 57, 61
Centre for Contemporary Cultural Studies, 23
Children of Men (movie), 38
Chile, 55
China, 20, 29, 60, 87, 100
CHiPs (TV show), 138
civil rights, 85, 89, 114, 138
climate change, 6
Clinton, Hillary, 74
Cloverfield (movie), 2
coding, 40
Cohen, Saul, 8–9
Cold War: Biblical prophecy, 128; classical geopolitics, 5, 8; diversion from problems of global inequality, 31; popular culture, vii–ix, 12, 16, 39, 42, 59, 61, 63, 83, 86; study of subcultures, 117
colonialism, 53, 56–58, 136, 138
Commonwealth of Nations, 59
compositional analysis, 39–41
consumption and consumers: affect, 98; identity and globalization,

26–27; mass, 23–24, 61; methods of studying, 40–42, 44; nationalism, 17, 20, 79, 90; new media, 143, 155; power, 67–68 (*see also* active audience); theories of, 29, 32–34, 37–38
contagion, 94, 109
content analysis, 40–1
continuity, 84–86
critical geopolitical eye, 64–65, 68
critical realism, 51
critical security studies, 95
CSI (TV show), 84, 138
Cuba, 16, 55–56
cultural capital, 128
cultural imperialism, 26. *See also* Americanization
cultural power, 12
cultural studies, 23, 29–30, 32–34, 37, 84, 98, 116–18
culture industry, 28. *See also* Frankfurt School
Czechoslovakia, 60, 63, 80

Daily Show, The (TV show), 1, 65
Dallas (TV show), 26
Daniel, Book of, 121
Darfur, 116
de Certeau, Michel, 29, 33–34, 111
DeMille, Cecil B., 102
democracy, 134
Descartes, Rene, 157
dialogism, 159
digital divide, 145
discourse, 10–19, 44; and affect, 91, 96; and anti-geopolitics, 134–36; and identity, 26, 75; relationship to representation, 49, 56, 68; theorizing, 32–36
discourse analysis, 41–42
Dominican Republic, 34, 56
domino theory, 8
Doom (video game), 104, 106–7
Doonesbury (cartoon), 64–65

Eisenhower, Dwight, 99
embedded reporting, 101

emotions, 92–95, 97
Enlightenment, the, 50, 56
environmental determinism, 5–6
eschatology, 121, 129
essentialism, 72–73, 142
Eternal Jew, The (movie), 103
Ethiopia, 129
ethnography, 42–44, 118
Evangelicalism, 33, 118–19, 121–25,
   127–28, 131–32
extraordinary rendition, 84
Ezekiel, Book of, 121, 127–29

Facebook, 21, 24, 146
Falkland Islands, 63–66
false consciousness, 30
fandom, 117–18, 125
fanfic, 118
Fascism, 63, 87, 89, 103
feminism, 36, 42–44, 63, 97
first-person shooter, 99, 104, 106–9
Fisher, Walter, 70
Fleming, Ian, 39
focus groups, 42–44
formal geopolitics, 13
Foucault, Michel, 29, 32–33, 41, 111
France, 17, 20, 54, 57, 60, 93, 140
Frankfurt School, 27–29, 31, 33, 40, 111,
   115
free trade, 11, 26, 55–56, 135–36
"freedom vs. fascism", 87, 89
Freud, Sigmund, 34–36, 157
From Russia with Love (movie), 60–61
Future Objective Force Warrior, 109

genre, 40, 45, 68, 84, 102, 105–6, 108
geopolitical imaginations, 18–19, 22,
   122
geopolitics, xvi, 21–22; and active
   audience, 118–19, 121–23, 125, 127,
   129, 131; and affect, 91, 95–98, 100,
   105; concepts, 16–17, 19–20; history
   and theories, 1–15; methodologies,
   36, 38–39, 41–45; and narrative, 72;
   and representation, 48, 50–52, 57, 63
Geopolitik, 4, 7–8
Germany, 29, 54, 77–78, 136; and

classical geopolitics, 3–4, 6–8, 18;
   and World Wars, 24, 48, 63–64, 67,
   80–81, 83, 103
globalization, 25–26, 140, 143
Glory (movie), 73
GoldenEye (movie), 63
Google, 2, 144, 148
Gramsci, Antonio, 29, 30–33, 111, 133
Grand Theft Auto (video game), 106
Grenada, 56
Guardian, The (newspaper), 21, 64, 152
Guatemala, 56
Guyana, 59

Haditha, 108
Haiti, 56
Hall, Stuart, 29
Hartshorne, Richard, 8
Haushofer, Karl, 4, 7–9
hegemony, 30–33, 79, 133–35, 137, 139,
   141, 143
Heritage Foundation, 13
Hess, Rudolf, 4, 59, 63
heteronormativity, 33
high culture, 23–25, 27–28, 117
Hitler, Adolf, 4, 8, 14, 80–81, 102–3
Hobsbawm, Eric, 76–78
Hoggart, Richard, 29
Hollywood, 1, 24, 26–28, 37, 102–3,
   139, 143
Holocaust, the, 71, 114
homosexuality, 114, 118, 152
Hoover, J. Edgar, 13
Horkheimer, Max, 28
Hotel Rwanda (movie), 116
House Un-American Activities
   Committee (HUAC), 13
human rights, 56, 132
Hungary, 30
Hussein, Saddam, 149–53
Huston, John, 102
hybridity, 25, 109, 139–42

Ibo, 75
identity, xv, 7, 155–60, 162; and
   consumption, 115, 118; and
   globalization, 26–27; and Lacan,

35–36; and narrative, 70–79, 85, 87, 90; national, 18, 20, 34, 64, 66; and postcolonialism, 140–42, 146
identity politics, 73–74
imagined communities, 16–17, 19, 113. *See also* Anderson, Benedict
imagined geographies, 18, 57
immersion, 43, 104–6, 109
imperialism, 10, 20–21, 26, 53, 55–57, 68
In Which We Serve (movie), 102
Independence Day (movie), 2
India, 7, 59–60, 78, 134
industrial revolution, 54
internal orientalism, 141
Internet, 2, 15, 24, 90, 108, 134–35, 143–47;
Internet Movie Database (IMDb), 44
intertextuality, 42, 44–45
interviews, 42–4, 125
Iran, 14, 61, 129
Iraq, 10–11, 14, 59, 61, 124, 136; First Gulf War, 107; Second Gulf War, 1, 29, 100–3, 105, 108, 143, 145, 149–53
Iron Man (movie), 103
Islam, 15, 19, 21, 44, 128–29, 132, 148–49
Islamism, 129
isolationism, 102
Israel, 10, 26, 120–22, 124–25, 127–30, 136, 144
Istanbul, 44, 60–61, 67

Jamaica, 59–60
Japan, 4, 26, 55, 60, 80, 83, 113, 139
jazz, 27
Jenkins, Jerry, 123. *See also Left Behind*
Jesus, 119–23, 125, 129, 131
Jews, 71, 80, 103, 120–21, 124–25, 136
Jordan, 125–26; Abdullah, King of Jordan, 21

Kazakhstan, xv
Keith, Toby, 1
Kerry, John, 31, 55
King, Jr., Martin Luther, ix, 114
King, Rodney, 138

King, Stephen, 25
Kirby, Jack, 80
Kissinger, Henry, 8
Kjellén, Rudolf, 3–4
Korean War, 83
Kosovo, 101
Kyrgyzstan, 43

Lacan, Jacques, 34–36
Lacoste, Yves, 9–10
LaHaye, Tim, 123. *See also Left Behind*
Latin America, 54–56, 64, 139, 142
League of the South, 141–42
Lebensraum, 4
Left Behind (books), 118, 122–25, 127–29, 131–33
Libya, 129
license plates, 34
Logos, 70, 74
London, 5, 11, 63–64, 117, 141
Lord of the Rings (movies), 118
Louima, Abner, 138

Mackinder, Halford, 4–7, 9, 12
Mahan, Alfred, 4–6, 12
Maibaum, Richard, 39
Malawi, 59
Malcolm X, 114
Mansfield Park (novel), 57–58
Marxism, 9, 28–30, 32–33
Matrix, The (movie), 48–49
McCarthy, Joseph, 13, 86–87, 89
Megiddo, 120, 125
mercantilism, 53–54
metanarrative, 71
methodology, 36–38, 40, 44
Mexico, 134–36, 143
Middle East, 2, 10–11, 18, 20–21, 108, 139
military-industrial complex, 99–101
military-industrial-media-entertainment complex (MIME), 98–99, 101, 104, 106, 110
mimicry, 140
Minority Report (movie), 84
mirror stage, 35–36
modalities, 37–39

modernity, 76–77
Mogadishu, Battle of, 109
music, xiii, 1, 26–27, 37, 43, 107, 112, 117
MySpace, 21, 24
Mythos, 70, 74

Napoleon, 57
narrativity, 70–71, 75, 80, 89
national interest, 11–13, 63, 65, 135
nationalism, 17, 19–21, 30–31, 75–80
Native Americans, 74, 78
Nazarbayev, Nursultan, xv
Nazi Party, 4, 63–64, 67, 80–81, 83, 86–87, 89–90, 102–3
neo-Confederate movement, 73, 141
neoliberalism, 135, 143
new media, 133, 142–43
Nicaragua, 16, 55–56
Nigeria, 59
Nixon, Richard, 8, 87
nonrepresentational theory, 51–52, 91, 96, 105
North American Free Trade Agreement (NAFTA), 135
North Atlantic Treaty Organization (NATO), 2, 8, 13, 29, 81, 86
Northern Ireland, 64
nuclear weapons, 100, 105, 129, 132

Obama, Barack, 74, 122
Obama, Michelle, 31
oil, 2, 4, 20, 61, 75, 99–100, 125
Olympics, 20
ontological narrative, 71, 74, 85
organic theory of the state, 3
Orientalism, 18–19, 26, 48, 57–58, 61, 68, 72, 80, 136, 138–39, 141
Ottoman Empire, 48

Pakistan, 59
Palestine, x, 129–30, 144
Panama, 56
Paris Review (magazine), 25
Parker, Trey. *See Team America: World Police*
patriarchy, 32

Pavarotti, Luciano, 25
Pax, Salam, 149–53, 159, 162
Pearl Harbor, 4, 82; 2001 movie, 113
performative consumption, 118, 128
Petra, 125–26
Pleasantville (movie), 87
plot, 4, 61, 70–72, 86, 90, 114, 122, 127
Poland, 14, 63, 80
polyphony, 159–60
pop art, 24–25
popular culture, 1–2, 15–16; active audience and, 111–14, 116–18; affect and, 91, 94–96, 98–99; British Empire and, 59, 67; Evangelicals and, 122–23, 128, 131–32; importance, xv–xvi, 20–22; narrative and, 80, 83–85, 90; nationalism and, 73, 77, 79–80; representation and, 47–48; subaltern and, 133–34, 136, 138–39, 141, 143; theories and methods of study, 23–45; video games and, 105–6
popular geopolitics, 14–17, 21–22, 50, 52, 57, 100, 105, 136; and affect, 96–98; and methods, 36, 38, 41–44
Port Stanley, 64
postcolonialism, 136, 138
post-Marxism, 32
postmillennialism, 121
poststructuralism, 10, 32, 35
practical geopolitics, 13–14
premillennial dispensationalism, 119, 122, 131–32
primordialism, 17–18, 75–77
printing press, 17, 24, 77
production, 29, 34, 103, 112, 133, 143; sites of, 37, 39, 41–42
propaganda, xiv, 4, 24, 40, 81, 102–3
Protestant Reformation, 24
psychoanalysis, 34, 36
public narrative, 71–74, 80, 83

R&B (rhythm and blues), 24
racism, 18, 87, 89
Rapture, the, 119, 121–24, 127
Ratzel, Friedrich, 3–4, 6, 9, 11, 18
Reader's Digest (magazine), 12–13, 42

Reagan, Ronald, 13, 16, 38
realism, 38, 50–51, 108–9
Red Dawn (movie), 16
Redacted (movie), 101
red-baiting, 13, 85–87
Rendition (movie), 101
representation, 44, 47–53, 134, 141–42;
    and British empire, 56–57, 59–61,
    63–64, 66–68; and the United States,
    80, 82–83, 87; and video games,
    104–105
resonance, 62, 64, 94
retcon, 85–87
Revelation, Book of, 114, 121, 123, 129
Rice, Condoleezza, 13–14
Rolling Stone (magazine), 25
Roman Empire, 122
Russia, x, 2, 5, 7, 57, 60–61, 86, 124,
    128. *See also* Soviet Union
Rwanda, 41, 116

Said, Edward, 18, 57, 136
Scofield, Cyrus,119
Scotland, 64, 66
Second Life, 143, 147
September 11, 2001 attacks (9/11): and
    American narrations of innocence,
    72; and cinema, 2; and importance
    of affect, 84, 94–95, 110; and *Left
    Behind*, 129; and SUVs, 112–13; and
    video games, 107–8. *See also*
    Al-Qaeda
serial narrative, 80, 84–85, 87, 89
"shock and awe", 95, 102
Sierra Leone, 59
Simon, Joe, 80
sites, 37–38, 40–41, 57, 108, 143
"slash" fiction, 118
slavery, 57, 73, 78
Smith, Kevin, 117
social capital, 128
social constructionism, 50, 157–59
somatic marker, 94
South Ossetia, 128
Southeast Asia, 139
Soviet Union, vii–ix, 5, 8, 12–14, 61, 83.
    See also Russia

spatial science, 9
Special Operations Command, 2
Special Relationship (between U.S.
    and U.K.), 62
Spykman, Nicolas, 9
Star Trek (TV shows and movies), viii–
    xi
Star Wars (movie), 117
state, the, 3, 8, 13, 17, 20, 31, 106, 134–
    36, 140;
state-centrism, 11, 95
Stewart, Jon. *See Daily Show, The*
Stone, Matt. *See Team America: World
    Police*
strategic essentialism, 142, 152
strategies, 33–34, 55–56, 73, 101
subaltern, 133–39, 141–43
subculture, 116–17, 131
subjects and subjectivities, 36, 97, 105,
    140, 146, 156–60
Superman, 81, 83, 85
SUVs, 112–113
symbolic capital, 128
Syria, 61

tactics, 33–34, 95, 102, 136, 141–42
Tanzania, 59
Team America: World Police (film), 1
terrorism, 14–15, 18, 84, 94–95, 128–29,
    132
Thatcher, Margaret, 65–66, 117
time/space compression, 25
Top Gun (movie), 2
Training Day (movie), 138
Treaty of Versailles, 48, 102
Tribulation, the, 119–23, 127–28,
    132
Tribulation Force, 124–25. *See also Left
    Behind*
Triumph of the Will (movie), 102–3
Trudeau, Garry. *See Doonesbury*
Trujillo, Rafael, 34–35
Truman, Harry, 5, 8
Tswana, 75
Turkey, 60–62, 136–7
Twitter, 146
Tyndale House, 123

U2, 25
Uganda, 59
Unforgiven (movie), 73
United Kingdom: British Empire, 5, 44, 52, 54–55, 57–67; and classical geopolitics, 4–5, 7; and cultural studies, 29, 117; and Orientalism, 18–19; in World War II, 81–82, 102
United Nations, xiii, 124
United States: American South, 73, 141–42; Department of Defense (the Pentagon), 2, 14, 81, 99, 107–8; Department of State, x, 99; development of geopolitical theory, 4–6, 8–9; and empire, 54–56; and evangelical geopolitics, 122, 129, 132–33; and the media, 12–16, 26, 99–104, 107–10, 136; and national narrative, 71–73, 78–87, 90; popular culture and domestic politics, 31–33, 65
Uzbekistan, 43

Valley of the Wolves (movie), 137
video games, 1, 91, 99, 101, 103–6, 108–10, 112
Vietnam War, 8, 37, 101, 109
virtuous war, 100–1
visual turn, 105
visuality, 36, 64, 105

Wales, 64
War on Terror, 94–95
Web 2.0, 146–47, 153
Wedding Crashers (movie), 28
welfare state, 31–32
Whedon, Joss, 117
Why We Fight (movie), 102, 104. *See also* Capra, Frank
Wikipedia, 146
Williams, Raymond, 29
Windtalkers (movie), 74
Wings (movie), 103
World Cup, 25
World Is Not Enough, The (movie), 60
World War I, 4–5, 7, 10, 48, 102
World War II, 24, 40, 55, 59, 99, 102–3; and Captain America, 80–81, 83; and classical geopolitics, 4, 8–9; importance to contemporary geopolitical discourse, 14, 63–64, 67, 74

X-Files (TV show), 118
X-Men (comics and films), 114

Yoruba, 75
You Only Live Twice (movie), 60
YouTube, 2, 21, 146

Zambia, 59
Zapatistas, 134, 136
Zimbabwe, 59

About the Author

Jason Dittmer is Lecturer in Human Geography at University College London. His interests lie in the cultural framings of geopolitics, in particular those accomplished through the tropes of the superhero genre and evangelical Christian eschatology. He is coeditor of *Mapping the End Times: American Evangelical Geopolitics and Apocalyptic Visions* and of *Aether: The Journal of Media Geography*.